KU-630-139

THE HOME FRONTS

By the same author

A soldier leaving home

JOHN WILLIAMS

THE HOME FRONTS

BRITAIN, FRANCE AND GERMANY
1914–1918

CONSTABLE
LONDON

First published in 1972
by Constable and Company Limited
10 Orange Street, London W.C.2
Copyright © by John Williams 1972

ISBN 0 09 457770 6

CENTRAL RESOURCES
LIBRARY

HERTFORDSHIRE
COUNTY LIBRARY

940.342

5421017

Set in Monotype Baskerville
Printed in Great Britain by
The Anchor Press Ltd, and bound by
Wm Brendon & Son Ltd, both of
Tiptree, Essex

FOR HAZEL

CONTENTS

CONTENTS

Part Five

1918: THE FINAL EFFORT

ILLUSTRATIONS

FOREWORD

While the military history of the First World War has been exhaustively recorded and its political and other aspects covered at length, no comparable comprehensive account has appeared of life on the Home Fronts of the belligerents, from the viewpoint of the ordinary civilian. Yet the impact of the war on the civil and domestic life of the nations involved was nothing short of revolutionary. The wholesale dedication of the belligerent powers to the waging of war brought changes to the civilian scene unprecedented in any previous conflict. War was no longer a matter almost exclusively for the fighting man, an isolated affair of clashing armies on some distant battlefield. The wearing of a uniform ceased to be virtually the sole criterion of service, privation or suffering. It was now, indeed, that the phrase 'Home Front' was first coined. This book aims to tell how the civilian populations of Britain, France and Germany fared during the four years of struggle, and how they reacted to the needs, pressures and ordeals of these years.

In a chronological treatment that takes account of the military progress of the war (the events of each year being prefaced by a brief summary of military operations) and covers as necessary the political and other background, the book attempts to deal in detail with all the varied facets of life on the Home Fronts of the three belligerents as they affected the people in the rear. Year by year, and country by country, it describes the social scene, the subjection of the populations to unheard-of regulation and regimentation, the impact of censorship and propaganda, the fluctuations of morale, the

I

conflicting trends of bellicosity and pacifism, the growing war-weariness, the insidious inroads of defeatism, the mounting discomforts and difficulties of everyday living, and in particular the dire effects of increasing food shortage – which in blockaded Germany produced near-starvation.

It narrates how the Home Fronts experienced the novel dangers of air-raids and long-range bombardment. It records too perhaps the most far-reaching social change caused by the war: the emancipation of women from their traditional status of inferiority, the result of their mobilisation for the war-effort and assumption of tasks hitherto the province of men. It also notes a phenomenon that increasingly affected all three belligerents as the war progressed: the alienation of the fighting soldier – who was, after all, only a civilian in uniform – from the citizen at home. All these factors, social and psychological, combined – along with the striking advances in industrial techniques and processes stemming from the demands of war – to transform in a few short years the face of these belligerent nations. They confirmed that the Home Front was as inseparable from total war, and as indispensable to it, as the fighting armies.

Most of the research for this book has been carried out in the London Library and the libraries of the British Museum and Imperial War Museum. Among the various people from whom I have sought and received advice and help I would mention Mr Correlli Barnett and Miss Margery Weiner, who provided me with valuable material, and Mr Eric Whelpton and Mrs Irene Soltau. To all of these my special thanks are due.

JOHN WILLIAMS

NOTE ON SOURCES

The potential bibliography of the non-military side of the First World War is enormous. Almost every non-specialised publication relating to the years 1914–1918 has some bearing on civil conditions on the Home Fronts of the belligerents; and there is a vast accumulation of works covering the war's political, economic and industrial aspects. But since my main purpose has been to describe everyday life on the Home Fronts and show how the war affected the ordinary non-combatant civilian, I have not dealt with these political and other facets any more deeply than is necessary to make intelligible what is predominantly a social history of the period. Nevertheless, a basic and essential foundation for any non-military history of the war is the *Economic and Social History of the World War*, the many-volumed and very comprehensive series sponsored by the Carnegie Endowment for International Peace. Another invaluable work is *The War behind the War: a History of the Political and Social Fronts*, by Frank P. Chambers, which covers in a masterly way, but largely at government level, the civil affairs of all the main belligerents.

These apart, I have mostly had recourse to a wide array of material, contemporary where possible and reflecting the day-to-day course of wartime events, ranging from newspapers and other periodicals to diaries. Among the latter can be mentioned: for Britain, *In London during the Great War*, by the journalist Michael MacDonagh; the *War Diary* of Lord Riddell; *From Day to Day*, by Lord Sandhurst. For France, I have found useful *The Paris Front*, by Michel Corday; *Histoire d'une Vie*, by Henry Bordeaux; *Journal d'une Ouvrière Parisienne*, by Louise Delétang. For Germany, there are Princess Blücher's *An English Wife in Berlin*; Mrs E. D. Bullitt's *An Uncensored Diary from the Central Empires*. There are also a number of memoirs from all three countries, such as Stephen McKenna's *While I Remember*, Mrs Sylvia Pankhurst's militantly anti-war *The Home Front*, Mrs C. S. Peel's *How We Lived Then*, and Caroline Playne's *Society at War* and *Britain Holds On*, Ernest Gay's *Paris Héroique*, J. M. de Beaufort's *Behind the German Veil*, the Duchess of Pless's memoir *By Herself*, and James Gerard's *My Four Years in Germany*.

Political diaries and memoirs I have not greatly used, but some, like Lloyd George's *War Memoirs*, Raymond Poincaré's *Au Service de la France*, and Prince Max of Baden's *Memoirs* have provided me with useful impressions. Among more general works I have found very illuminating the twelve-volume *The Great War*, edited by H. W. Wilson and J. A. Hammerton, with its contemporary articles covering the war in detail at both front and rear, in various countries. There are, too, revealing glimpses of the Home Front from the writings of some serving soldiers, like Robert Graves's *Goodbye to All That* and Edmund Blunden's *Undertones of War*.

On a wider historical level, there are the valuable *The Deluge: British Society and the First World War*, by Arthur Marwick; *English History, 1914–1945*, by A. J. P. Taylor, *The Development of Modern France, 1870–1939*, by Denis Brogan; and the German work of A. Mendelssohn-Bartholdy, *The War and German Society*.

The illustrations are all reproduced from originals in the Radio Times Hulton Picture Library.

Prologue

THE END OF PEACE

JULY 1914: in Britain, France and Germany it was a time of holiday. The 'season' was ending and fashionable folk were leaving town for spas, country estates and smart resorts. On the beaches of Brighton, Boulogne, and the Baltic, ordinary people were basking in the golden sunshine of the most brilliant summer for years. Superficially, the general mood appeared as carefree and the scene as pacific as in any previous July. It was as if this were just one more summer in Europe's long span of unbroken peace. But appearances belied the reality. Since the end of June, when the Austrian Archduke Franz Ferdinand and his consort had been shot down by a Bosnian student on a street corner in the Bosnian town of Sarajevo, European peace had been in growing jeopardy. Trouble in the Balkans was nothing new, and at first the gravity of the affair had been largely discounted in the West, where in any case each nation had its own internal preoccupations. There were optimistic hopes that it would blow over or be settled by diplomatic means. But instead, amid growing anxiety in the Chancelleries of Europe, it had swiftly intensified into a major crisis until, in the last days of July, its fateful issue had become unavoidable. While the people played on and their leaders strove belatedly but impotently to avert the coming catastrophe, Europe was plunged from peace into war.

With Europe's nations linked by alliances and understandings or alienated by rivalries and conflicting interests, war, like peace, was indivisible.[1] So the war moves, once started, spread across Europe like an epidemic, involving country after country and gathering speed in their course. On the 23rd July

Austria-Hungary, backed by Germany, presented Serbia (alleged to be responsible for the assassinations) with an ultimatum; on the 28th Austria declared war on Serbia; on the 1st August Germany declared war on Serbia's ally, Russia, and invaded Luxembourg; on the 2nd Germany presented an ultimatum to Belgium; on the 3rd Germany declared war on France; and on the 4th Britain declared war on Germany. As the armies mobilised and began to march – committed now to irreversible plans and time-tables – Britons, Frenchmen and Germans awoke, half incredulous, to the grim truth. Nowhere had the man-in-the-street thought it would really come to this. Even the national leaders seemed caught unawares. In late July the German Emperor was on a yachting trip in the Norwegian fiords; the French President and Prime Minister were visiting St Petersburg; and on Saturday 25th Sir Edward Grey, British Foreign Secretary, and all his colleagues left London for the country, more concerned with the imminent threat of civil war in Northern Ireland than with the international crisis. According to David Lloyd George, then Chancellor of the Exchequer, the British Cabinet had not even discussed the crisis before 24th July.[2]

The mounting tension brought with it a surge of war-fever – the hysteria and jingoism that filled the streets with cheering crowds, the fears that set prices soaring, closed the stock exchanges and precipitated a rush of food-hoarding. First to be affected was Germany, more immediately involved in the crisis than France or Britain. On the night of the 25th July, when Austria's ultimatum to Serbia expired, huge throngs paraded Berlin's Unter den Linden and demonstrated outside the Reichstag and Austrian Embassy. Serbian flags were burned and Serbian residents attacked. Two days later the Emperor returned to Potsdam from his cruise, to be greeted by cheering thousands. At night the streets echoed to the strains of 'Deutschland, Deutschland über Alles'. Silver and small change began to disappear, and bank depositors made large withdrawals of gold. Customers queued to remove their savings from the municipal banks, Stock Exchange values slumped disastrously and by the 29th, when paper money was refused in the provinces, people were crowding to Berlin in search of gold. That evening several private banks suspended payment. Meanwhile food prices rose steeply as anxious citizens rushed to buy provisions.

France began to be fully alerted on the 29th, when President Poincaré and the Premier, M. Viviani, returned unexpectedly to Paris from their curtailed State visit to Russia. Welcomed like the Kaiser at Potsdam, they drove to the Elysée Palace through cheering crowds. As in Germany, there was a sudden run on the banks and a shortage of gold and small currency; and as a precaution the Paris Bourse closed. But in Britain, though the press had issued sober warnings on the crisis from 25th July onwards, the reaction had been slower. As always, the Channel seemed to be isolating the country from continental dangers. Austria's declaration of war on Serbia caused deepening concern; but only on the 31st, with the raising of the Bank Rate to 8%, the closing of the London Stock Exchange and an announcement about possible currency regulations, was the public shocked into the realisation that war might be imminent.

Meanwhile, in Germany, events were approaching a climax. That same day a special early edition of the afternoon papers announced that the Kaiser had decreed a state of siege throughout all Germany except Bavaria, and that he was returning at once from Potsdam to Berlin. He reached his palace at 3 p.m., his car surrounded by wildly cheering crowds. Within two hours Germany's civil government had disappeared and the military had taken over. All banks and public buildings were guarded by sentries with fixed bayonets, and armed police moved in to close food shops that were contravening the price-regulation orders and to enforce the acceptance of paper money. Soon after six the Kaiser, with all his family, appeared on the balcony of his palace to make an address. When the thunderous acclaim of the waiting crowds had died down, he gave a short but ominous speech. 'This is a dark day and a dark hour', he said. '... The sword is being forced into my hand . . . This war will demand of us enormous sacrifice in life and money, but we shall show our foes what it is to provoke Germany.'[3]

As the German ultimatum to Russia, presented a few hours before, was due to expire before midnight, this was a virtual announcement of war. Throughout that night and next day, the 1st August, Berliners crowded the streets, waiting tensely for the next move – the order for general mobilisation. Nothing significant happened until 5.30 p.m. when the Imperial Chancellor, Herr von Bethmann-Hollweg, was seen to emerge from the Foreign Office in the Wilhelmstrasse carrying a white paper and drive with the Foreign Secretary, Herr von Jagow, to the Royal Palace. Taking this to be the mobilisation order, expectant crowds flocked around the palace entrance, while from the nearby cathedral in the great square fronting the palace the bells tolled for war service as on the outbreak of the Franco-Prussian war in 1870. Soon after, a policeman appeared at the gates to announce mobilisation. The massed assembly thereupon broke into the hymn 'Now thank we all our God'. Meanwhile the news was carried down the Unter den Linden by officers standing up in cars, brandishing handkerchiefs and shouting 'Mobilisation!' to the cheering crowds. Special news-sheets were rushed on to the streets bearing the proclamation 'The Emperor has ordered a general mobilisation of all the armed forces of the Empire'.

Next day, Sunday the 2nd, 30,000 civilians and called-up reservists gathered at an open-air service in the Konigsplatz. As the Lord's Prayer was recited, the congregation following the chaplain sentence by sentence, emotions overflowed. Women wept and men hid their faces. Then, accompanied by the military band, the vast crowd sang the famous hymn 'Niederlaendische Dankgebet', which one hundred years before had celebrated Napoleon's defeat on the field of Waterloo. At the end of the service the congregation had to depart on foot as all public transport and even taxis were besieged by reservists travelling to their depots. But now at last the tension of recent days was relaxed. That night a brittle gaiety prevailed and

Berlin's cafés, dance halls and theatres, almost empty for a week, were as full as at the season's height. Yet, to mark the underlying uncertainty, gold and silver were now being hoarded to the point where they practically vanished from circulation.

In France, meanwhile, the crisis atmosphere had heightened ominously. Her involvement in war now seemed certain, as on the 31st July, she, like Russia, had received Germany's ultimatum. Next day the French President answered the challenge by proclaiming to a grave and sober nation a state of siege throughout France and Algeria; and in the afternoon, on the walls of town halls, post offices and schools throughout the country, policemen and municipal employees fixed the orders for general mobilisation – matching Germany's order, made almost simultaneously. Though this was not to take effect until midnight, already that evening groups of Frenchmen, bundles on their shoulders, were marching to the railway stations and depots, watched by weeping women. As in Germany, the order wrought an immediate and total transformation. Next day, with mobilisation in full swing, France's able-bodied males were flocking to the colours from shops, offices, factories, farms and the public services. In Paris, notably, transport came almost to a halt. One observer described the whole town as on foot, queuing outside food shops or banks, or accompanying reservists to the Gare de l'Est, the rail terminal that was the capital's chief gateway to the front.

Unlike Berlin, Paris on the brink of war saw no huge demonstrations and cheering crowds. For a few nights bands of young men paraded the boulevards chanting the Marseillaise, but in general there was little of the hysteria that marked the start of the Franco-Prussian war of 1870. Only at the leave-takings with the troops did real enthusiasm erupt. In the streets marching columns were pelted with flowers, and the 'Farewells of the Gare de l'Est', with their songs and war-slogans, were a feature of these hours. But in the country districts the mood at the troops' departure, it was recorded, was strangely different. No crowds or bands saw off the small contingents of village reservists: instead those remaining asked themselves anxiously who would finish the harvest now that almost all the able-bodied men had gone.

Across the Channel, Saturday, 1st August, marked the start of Britain's Bank Holiday week-end. But with Germany's ultimatum threats to Russia and France, and France and Germany mobilising, the usual festive spirit was sadly damped. One reaction to the grave news, perhaps encouraged by the report that provision prices in Germany had risen by 75%, was a rush to buy up food. People were seen loading cars and taxis with provisions, and one London firm reported eight days' business done in one day. In consequence prices were rising and some shops began rationing goods. Alarm in the money markets mounted and the Bank Rate now soared to 10%. Outside the Bank of England customers were queuing to get gold, and ready cash was becoming short. Sunday was a day of ever-sharpening tension. The daily papers issued special editions, and in Piccadilly Circus avid readers snatched the copies from the newsboys' hands. By mid-day it was known that the Germans had invaded Luxembourg. There was shocked speculation as to where Britain stood now, and all attention was concentrated on the Prime Minister, Mr Asquith, and his Cabinet, in session in Downing Street since early morning. At an emergency meeting of financial leaders, called by the Chancellor of the Exchequer, the Bank Holiday was extended by three days. That night, spurred by patriotic fervour in the face of the gathering storm, the first crowds assembled outside Buckingham Palace to sing Rule Britannia, the Marseillaise and the National Anthem.

Bank Holiday Monday saw Britain tensely poised between peace and war. Overnight Germany had delivered another shock – her ultimatum to Belgium demanding free passage of her troops. At their picnics on the beaches and in the parks the holiday thousands discussed the sombre tidings and wondered what would happen next. The outgoing trains were filled with aliens recalled to their own countries, an exodus which left many hotels and restaurants suddenly bereft of their staffs.

At Buckingham Palace the King said goodbye to his foreign chef. Sporting events like Cowes Regatta were abandoned and a general moratorium was announced. But the central scene of that sunny summer day was London's Parliament Square, where in the afternoon a cheering multitude greeted members of the Government as they arrived to hear the Foreign Secretary deliver the fateful speech which would state Britain's attitude in the crisis and define her commitments to threatened Belgium. Crowds in light holiday garb packed Whitehall, through which threaded taxi-loads of young men chanting the Marseillaise. Street traders did a roaring trade selling Union Jacks. And that evening the Prime Minister, on his way to the House of Lords, was cheered to the echo.

Meanwhile the sands had run out for France. At 7 p.m. she received Germany's declaration of war. In Paris, as the news broke, angry crowds attacked German and Austrian shops; but soon, with a curfew placed on all cafés and restaurants and the banning of loiterers from the streets, an uneasy quiet descended on the city. By contrast, Berlin was in jubilant mood, its brasseries and entertainment places thronged late into the night, its streets filled with excited, singing crowds whose war-fever had mounted steadily since the proclamation of a state of siege three days before.

On Tuesday, 4th August, came the last moves in the drama that sealed the doom of European peace. At a ceremonial session of the Reichstag in the Imperial Palace, Berlin, the Emperor – a short, slight figure in grey-green military uniform, wearing the Prussian pickel-haube helmet – read a solemn address justifying German actions and appealing for German unity in the face of the coming danger. In Paris, amid scenes of great enthusiasm, President Poincaré addressed the National Assembly, announcing an *Union Sacrée* (a truce between opposing political parties) and implementing the state of siege, which meant the assumption by the Government of unlimited powers. Finally, from London went Britain's ultimatum to Germany respecting Belgium – for whose inviolability Britain stood guarantor – with the demand for a reply by 11 o'clock that night.[4] As Big Ben boomed the hour and no sign came from the Ministers gathered in No 10 Downing Street, the waiting crowd outside delivered its own declaration. Quickly dispersing, it ran into Whitehall shouting almost hysterically 'War! War! War!'

So after a brief thirteen days of threats and ultimatums, demands and démarches, a mounting intransigence which defied all conciliation efforts, Europe was engulfed in war. The longest peace the continent had known for centuries was shattered. But in the last decade that peace had become increasingly precarious. Clashing ambitions, piling armaments and the sabre-rattling of power politics had produced a dangerously inflammable situation. The strains and stresses between the nations were matched by discords and unrest within them. Beneath the deceptively smiling surface of this last summer of peace, disruptive forces were on the move everywhere. But if European war, when it actually came, seemed unexpected and was even unwanted, once the gauntlet had been thrown down the challenge was eagerly accepted. Yet even as the cheers rang out in Berlin, Paris and London, there was a woeful ignorance among the belligerents, disarmed as they were by long years without conflict, of what twentieth-century war between industrialised nations would involve, for civilians as well as armies in the field. In the general euphoria of the war's first hours there were few who did not think it would be over by Christmas. No one realised that it would bring the end of an era.

Part One

1914: 'HOME BY CHRISTMAS'

Chapter 1

GOD IS ON BOTH SIDES

THE German Army invaded Belgium in the early hours of 4th August. Operating according to the 'Schlieffen Plan', it aimed at cutting into Northern France, west of Paris, by-passing the capital and encircling the French forces. But as the German drive neared the capital the plan started to miscarry; and the French were saved by the Battle of the Marne early in September. The initial war of movement was halted, and through the autumn the opposing sides settled into a static trench-bound front stretching from the Channel to the Swiss border.

In East Prussia, the Germans scored a resounding victory by defeating the advancing Russians at Tannenberg at the end of August and at the Masurian Lakes at the beginning of September. Farther south the Russians occupied all Austrian Galicia before the Austro-Hungarian Army was able to form a stable defence line.

Everywhere the onset of war had started a great homeward trek of holiday-makers, emptying the crowded beaches and country haunts almost overnight. In Germany, under military rule since 31st July, returning travellers received short shrift. Trains were seized and luggage unceremoniously thrown out, leaving wayside stations strewn with holiday trunks, folding prams and bundles of spades. Meanwhile at her gay summer resorts, with guests, waiters and hotel-keepers gone, life seemed to stop. In riverside retreats the fleets of small pleasure boats lay idle, their cushions piled and engines tarpaulin-covered.

The countryside itself, without either visitors or workers, looked abandoned. Half-laden wagons stood in the fields, here a ladder stood against an unfinished rick. Often the sole sign of activity was an armed sentry guarding a bridge or level crossing. Within a week the inertia had spread from farms to factories, forced to close through lack of men and transport.

A vivid picture of Germany in these hours is given by Princess Blücher, an Englishwoman married to a German nobleman, who travelled from England to Germany on 6th August: 'A confused vision of . . . anxious-eyed travellers, yellow corn-fields and groups of sunburnt peasants, women pausing in their work and staring with hand-shaded eyes, as again and again we were forced to stop to let the never-ending procession of troop-filled trains hurry by on their way to the West; shouts of enthusiasm, fluttering of handkerchiefs, bursts of song, flushed eager faces of soldiers, field-grey uniforms, white-robed girls and women with the Red Cross on their arms, offering food and drink to the thirsty men. And all this, which might be some great national festival, means but the entry of death and foul disaster.'[1]

In France the general scene was similar, though perhaps less wildly enthusiastic. With the railways commandeered and packed troop trains rolling eastwards day and night, home-going civilians waited hours for almost non-existent transport. No Frenchman, in town or country, could be unaware that civil life was being rigorously subordinated to military needs. And in Britain, if the move to a war footing was less drastic and immediate, the staring newspaper headlines of 5th August – 'Britain at War!' – shocked returning holiday-makers and people going to work into full realisation of the catastrophe that had struck them. That day, while the first emergency legislation that would fundamentally change and restrict their lives was already taking effect, there was a renewed and almost panic rush of food hoarding. Though the King and Queen set an example by ordering simple living at the royal table, London stores were besieged by women with long shopping lists, and in the suburbs women loaded with parcels were stopped by others and roughly deprived of their purchases. Food delivery-vans were held up and their contents rifled. It was a typical reaction on the part of people long accustomed to peace, who did not know what the future would bring but were preparing for the worst.

If neither Britain, France nor Germany had actually desired war, all three countries were buoyed by the conviction that their cause was right. To the British it was largely a matter of 'honour' and 'justice'. Finally stirred to fighting pitch by Germany's violation of Belgian neutrality, they looked on Germany as an aggressor determined on world domination, an enemy that must be confronted and beaten. The French, traditional foes of their stronger and more populous neighbour Germany, and ever mindful of their humiliating defeat in the war of 1870, now saw their chance for the revenge (*revanche*) for which they had waited and prepared ever since. For them the mystical concept of '*La Patrie*' dominated everything. The Germans, so far from feeling themselves the aggressors, believed that they were fighting for their existence as a people, a belief strengthened by what they regarded as perfidious intervention against them of the British, a people of similar race to themselves.

To support their arms, both sides unhesitatingly invoked the Deity. The attitude of Britain's Established Church was one of total acceptance of the war. Britain was imbued with the idea that she was somehow acting as the agent of a divine power in a struggle from which she would emerge spiritually stronger and more united than before the war. According to the militant feminist, Mrs Sylvia Pankhurst, the clergy were even circularised regarding the line their serious sermons should take.[2] In October the Archbishop of York declared that every man who respected his conscience must 'stand to his place until the war was ended'.[3] In Germany the Protestant Church, being dominated by the State, especially in Prussia, was automatically aligned with the war leaders. Pastors of the Prussian State Church, having on entry sworn an oath of equal allegiance to their King (who was also the German

Emperor) and State, had no alternative but to proclaim that the Almighty was on the side of Germany, and this they did with strong and unanimous voice. As the war progressed, their preachings against Britain – and the United States – were to increase in bloodthirstiness and venom.

In each country the immediate effect of war was to banish internal differences and unite dissenting elements in a common bond of loyalty: in face of the danger without, party conflicts were shelved and current political issues put aside. This sudden closing of the ranks was achieved against a background of profound social change and ferment, even instability, that over recent years had affected all three countries and to some extent left them with a potential weakness. How far the new-found unanimity would stand the test of total war, with its promise of unprecedented ordeals, privations and reverses, remained to be seen.

Britain had just emerged from the Edwardian era. So far from being the tranquil golden age of nostalgic legend, this was a time of social ferment and restless doubt and questioning. Across the whole national spectrum old ideas were giving place to new. Though pride in King and country were still as strong as ever, traditional faith in the more jingoistic brand of British imperialism had been shaken by the Boer War of 1899–1902. The social conscience was stirred by the continuing contrasts between wealth and poverty, the lavish luxury enjoyed by the few and the grinding want endured by the more depressed industrial workers. There was a sharpening awareness of class inequalities, concepts of morality were changing, agitation was mounting on behalf of women's rights, the Labour movement was gathering strength and militancy and political freedoms were hotly debated. This controversial campaigning atmosphere had persisted into the reign of Edward's successor, George V, preoccupying ordinary Britons virtually to the exclusion of foreign affairs. In 1914 the public was currently exercised by problems of Trade Union unrest, women's suffrage and Irish Home Rule. But when war erupted, these issues were immediately forgotten. Apart from the anti-war attitude of certain Government members, some sections of the Liberal press and a small pacifist minority, Britain stood united against the enemy.

France was in worse case than Britain. After her defeat in 1871 she had risen with a reborn national pride as embodied in her newly-created Third Republic. To ensure that she should never again be invaded by Germany she had introduced universal conscription. Military service had been invested with an almost mystical aura of patriotism. It was France's dream that one day her army would recover the provinces of Alsace and Lorraine, lost in 1871. But over the years, with the opportunities for military activity few and far between, pride in the army had wilted – and with it patriotic fervour. Anti-militarist feeling had grown, fostered by the Dreyfus affair (in which the army, wrongly accusing a Jewish officer in 1894, of treason and ruining his career, was badly discredited) and the growth of international socialism. The first decade of the twentieth century had seen grave social and labour unrest. A chronic weakness of political leadership led to a run of ten ministries between 1909 and 1914. And as war approached, France was a country beset by party conflicts, tainted by revolutionary anarchism, lacking firm government and with her national finances severely disordered. In 1914 she was deeply split on the issue of three-year military service, a measure violently opposed by the Socialists. But this, along with all other differences, was swept aside in the *Union Sacrée* of August 1914. As a token of the solidarity of this truce, there was no implementation of the notorious Carnet B, by which 3,000 known anarchists and agitators were to have been detained in the event of war.

Germany, since her victorious war of 1870, had been an Imperial State (consisting of Prussia, three other kingdoms and a collection of duchies and principalities) ruled by an Emperor who was also Supreme War Lord and King of Prussia, and by his all-powerful Imperial Chancellor. Welded together by the Imperial constitution of its first Chancellor,

Bismarck, the country had progressed under a regime that was rigidly autocratic compared with those of France or Britain. But changing times had altered the predominantly agricultural pattern of the national life. Industrial development had increasingly drawn Germans from the land, creating a new class of workers, who had become unsettled by their conditions and discontented at their relative lack of representation in an electoral system which favoured the old rural constituencies. In the first decade of the twentieth century, only Germany's booming prosperity had averted a social crisis. Meanwhile the industrial workers' cause was being championed by the Social Democrats, who had become the chief opposition in the Reichstag and in 1912 represented a third of the German people. Campaigning on a radical programme, the Social Democrats demanded democratic reforms, new suffrage laws, relief from the heavy burden of militarism. In this divided mood Germany reached the eve of war. Within days of its outbreak there was a massive Socialist anti-war demonstration in Berlin. But again, war itself brought a solid front of political unity. In the Reichstag there was a unanimous vote for war-credits – the only concession of the Social Democrats to their previous anti-war attitude was the stipulation that the war should be strictly one of defence.

On both sides the outburst of patriotism was accompanied by a wave of xenophobic spy-mania. Suddenly every foreigner seemed to be a sinister enemy agent. In early August German police stations were crowded with aliens, most of them tourists caught by the outbreak of war and arrested as spies. It was said that the possession of a well-cut coat, a well-filled wallet and notably a motor-car was enough to ensure immediate imprisonment as a spy. Englishmen in particular were ill-treated by police and threatened in the street, and many were sent, regardless of age or sex, to the dreaded Spandau fortress. Even if not arrested and interned, hundreds of English teachers in Berlin were left stranded and penniless.

The fever was equally rampant in Britain, whose large

German communities in London and elsewhere made a happy hunting ground. Many Germans had left at once for Germany, and those remaining had to register, a large number being interned then and later. Meanwhile, as the Government acted to arrest suspected spies, everywhere German tradesmen became targets for attack. There were wild stories that grocers were lacing their provisions with poison and barbers liable to cut their customers' throats. Suspicion fell on faithful and long-serving governesses, who were said to have bombs hidden in their trunks. In one case a child, hearing her parents discussing her German governess, was said to have asked anxiously: 'Oh Mummy, *must* we kill poor Fräulein?' Innocent people were harried – like the Swiss waiter who had sketched on a menu-card a plan of the dining-tables in a hotel dining-room and was hustled to Scotland Yard in the belief that he had been drawing a plan of military installations; or the West Country artist and his wife, arrested because he wore a soft, wide-brimmed hat and she an unfamiliar-looking coat. But occasionally suspicion appeared well-founded as in the case of the 'nurse' in the railway-carriage who, when she removed her gloves, was noted by a travelling-companion to have hands 'like a butcher', and was forthwith denounced and arrested.

It was widely reported that hard tennis courts and paved back gardens were in reality gun emplacements. And railway signalmen in their boxes, it was said, were being overpowered by roving bands of Germans. Most bizarre was the tale that the enamelled advertisement-plaques for the popular Maggi Soup, displayed on the hoardings in Belgium, concealed military information supplied by local traitors, which was being used by German officers.

Another current phenomenon was the spate of name-changing. In Britain many Germans, albeit naturalised, quickly adopted English names (Bernstein becoming Curzon, Steineker Stanley, Stohwasser Stowe, Rosenheim Rose, Schacht Dent). In France the Parisian thoroughfare Rue d'Allemagne became Rue Jean Jaurès, and it was proposed to alter the name Eau de Cologne to Eau de Provence. The movement went furthest in Germany, where the Berlin police chief, von Jagow, ordered the elimination of all foreign names and words. Many famous English designations disappeared, like Hotel Bristol and London Bar: the Hotel Westminster became Lindenhof and the Café Piccadilly became Vaterland. *Chauffeur* was transliterated to *schauffoer, reine claude* (gooseberry) became *raenekloder*. A large Berlin draper ran a competition for germanising the words confection, covert-coat, cheviot, *saison*, but most were found impossible to change satisfactorily. In Breslau the military governor ordered a confectioner to stop using the word *bonbon* – to be told that this would gladly be done if the officer would stop calling himself *general* (this too being a French word). Germany's wildest gesture was to come in May 1915, when Italy joined the Allies, and menus in Berlin restaurants changed 'Italian salad' to 'Traitors' salad'.

With the coming of war, the economic life of each country underwent a vast upheaval. The sudden disruption of normal financial dealings – banking, credit, foreign exchange – and overseas trade massively affected business, causing the closure of firms and factories and consequent unemployment, especially among women workers. Further dislocation was created by the reduction of the national labour forces through mobilisation, which itself left broken homes, deprived of bread-winning husbands, fathers and sons. This manpower drain was most serious in Germany and France, with their universal conscription. Within a few days some five million Germans and four million Frenchmen had reported for military service. In Britain, relying initially on her small voluntary regular army and territorial force – totalling 750,000 men – the loss was less wholesale. Meanwhile all three countries, in a mammoth drive to muster their resources for war, were taking urgent steps to control and direct industry, labour, food production and distribution, financial resources, prices, transport, the press, propaganda – and indeed the very lives of the civilian populations.

In Britain the emergency wartime measures were to be most

Newspaper placards in London, August 1914

Mobilisation of the French Army

Unter den Linden, Berlin, 4 August 1914

A run on the Berlin Savings Bank

drastic in the field of individual liberty, a historic privilege more jealously prized and guarded than in autocratic Germany or even Republican France. The state-of-siege proclamations of both the latter countries, which abolished democratic rights and established martial law, were for them less revolutionary than the measure that, along with the rest of the war legislation, affected British citizens in the first days of the war: the Defence of the Realm Act. In this enactment of the 8th August, passed by a tense House of Commons in all its stages in five minutes, the traditional freedoms of Britons were signed away at the stroke of a pen. 'DORA' as it was half-jocularly called, virtually suspended civil rights for the duration and put Britain too under martial law. It gave the executive almost unlimited powers, notably that to court-martial persons charged with breaking the many security regulations. By a subsequent provision it empowered the police to stop and question suspects, who could be imprisoned on refusal to answer, and arrest without warrant. As the war continued, DORA was to encroach, in a manner totally unprecedented, into every activity of British citizens, affecting their eating and drinking, their work, their freedom to go where they pleased, to write or speak as they wished.

But in one vital sphere personal liberty remained inviolate. Though Britain's most immediate need was for a greatly enlarged army to fight on the continent alongside her ally, France, Parliament firmly ruled out conscription. No Briton was to be forced to join the colours. Instead, sanction was given for an additional force of half a million volunteers. Soon, on the 6th August, appeared on British hoardings the classic poster 'Your King and Country Need *You!*', dominated by the frosty-eyed, heavily-moustached features and accusatory pointing finger of a British Field Marshal, Lord Kitchener. Straightaway the call was answered. From that day onwards throughout the autumn, the recruiting stations were besieged by thousands of young men, straw-hatted and cloth-capped, clerks, shop-assistants, factory workers, farm-hands, eager to enlist. In little over a month, 100,000 volunteers had been enrolled. It was a scene peculiar to Britain: in France and Germany, where compulsion reigned, mobilisation of the great conscript armies of trained reserves was completed with machine-like efficiency within a fortnight.

These first days of war were days of wildest rumour, bred of the same popular hysteria that saw spies everywhere. Britain buzzed with the story that a great battle had been fought in the North Sea and that the German Navy was at the bottom, or – alternatively – that all our own dreadnoughts were sunk. Likewise there was the famous 'snow-on-their-boots' myth of train-loads of Russians crossing England en route for France. In Germany it was said that French gold was being smuggled in cars through the country to Russia, and bands of armed villagers turned out to attack suspicious-looking vehicles. A married Englishwoman resident in Berlin was to note in mid-September that odd reports were circulating in the British press, as that the Russians were already near Berlin, while Berlin itself was in flames and in a state of starvation, panic and revolution. To some extent all this was due to the initial lack of firm war news. But even then the national news and propaganda media, recognised as potent war weapons, indispensable for manipulating the truth so as to sustain Home Front morale and influence neutral opinion, were being rigorously harnessed in all three countries.

In Germany, the newspapers, like all else, were under direct military control. The publication of military news was restricted to bare statements by the Press Department of the General Staff, which met newspaper editors thrice weekly in a large hall of the Reichstag. On non-military matters editors were regularly directed by Government officials as to what they should or should not say. There was no free expression of opinion, and papers which defied official directives were liable to suspension or suppression. The dictated propaganda-line was that the war had been 'instigated' by England to crush Germany, her dangerous and hated commercial rival, and that if she did not fight she would be quickly over-run by hordes of Russians and Frenchmen. Foreign correspondents were fed with propaganda from the Publicity Service of the Foreign Office (*Nachrichtendienst*), and allowed to dispatch only what the Government approved.

The French press, like the German, was under military control. No war news could be printed beyond the three daily communiqués issued by the Staff. Papers were restricted to one edition a day and had to be submitted to the military censorship in the Rue de Grenelle, Paris. Big headlines were vetoed, and newsboys forbidden to shout their wares in the streets. Press correspondents were banned from accompanying the army, and soldiers themselves were forbidden to mention military matters in their letters. Thanks to the pre-war existence of various national and international societies with wide foreign connections, France had ready-made channels for foreign propaganda.

Britain's press censorship, though less directly military than the others, was in effect almost as stringent. It was handled by the Press Bureau, set up on the 10th August (first under F. E. Smith, M.P. – who became Lord Birkenhead – and then under the journalist E. T. Cook) in the Royal United Services Institution building in Whitehall. The Bureau had two functions: to issue to papers the official war news supplied by the War Office and Admiralty, and to censor such war news as the papers independently obtained for themselves and submitted to the Bureau. But insofar as the papers were not obliged to pass their material to the Bureau, there seemed to be a weakness in the system. However, they were governed by the ultimate sanction of DORA, under which they could be prosecuted – and faced suspension or suppression – for publishing any restricted military information as well as false statements regarding the war. This was a strong incentive to get preliminary clearance from the Bureau.

It was in the converted lecture-theatre of the Institution that representatives of London and provincial dailies attended day and night to receive and transmit the war news to their papers. But while all facts were at the mercy of the British censorship, the British press differed from the French and German in having no censorship of opinion. Thus far DORA did not go.

In the home propaganda field Britain started early and energetically. In a great pictorial poster campaign, spearheaded by Kitchener's famous appeal, the walls of Britain were placarded with calls for recruits by well-known artists – like that of Sir Frank Brangwyn, depicting Belgians walking among the victims of German violence. At the beginning of September the Prime Minister, Mr Asquith, in a rallying speech at London's Guildhall, told the nation why Britain was fighting. 'The conflict in which we are now engaged', he declared, 'is not merely a material but a spiritual one ... Responsibility for all the illimitable sufferings which now confront the world belongs to one Power, and one Power only, and that Power is Germany.' This was the commencement of a sustained effort by poster, newspaper, book, pamphlet and even song, that was to continue through the war. A vast amount of the output was unofficial, ranging from soberly written series of explanatory booklets like those of the Oxford Pamphlets and the publications of the Victoria League, to single sheets of patriotic verse such as that entitled 'The Day', reprinted (without date) from the *Daily Express*. Heavily edged with a margin of red, white and blue, 'The Day' declaimed against Germany in Kiplingesque style ('A poem such as this lifts its author to the rank of a national poet,' asserted the *Daily Express*). One verse ran:

> 'You have sown for the Day, you have grown for the Day;
> Yours is the Harvest red.
> Can you hear the groans and the awful cries?
> Can you see the heap of slain that lies,
> And sightless turned to the flame-lit skies
> The glassy eyes of the dead?'

Up to 1916, when military conscription was introduced, the campaign concentrated mainly on recruiting. The accent was powerfully on King and Country. It was in 1914 that 'God Save the King' was for the first time regularly played in theatres and cinemas, and 'Land of Hope and Glory' became almost a second national anthem. Recruiting committees sprang up everywhere, and typical of their appeals was that of the London

Parliamentary Recruiting Committee: 'There are Three Types of Men. Those who Hear the Call and Obey: Those who Delay: and – The *Others*. To Which Do You Belong?'[4] Military bands paraded the streets attracting columns of volunteers to the recruiting stations. Clergy from their pulpits called on young men to join the colours. Songs like 'We don't want to lose you, but we think you ought to go', feelingly intoned from the music-hall stages, became immensely popular. But in addition the press constantly featured advertisements for munition workers – calling on the patriotism of private employers. 'Have you a man serving at your table,' asked one, 'who should be serving a gun? Have you a man preserving your game who should be helping to preserve your country?'[5] Later, when the food position became difficult, a great drive would be mounted towards food economy.

British propaganda to the neutrals was managed by the War Propaganda Bureau, a Foreign Office department established at Wellington House in London before the end of 1914. In 1917 the Bureau was to be expanded and moved to the Foreign Office; but enemy-directed propaganda was not to be seriously organised until 1918, when Lord Northcliffe set up at Crewe House as Director of Propaganda in Enemy Countries.

Meanwhile, as the armies clashed in the first great battles and the people at home moved to war conditions, the civilian scene was being transformed. In Britain, the landing of whose Expeditionary Force in France was completed by 16th August, there were the recruiting posters meeting the eye at every turn, the increasingly familiar presence of khaki, the queues waiting to enlist, the squads of motley-garbed volunteers drilling on the commons and in the parks and squares, the bridges, tunnels and railway stations guarded by the new 'specials' – the volunteer special constables – with their blue and white armlets and whistles, the trenches dug on the coast. Cars and taxis were fewer in the streets. County cricket was no more and golf courses were mostly deserted – though professional football and racing continued. Unemployment, particularly of women and girls, was rising owing to the business slump. In the smart shopping areas firms like dressmakers and art dealers were notoriously hard-hit, and many hotel-keepers at the now deserted holiday resorts found their living suddenly gone.

September brought a compulsory dimming of street lamps and shop lights. London at night, seen from the Hampstead heights, now presented a subdued glow – the prelude to a later almost total blackness. The London theatres adapted themselves to the war mood with patriotic plays like *Tommy Atkins* and *England Expects*. With the passing weeks the women's papers, which had at first continued to feature extravagant peacetime fashions, turned to more sober themes like wartime economy and women's work in war. Smart clothes gave way to plainer garb. There were the growing casualty lists, and the daily sight of ambulances leaving Charing Cross with their wounded, greeted in the courtyard by the flower-women with bunches of violets and the cry 'God bless you, lads!', while across the Strand, outside Charing Cross Hospital, hung the banner, with its sobering injunction 'Quiet for the Wounded'. But elsewhere, peacetime traditions died hard. At the Lord Mayor's banquet at the Guildhall in November, turtle soup was served as usual, champagne flowed freely and white-coated stewards carved the time-honoured barons of beef.[6]

A month later Britain awoke to the reality of war with the bombardment of the North-East coast by enemy warships. On a grey morning in mid-December, shells rained down on Hartlepool, Scarborough and Whitby, causing seven hundred casualties. The nation was shocked and incredulous. It seemed unbelievable, as one writer put it, that an English girl at Scarborough should be killed by Germans while cleaning a doorstep! It was perhaps a salutary lesson for a population still, as evidenced by the absence of military conscription, making less than a total war effort; a people still, despite the strides being made in converting to war production, too much governed by the maxim 'Business as usual'.

In France and Germany, more totally committed and

regimented (to say nothing of France's own soil being a battleground), the war mood was sterner, the signs starker. Paris, in the sultry heat of that mid-August, was like a big provincial city, its gay Allied flags hanging listless, its tourists and foreigners departed, its daytime bustle stilled and with its night-life dead, its streets almost deserted after dark and echoing to the footsteps of the few late pedestrians. Transport was seriously reduced. A predominant sound in the general quiet was the klaxon note of speeding Red Cross ambulances. The big stores were empty, and behind the counters sat the girl assistants sewing shirts and bandages for the troops. Many smaller shops, here and in the provinces, were shuttered, their owners and staff mobilised. Though food was plentiful – at grossly increased prices – the worsening war news of late August produced a sudden access of austerity in the shedding of fashionable fripperies and cessation of social entertaining.

With September came fresh alarms, as the swiftly advancing Germans threatened Paris itself. While President Poincaré stoutly proclaimed '*Durer et tenir*' (Hold and endure), crowds of anxious refugees – fugitives from Northern France and Belgium mingling with Parisians – besieged the city's railway termini, struggling to make their way south. On the 3rd the Government left for Bordeaux, accelerating the mass exodus which now totalled one million. That same day a poster appeared on the city's walls, signed by the new military governor, General Gallieni: 'Army of Paris, citizens of Paris . . . I have received the order to defend Paris against the invader. This order I shall carry out to the end.' An iron military rule now descended on the capital. Its gates were barricaded, café terraces closed and a curfew imposed on places of entertainment. Processions were forbidden and the sale of absinthe – a popular French drink – prohibited. The big hotels were converted into hospitals, though these remained empty (the wounded being kept out of Paris at this time for morale reasons). The capital took on an air of vast emptiness. As an observer noted, it had become 'a city of women', many of them in deepest mourning. The only patrons of the cafés seemed to be nurses, soldiers and workers. With buses and even taxis commandeered to rush troops to the front, a few old horse-cabs plied the boulevards. At the end of September the first bombs fell on Paris, causing one casualty. Meanwhile uncertainties were increased by the rigid censorship which banned mention of all unfavourable news. The city's preparations to withstand siege were demonstrated by the strange sight of thousands of cattle grazing in the Bois de Boulogne.

While Paris and the nation waited tensely, a few score miles from the capital the crucial battle of the Marne had been fought and won; and by the end of October, with the enemy advance halted and the front stabilising, the city's worst emergency was over. Parisians started drifting back (though the Government remained in Bordeaux until mid-December), some shops and restaurants reopened and there were halting signs of returning normality. But Paris in late autumn was still a city darkly shadowed by war. Mourning was now widespread – worn by women for any relation, close or distant, killed 'on the field of honour' – and dressmakers displayed notices advertising the prompt delivery of mourning clothes. There was a big demand for mourning brooches and other trinkets in black beads or jet. The streets, ill-served with transport, were still half-empty and all public buildings, like museums, closed. Parties and social entertaining remained taboo, and evening dress was banished. A patch of lighter relief was provided by the recently reopened cinemas and theatres, the productions of the latter, whether revue, satire or comedy, being under strict military censorship. And now, whereas earlier there had been little sign of troops in the capital beyond the recruits drilling in the Place des Invalides, Paris began to be brought to life again by numbers of men on leave who filled the amusement places.

From the first the scene in Germany had reflected the nation's total mobilisation for war. Already in August, Berlin's trams were manned by women, electric street lighting was severely limited for the sake of economy, benzol was being used instead of petrol and traffic restrictions had almost ended night life.

As regards public entertainment, the heavy hand of censorship soon stepped in, insisting on the music of cafés and dance-halls being 'suitable' to the occasion: thus ragtime was banned and songs had to be serious or patriotic, while theatrical performances likewise had to show a warlike or patriotic spirit, musical comedy was virtually banned and pressure was brought on the popular *cafés chantants* and cabarets to close altogether. Along with these disappeared – in the name of the 'gravity' now being demanded of the German people – the Saturday and Sunday dances beloved of German maid-servants.

Unemployment was rife, especially in garrison towns where tradesmen had largely relied on army patronage. Lodging-house keepers, bereft of their numerous foreign working-class lodgers, found themselves penniless. As in France and Britain thousands of girl workers were suddenly unemployed, and cheap kitchens had to be set up all over Berlin to feed these and other unfortunates. Meanwhile, with farm workers everywhere called up, a nation-wide campaign was started for townspeople to gather the harvest. Free rail tickets were issued to take them to the farm areas, and even schoolboys were conscripted. Late in August, when normal rail services were partially resumed, Berliners and others were crowding to the country, their luggage a single blanket to supplement the rough straw bedding provided in the barns.

The public mood was almost extravagantly patriotic. In Berlin, troops marching to the station were joined in their singing of 'The Watch on the Rhine' by passers-by and people rushing from their houses, until the strains of the song rang through the streets. 'The whole life of the Germany of today' wrote an observer, 'seems to move to the rhythm of this tune.'[7] But with the patriotic enthusiasm grew another sentiment: a consuming hatred directed against England. Animosity towards the enemy was obviously an indispensable element in war, and thus the August ban against speaking English on the telephone or in public places – together with all the other anti-British gestures – was understandable. But German 'hate' went far beyond this: officially inspired and fostered, it was deliberately designed as part of the civilian-war effort.

The campaign started with the adoption of a virtually new National Anthem, the 'Hymn of Hate' against England. This was composed by a minor German poet named Ernest Lissauer, serving as a private in the army, and it soon earned him the Iron Cross. Spreading through Germany like wildfire, it was sung and recited in every café and music-hall, and for a time supplanted the traditional battle-hymn 'Deutschland über Alles'. Its first verse ran as follows:[8]

> 'French and Russians they matter not,
> A blow for a blow and a shot for a shot;
> We love them not, we hate them not,
> We hold the Vistula and the Vosges-gate,
> We have but one and only hate,
> We love as one, we hate as one,
> We have one foe and one alone –
> ENGLAND! . . .'

Along with Lissauer's hymn appeared the new greeting between Germans, 'Gott strafe England!' This quickly achieved nation-wide popularity. It was rubber-stamped on letters, printed on millions of postcards and engraved on scarf-pins, cuff-links, brooches and wedding-rings. It figured on buttons and badges, handkerchiefs and domestic utensils, pocket-knives and even on the Imperially-coloured black-red-and-white braces provided for soldiers at the front. All this engineered hate was a natural sequel to the distortions put out by the German propaganda-machine both immediately before and on the outbreak of war, which (incompatibly) asserted first that Britain, immersed in her own difficulties, would never fight Germany, and then that Britain had instigated the war to crush Germany. But apart from this it reflected the bitter chagrin of the German leaders that Britain had, against all their expectations, intervened and was now presenting such a dangerous threat against them. In any case the hate-campaign, so much in tune with doctored German opinion, was taken up by the Germans with avidity.

No such organised phenomenon existed in France or Britain. The French had no need of it: they already regarded the Germans with a spontaneous, deep-seated almost racial hate. Britons, for their part, treated the German ravings with derision rather than anger. Their own 'hate', such as it was, initially expressed itself in little more than the sporadic smashing of German-owned property (and, it is said, the kicking of dachshunds). It was hardly more than an offshoot of the spy-fever that reached its climax of senselessness in October in the hounding of Prince Louis of Battenberg from his post as First Sea Lord – though one stupid symptom of anti-Germanism did appear in 1915 with the banning from Sir Thomas Beecham's Promenade Concerts of all German music. Likewise there was an outcry against the performance by choral societies of German works, until it was realised that the 'Messiah', 'Elijah', and other classics could no longer be heard. In Nice the French banned German music, except for a performance of Handel which was justified on the grounds that Handel really counted as an English musician.[9]

But Britain and France were as ready as Germany to use one powerful hate-weapon: the atrocity story. Soon various horrifying tales of cruelty were circulating on both sides, to intensify German hatred and shock and outrage the hitherto easy-going British. No matter that most were false – like the notorious story appearing in a Scottish paper of the young nurse in the Belgian hospital who had had both breasts cut off by the Germans and was left to die while the hospital was burned down; all were eagerly reported in the national presses and widely believed. In France and Britain such tales had a basic formula, involving the raping of nuns, impaling of babies on bayonets, mutilation of Belgian girls. German stories were similar, of cruelties perpetrated by Belgian women on helpless German prisoners, the use of dum-dum bullets by British soldiers and – among the most gruesome – the systematic gouging-out of captured German soldiers' eyes. There was said to be a whole hospital-ward full of such cases at Aix-le-Chapelle. Thus once again, in war, did truth become the first casualty.

One truth, however, was plain and inescapable. This war would not, as all wars had virtually been hitherto, be just a man's war. Total as its demands promised to be, it would be impossible to wage without the massive help of women. Apart from their time-honoured role of nursing, for which they would be needed as never before, on them must now fall the vital tasks of producing war materials, helping to run the farms and public services, performing multifarious clerical and other jobs, all the vast range of essential war work for which there were, or soon would be, no men available. The wholesale absorption of women into the war effort – the ladies of leisure who had never worked before, the housewives occupied at home, and the thousands already employed who had been displaced at the start of the war – was to be a revolutionary chapter in the story of women's emancipation, for within half a decade women in all three countries had as a result largely thrown off the inferiorities and inequalities they had endured for centuries.

In Britain the initial recruitment, for nursing, canteen-running, provision of troop comforts and so on, was entirely through voluntary bodies. Not until the great munition-making expansion of 1915 was there any Government drive for women war-workers. From then on the movement gathered speed and volume, to cover almost every war activity short of fighting. A remarkable feature of its early days was the readiness shown by women to co-operate – remarkable in that right up to the outbreak of war they had been in bitter conflict with men over the burning issue of female suffrage. But now, to their credit, they immediately declared a truce and aligned themselves with their erstwhile male enemies against the common foe. Henceforth, in increasing numbers, they were to discard their clinging, foot-swathing empire robes, their elaborate high-necked coats, their theatrical hats and turbans, for the nurse's uniform and later the factory worker's rough overall and the uniforms of the various women's military, naval and agricultural services.

French women, at war once more with their traditional enemy, were more emotionally affected and fiercely patriotic than their British counterparts. (As they were far less concerned with achieving female independence, there had been no initial risk of their withholding their full womanly co-operation with the war effort through frustration or sexual hostility.) A large section of them – those living on the land – found themselves involved in war work from the start. On 3rd August they received a Government appeal to carry on in the fields, gathering the harvest and attending to the vintage. These frugal, industrious wives and mothers needed no bidding. With their menfolk gone, they set to work, often alone, with a dour determination that quickly hardened as they saw their own soil ravaged by the fighting. Meanwhile their urban sisters were enrolling for nursing and similar work, and would soon take on a whole array of men's tasks – making their greatest contribution in the munition factories.

One typically French project soon gained ground, the *Œuvre de mon Soldat,* by which better-off French women – calling themselves '*marraines*' or godmothers – undertook to adopt and look after troops from the invaded territories who were fighting at the front. They would write to them, send them little delicacies, entertain them when on leave in Paris. This was greatly appreciated by the '*filleuls*' or godsons, and a similar idea swiftly spread to England.

Germany's enlistment of women was the most far-reaching and efficient of all. In particular, the Government had foreseen the problem of the large initial displacement of female workers and had straightway recruited the head of one of the biggest women's rights bodies in Germany, Dr Gertrude Baumer, to organise German women for war work. By the end of September workrooms for the production of cartridge belts, bread sacks and the like had been set up in all the larger cities, and thousands of women had been sent to agricultural work and army equipment factories. This was the start of a comprehensive mobilisation of female labour in which, as the war progressed, Germany's women would engage enthusiastically in every form of employment, much of it heavy and essentially masculine work of the kind not undertaken by women in either Britain or France.

Behind the general move of the belligerents on to a war footing, the initial emergency decrees, measures and regulations for mobilising and utilising their resources, lay the vital matter of their actual capacity for war-making. Long or short, the prosecution of this war would depend fundamentally on the raw materials and industrial output essential to provide their armies with weapons and munitions, and on the ability to feed their populations. Industrially, Germany had the advantage over both Britain and France. With her economic strength founded on steel and coal, by 1913 she was exporting £100 million worth of iron and steel manufactures and machinery. She also had a flourishing overseas trade from her highly-developed chemical and electrical industries. Though all this business was at once cut off by the Allied blockade, Germany was left with invaluable ready-made facilities for her own war-production. Even more important, she already possessed a fully-operative armaments manufacture in the vast establishment of Krupp at Essen, with its 80,000 workers. On the other hand, her petrol supplies were immediately threatened by the stoppage of imports from the u.s. She was also badly short of rubber. At first it had seemed too that her cotton imports – necessary for shell-making – would be in jeopardy, but she managed to obtain continued supplies as Britain had not declared this commodity contraband.

With Teutonic thoroughness, Germany capitalised on her advantages by quickly creating a War Raw Materials Division, part of the Ministry of War, under one of her most able young businessmen, Dr Walter Rathenau. His task was to organise all existing supplies of raw materials needed for the war and arrange for their replenishment on the largest scale. Rathenau (as he was later to explain to the u.s. newspaper correspondent, Edward Bullitt) had virtually appointed himself to this vital role.[10] Realising on the outbreak of war that the German General Staff had made no plans to counter a British blockade, he immediately drafted plans for an 'Industrial General Staff' and submitted them to the German Chief of Staff, General von Falkenhayn, who approved them and ordered Rathenau to implement them at once. From his impromptu headquarters in one small room in the Prussian War Office Rathenau promptly called for a census of all Germany's raw materials – bullying the officials into producing it in three weeks after they had said that the job would take six months. Stringent orders had then gone out to manufacturers to use certain raw materials solely for military needs, thereby revolutionising their normal working overnight. Thus Germany's largest piano factory suddenly found itself converted into making shells – one among countless other plants similarly affected.

Compared with Germany's, Britain's industrial system in 1914 was old-fashioned, with few modern developments. Skills and techniques were unprogressive, and mass-production plants were hardly known. Her overseas income derived mostly from coal and investments. She had depended on heavy industry, like shipbuilding, had virtually no chemical industry and few light engineering factories which could be turned over to shell-making and -filling. For many vital products and components – ball-bearings, magnetos, optical goods, dyes and drugs – she had relied largely on Germany herself; and her machine-tool industry, such as it was, was inadequate to equip the vast new factories which would now be needed. All this was a measure of the enormous efforts Britain would have to make to gear herself to effective war-production. On the other hand, so long as she commanded the seas, she could, unlike Germany, count on making up her deficiencies from neutral countries across the oceans.

France was no better prepared than Britain. Her industry, still mostly a matter of small workshops, was equally backward (in 1913 her steel production was five million tons, compared with Britain's seven and a half million and Germany's seventeen million), and she too largely depended on Germany for many essential products. Moreover, having lost the iron output of Lorraine in 1871 she was now, in the war's early days, further deprived of the iron and coal of her invaded northern territories. But against these serious shortcomings, France could at least boast a sound food situation. Being basically an agricultural nation, she was self-supporting: under a kindly climate the fertile soil of her various provinces yielded ample grain and fruits, rich dairy products, meat and wine enough for all her forty million inhabitants.

Britain's food position, though she imported much of the foodstuffs needed for her forty-five million population, was secure as long as her navy could ensure the safe transit of supplies from overseas. There was no sign yet that this could not be done. More vulnerable than either France or Britain was Germany. With a population of some sixty million, not only did she have to import food; she also had to import by sea the chemical manures needed to treat the very light soils that produced her own home-grown grain and fodder for her animals. When, as soon happened, the Allied blockade cut off the manures as well as the sea-borne foodstuffs, Germany faced a problem that would intensify throughout the war: she would have to increase her home cultivation or risk starvation.

An element more imponderable but hardly less vital than food or war *matériel* was morale. In the euphoric days of August, when the armies joined battle in what everyone expected would be a fast-moving conflict that would be over by Christmas, morale on both sides was boundingly high. In Germany the fighting men were almost suicidally dedicated. 'There is hardly any thought of love and life and relations in the young men going away', noted Princess Blücher, 'but a sort of reckless joy in the certainty of the near death awaiting them.'[11] The civilian mood, inflamed with the hatred against Britain, was almost as exalted – even among the millions of Socialists, who saw Germany fighting for her existence against the Russian Czar's destructive hordes. The French, suddenly and miraculously united in the common effort, had unbounded faith in their glorious armies who after forty years would recover the lost provinces and finally subdue their historic enemy. The British were unanimously confident of speedy victory as soon as their new army could take the field, and unshakably convinced of the invincibility of their navy.

Much of this ebullient morale stemmed from an almost

hero-worshipping trust in the national leaders. Predictably in each case the chosen figure was not a frock-coated politician (though it was generally the politicians whose voices were loudest in the matter of patriotic speeches and appeals) but a soldier. In Germany the fount of all warlike spirit was fifty-five-year-old Wilhelm II, Emperor and Supreme War Lord. Martially-helmeted, with his fierce upturned moustaches and the withered arm he had had from birth, the Kaiser was venerated as the warrior-chief who would lead the nation to victory. Everywhere he went, he was wildly greeted by subjects whose enthusiasm demonstrated their whole-hearted loyalty to him and support for the struggle he was conducting. Similarly in France the man to whom the people looked was no civilian Minister but General Césaire Joffre, French Commander-in-Chief and Allied Supreme Commander. Burly and white-haired, at sixty-two placid 'Papa' Joffre, in his baggy blue Engineers' uniform, towered above all others as the embodiment of France at war, his prestige enormously enhanced by the September victory of the Marne which had turned the tide of the German advance. Britain's hero was sixty-four-year-old Field Marshal Lord Kitchener, the military chief whose features, adorning the recruiting posters on every hoarding, were familiar throughout the land. The stern and taciturn Lord Kitchener – appointed Secretary of State for War in late August after distinguished service in Egypt and the Sudan – enjoyed an almost mystically exalted reputation as Britain's fighting leader.

It was Kitchener who already in August was quietly forecasting that the war would last twelve months. And as the year moved into winter and Christmas approached, the fact that it would have no speedy ending became obvious to all. The civilian fronts were now starting to settle materially, industrially and psychologically to a conflict that must persist well into 1915 or beyond, and if the first rosy flush of war-fervour had worn off, on both sides morale remained strong. Christmas-time scenes in the capitals revealed a mixture of wartime austerity and seasonal gaiety. In Covent Garden

Christmas trees and turkeys were plentiful; the city's shops were full of goods and its theatres doing good business. The chief West End hotels staged dinners and dances, their rooms bright with lights and decorations, their tables crowded with revellers – many in khaki. Outside was a dimmed and darkened town, with the sky overhead pierced by two lone searchlights. Paris at night was less dark than London, but it too was celebrating, though in a quieter way, and in a mood that betokened the near presence of war. Mourning was everywhere, and now the limping figures of the wounded were a common sight in the streets and theatres.

Part Two

1915: THE LENGTHENING STRUGGLE

Chapter 2

THE GENERAL SCENE

Attrition, food and politics

IN the West, the Germans were this year on the defensive, concentrating their main efforts against Russia. Of the eight Western attacks launched in 1915, seven were made by the French or British, who sought but failed to secure a breakthrough. In the East, in a campaign lasting from May to September, the Germans rolled back the Russian front in Poland and Austria, to advance two hundred miles and free all German-Austrian territory. Meanwhile, in an attempt to by-pass the stalemate in the West, the Allies had opened a new front. In February they attacked the Dardanelles with the strategic aim of knocking Germany's ally, Turkey, out of the war and keeping open the supply line to Russia. This campaign, fought as a sea-and-land operation, proved a failure, and by the end of the year the Allied forces were evacuated. In May Italy, repudiating her membership of the Triple Alliance, declared war against Austria-Hungary.

As 1915 dawned, with trench-bound stasis on the battle-fronts and hopes of an early breakthrough shattered, there was no prospect for the belligerents but to intensify their efforts and muster every available resource for a prolonged struggle. Germany (though herself not organised for a long war) was in the best position to do this. Her highly-centralised autocratic government and rigid military regime were more adapted to achieving quick decisions and rapid and unified action than the slower-moving democratic systems of France or Britain. Her pre-war industrial ascendancy had given her a valuable start over her enemies, and she was already mobilising her civilian population more rigorously and efficiently than either of them. Britain, while industrially better-equipped than France, had, like France, only begun to put her production on a full war footing. Moreover, she lagged seriously behind France in the vital matter of fighting manpower – being still opposed to military conscription. Amid the increasing pressures of the coming year, this policy would be gravely questioned: and as the first fine ardour of national unity began to cool, in all three countries other issues would arise that showed up greater or lesser weaknesses. Meanwhile, for the civilians on both sides the closest and most immediate concern was in the matter of food.

Food – the basic daily necessity – was an ever-present preoccupation that, like nothing else, brought the reality of war right into the home. This had been shown by the universal panic of provision buying and hoarding at the start of the war. Government maximum-price schemes had quickly stopped the rush, but food costs had later risen notwithstanding, and in Britain at least, the price-fixing had been abandoned by the end of 1914. While Britain had during that year seen no actual food restrictions, certain limitations had appeared in both France and Germany. Parisians had suffered a hardly more than symbolic embargo – the banning of the famous French rolls. But Germans, though their harvest had been above average, had already been subjected to the adulterated 'War Bread', with its admixture of rye and potato flour; and in November restrictions were imposed on the hours of baking and selling bread. Fearing riots, the Berlin authorities had appointed 'bread constables' to protect bakers' shops – a precaution that proved unnecessary. On the other hand, Germans had enjoyed an unexpected bonus in the massive quantities of meat and sausages suddenly thrown on the market, the result of a misguided order that had decreed the hasty and wholesale slaughter of pigs and cattle because of a fodder shortage.

But from now on, the general pattern of food provisioning

among the belligerents was to vary from a gradual slight tightening of the belt in France to a desperate state of shortage in Germany, with Britain somewhere in between.

Germany's first serious move to husband her food resources came in January 1915, when she introduced bread rationing. Every citizen was issued with a bread card, which initially allowed a daily quota of 225 grammes (nearly eight ounces), with modifications according to age, sex, type of work and so on. Cards had to be presented at the baker's or to obtain bread with a restaurant meal. Potato and meat supplies were also rigorously controlled. Meat indeed, scarcer than flour or potatoes, was causing some concern. Though local communities were ordered to buy and store preserved and smoked meats, no fresh meat was reaching the market. With demand far exceeding supply, prices soared. Powerful appeals were made to the public to be thrifty and frugal. At a meeting at Dortmund, the Burgomaster suggested that all true Germans should adopt the motto: 'I am proud to thirst and hunger for the Fatherland.'[1]

But in 1915 Britain on the other hand – with no rationing – did not know the meaning of real scarcity. At the start of the war she had enough meat, together with crops then being harvested, for four months' consumption.[2] Since then her only food difficulties had appeared in the form of steep price-rises. By July average prices had increased by 34% compared with August 1914. Meat cost 40% more, fish 60%, bread nearly 40%, flour 45%. Sugar, which had risen by 68%, was taken under Government control.[3] In May *The Times* had noted a general tendency to eat more vegetables and salads, with the 'hitherto despised mutton-bone' becoming popular as the basis for soups. The situation was no worse in France, likewise unrationed. Here too, in April, sugar prices rose sharply owing to a scarcity caused by the destruction of beet sugar factories in northern France. But by August, lack of price control was allowing general food costs in Paris to soar alarmingly: at the Corbeil market the average increase was said to be about 300%.[4]

If the food situation was nowhere presenting serious problems as yet, all three Governments were now faced with other issues that threatened the political unity so notably achieved in August 1914. In view of the widening scope of the war and the ever-growing demands it was making on the national resources, this was hardly surprising. In France and Britain there was criticism of the way the Governments were running the war, while in Germany the Socialists were questioning the very nature of the war the Government was waging.

As early as September 1914 there had been French concern at the munitions shortage, to overcome which the War Minister, M. Millerand, had promptly set about organising increased supplies. And in December, deputies had protested against the almost dictatorial control of affairs exercised since August by Viviani's government and the vast French General Head-quarters (GQG) presided over by General Joffre. The mounting agitation, supported by the redoubtable patriot Georges Clemenceau in his journal *L'Homme Libre* (which was quickly suppressed by the censor and reappeared under the name of *L'Homme Enchaîné*), was strong enough to threaten ministerial crisis. With confidence in it further shaken by the military frustrations and failures of 1915 (no less than four French Western offensives were to end in costly stalemate) and questionable Allied diplomacy in the Balkans, Viviani's Ministry was to continue uncertainly until October, when it resigned and was replaced by the Government of Aristide Briand, the veteran Socialist, who instilled fresh encouragement with his call 'Peace through Victory'.

In Britain, likewise, it was dissatisfaction over the munition shortage, together with the feeling that the war was not being prosecuted with sufficient vigour, that brought the Asquith Government under fire early in 1915. Political harmony was further disturbed by the acrimonious dispute between Winston Churchill, First Lord of the Admiralty, and Sir John Fisher, First Sea Lord, concerning the handling of the recently launched Dardanelles campaign. There was talk of a Coalition to replace the Liberal Ministry that had held office under Asquith since the start of the war. Then in early May the munitions question leapt into new prominence following the abortive British attack at Festubert (Aubers Ridge) in France, which resulted in heavy losses owing, it was asserted, to a lack of shells. On the 14th *The Times* published a sensational dispatch from its war correspondent, Colonel Repington, headed: 'Need for Shells: British Attacks Checked: Limited Supply the Cause.' The pith of the dispatch lay in the grave allegation: 'The want of an unlimited supply of high explosive was a fatal bar to our success . . .' Soon after, the *Daily Mail* (owned, like *The Times*, by the press baron Lord Northcliffe) violently assailed the man held to be responsible for the shortage, Lord Kitchener, Secretary of State for War – and, along with *The Times*, was burnt for its pains by indignant brokers on the floor of the Stock Exchange.

But while Kitchener's immense public prestige remained unshaken, the 'shell scandal' sealed the fate of Asquith's Liberal Government. On the 25th May he announced the formation of a Coalition Government, which included eight Conservative and one Labour Minister. The new Government's great innovation was the creation of a Ministry of Munitions, headed by the late Chancellor of the Exchequer, the brisk, dynamic Welshman, David Lloyd George. This was to prove one of the most significant political moves of the war.

Signs of a rift in Germany's political unity came, as was predictable, from the Socialist camp. At the start of the war the Social Democrats, champions of peace and even pacifism, had made it clear that their support depended on the 'defensive' nature of the war. This had followed a pre-war warning that should Germany wage an 'aggressive' war they would institute a general strike. But, having voted the initial war-credits, they had appeared to range themselves loyally behind the national war effort. This attitude did not last long, and in April 1915 the Socialist leader, Herr Haase, backed by his colleagues Bernstein and Kautsky, bitterly opposed the call for further war-credits, declaring that the Socialists now realised they had been duped by the Government. In June they repeated their protests in a Leipzig left-wing paper, and the ultra-radical Karl Liebknecht went even further, angrily telling the Prussian Diet that the German masses wanted peace. In July the peace cry was taken up by the Social Democratic party's National Executive in a manifesto pressing for the end of the war.

But even though the Social Democrats were backed by over four million votes and were the largest political party in the Reichstag, holding 111 out of the 397 seats, their protests amounted to little. (As a factor to influence events the Reichstag itself amounted to little: all the real power lay with the Emperor and Supreme War Lord, and his Imperial Chancellor and Secretaries of State – none of whom were members of the Reichstag but appointed by the Chancellor – heading a military regime whose grip on the civil population was absolute.) So immaterial, in fact, was the Socialist opposition in face of the still-unquestioning loyalty of the German masses that, beyond suppressing the Socialist paper *Vorwarts* for making 'treasonable' peace demands, the authorities hardly bothered to curb it. But throughout 1915 the left-wing threat persisted, a potential Achilles' heel in the German body-politic.

Chapter 3

BRITAIN

The nation awakens

THE political shake-up in Britain in May 1915 was providential in that it paved the way to her becoming at last
a nation in arms. When Lloyd George walked into his office in
Northumberland Avenue – unfurnished except for a table and
one chair – in June, he was inaugurating a new era in the
national war-effort. Despite the number of committees,
conferences and consultations that had been promoted to
accelerate the output of arms, the country had so far been
signally lacking in the basic industries and techniques necessary
for full war production – to such an extent that while the
Germans were making 250,000 high-explosive shells daily and
the French nearly as many, British production was only 700.[1]
But now, under Lloyd George's driving energy and thanks to
the formidable powers accorded him under the new Munitions
of War Act, the wasteful inefficiencies and the old piecemeal
industrial methods that largely depended on private initiative
were to be swept away and replaced by a system of national
direction and compulsion. The nation's plants, factories and
civilian work-force were to be marshalled and co-ordinated
into a gigantic arsenal for the paramount task of producing
the guns and shells sufficient to meet the voracious and ever-
growing demands of the battlefronts.

The economic and industrial picture of Britain from August
1914 to May 1915 had been one of war and prosperity going
hand in hand. The initial rise in unemployment and poverty
had been brief, so that by September there were few workless
and little working-class distress. At the end of 1914 the per-
centage of unemployed was 2·5, about the lowest on record.

The demand for labour had pushed wages up, though by the end of December the cost of living had also risen, by nearly 20%.[2] Predictably, strikes and labour troubles had almost disappeared, the number of disputes from August to December being less than one sixth of those from January to July. The overall trend was continuing to mid-1915, with high employment and good wages offset by increased living-costs. It was a boom situation due mainly to labour shortage and the enormous expenditure on the war, which was by now running at more than £3 million a day.

In conditions where at least three civilian workers were said to be necessary to equip and maintain one man at the front, Britain's Trade Unions were in a strong position. At the beginning of the war they had responded to the needs of the time by declaring an industrial truce, and early in 1915, in answer to an appeal from Lord Kitchener, had agreed to waive their established rules and customs to increase munitions output. But still, increased armaments production had been hampered by sheer labour shortage, due partly to essential operatives in the large industrial centres volunteering for the forces, and partly to the numbers of workers who continued in inessential employment. Consequently the great shipbuilding yards on the Tyne and Clyde and at Belfast found themselves overwhelmed with orders which they had not the hands to fulfil, and at Newcastle armaments firms like Armstrongs had to bring miners from the coalfields to help build new sheds, and employ women for shell-filling and other work. In Glasgow, manufacturers were forced to advertise for men to undertake Government work, but often the difficulties were aggravated by the reluctance of workers to move from their homes. The extent of the labour shortage in April 1915 was shown by the columns of 'situations vacant' advertisements for work of almost every kind in the national papers.

This was the situation facing the new Minister of Munitions when he took office in June. The Munitions of War Bill, introduced by himself, was his answer to the problem. In his own words, 'it dealt with the settlement of labour differences, the prohibition of lock-outs and strikes, the controlling of establishments engaged in production of munitions and the limitation of their profits, the control of munition workers and the issue to them of badges; and it also provided for the voluntary enrolment of a body of munition workers to be at the disposal of the Ministry and work where the need for their services was greatest'.[3] In its total turning-over of war production (hitherto in the hands of the purchasing departments of the War Office and Admiralty) to a single all-powerful authority, and assumption of arbitrary control over the workers – including the suspension of their cherished right to strike – the Bill signified nothing less than an industrial revolution. But industrial revolution was the only method by which Britain's potentially great but still under-exploited capacity could be welded into an effective war-machine. And soon the results of the transformation began to be seen. A network of munitions committees and sub-committees was established which distributed orders to the large establishments and advised the smaller ones how to adapt themselves. Engineering shops sprang up everywhere, and railway construction depots, big electrical works, motor and bicycle works and agricultural factories became busy turning out war material. Sizeable towns appeared in quiet country districts, housing miles of workshops and temporary dwellings, with populations of workers amounting to tens of thousands. By the end of the year there were over 2,000 controlled establishments working at full blast.

At the same time Lloyd George battled with the War Office for the release of skilled workers who had joined the army, and managed to obtain the recall of some 40,000, for placement in munitions work. But still a shortage persisted which could be alleviated only by dilution of skilled workers by unskilled and semi-skilled. This was secured by special agreement with the unions, whose traditional fears of 'blackleg' labour had to be overcome.

That Lloyd George's Act had 'teeth' was soon apparent from the penalties imposed on defaulting workers by the new

Munitions Courts. Sylvia Pankhurst quoted sundry cases: a fitter fined £3 and costs in North London for leaving his employment; seventeen striking workmen in Glasgow fined £10 each with the alternative of thirty days' imprisonment; employees at Cammel Laird's, in Liverpool, fined up to £3 when late for work on Monday morning after working long hours through the week-end.[4] Mrs Pankhurst also cited the Act as being invoked to prevent workers from changing their employment to secure higher wages or more responsible employment, or to work nearer home. But the measure did not go through entirely smoothly. Its passing coincided with simmering unrest in the coal-mines over wages, which in mid-July came to a head with a strike of 200,000 miners in South Wales – in defiance of the Act. To achieve a settlement Lloyd George himself had to visit Cardiff. For a time the latent industrial discontent was to cause the Government anxiety and threaten to impede Lloyd George's arms programme. Nevertheless, for all the radical readjustments demanded of industry in this difficult year, trade disputes in 1915, totalling 674, were to prove the fewest since 1910.[5]

But – to the dismay of Labour and Liberal militants who saw British freedoms speedily being whittled away – the regimentation of Britons was soon to go yet further. In July, close on the heels of the Munitions Act, came another move towards total war-effort: the National Register Act. This provided for the registration of everyone between the ages of fifteen and sixty-five, with particulars of residence, marital state and dependents, and other details including a statement of willingness or otherwise to undertake war work. All registered persons had to carry a registration card, and anyone falsely claiming to have registered was liable to three months' hard labour and a fine of £20. It was clear that a new and sterner mood was now possessing Britain's leaders, directed at pulling in the slack which had persisted for too long, and streamlining and utilising the national resources, human as well as material, to the utmost. To this end a powerful propa-

ganda campaign was mounted, appealing for economy as a
patriotic duty.

Already in April there had been a concerted call to the
workers for greater efforts, and Mr Asquith had personally
invoked the patriotic support of the Tyneside shipbuilders.
The King, too, was visiting factories and shipyards, addressing
and exhorting the workers. Likewise Lloyd George and Mr
Henderson, President of the Board of Trade, were busy
speaking in public and private. Now, in speeches, press articles,
even sermons, there were calls to cut out manpower waste.
People were urged to do without gardeners, gamekeepers,
chauffeurs, not to buy cars. To relieve pressure on the labour
market, economy in food and dress was advocated. If many of
the recommended economies hardly applied to the majority
of the population, the campaign did succeed in curbing luxury
spending. There was less travelling; the London branch of
Worth's, the famous dressmakers, was closed; well-to-do ladies
started carrying home their own purchases; and shops shut
earlier, thereby employing fewer assistants.

But there was another aspect of manpower that now caused
the authorities increasing concern: recruitment for the armed
forces. From the moment of Kitchener's clarion 'Call to Arms'
at the start of the war, men had come forward in droves – the
recruits of 'Kitchener's Army'. The numbers had been swelled
by the appeals of political leaders who had toured the country
calling for volunteers. On one September day, 33,000 men had
enlisted. By mid-November 700,000 had joined up (while
hundreds had been rejected as physically unfit), bringing the
strength of the army to 1,100,000 men. But the heavy casualties
in the earlier battles of 1915 soon made it clear that the
voluntary system would be insufficient to maintain the necessary forces: it was also seen to be wasteful and indiscriminating
in that it deprived the essential war industries of key men who
had enlisted. The situation had been foreshadowed in a House
of Lords debate in January, but the Government had not then
accepted the uncomfortable alternative – conscription – as a
practical possibility. Kitchener himself had continued to

oppose the idea of compulsion, though by now popular feeling, despite growing anti-conscription propaganda by minority groups, was veering in favour of it, if it were necessary to secure Allied victory.

The common sight of numbers of fit young men in the streets, still in 'civvies', raised uneasy questions. 'As I walked from St Bart's yesterday,' noted a peer, Lord Sandhurst, in mid-May, 'in a little over ten minutes I counted one hundred young men who might all have been soldiering and did not have the appearance of being busy or in a hurry; of course some may have been incapacitated, but they didn't look it. I also see any quantity of very good male material on the move after shop hours, hurrying towards the stations. I wonder if we shall have to come to some sort of conscription.'[6]

But Mr Asquith remained complacent. In July he pronounced recruiting to be 'highly satisfactory', stating that the latest figures were the best for a long time. It was a calumny, he said, to claim that people had not risen to the occasion: no less than three million men had already offered themselves for service. However, this complacency was not echoed in the report of a Cabinet committee appearing in September, which showed that the weekly intake of recruits was inadequate to maintain the strength of the new British Army of seventy divisions (in August 1914 the army had numbered twenty-six divisions). By now Lord Kitchener himself had come round to admitting the need for compulsion, while the Cabinet was divided on the issue, an intermediate group standing between those firmly in favour and those firmly opposed. So, in a final effort to save the voluntary system, the Government introduced a plan known as the Derby Scheme.

Under this scheme, the Under-Secretary for War, Lord Derby (a convinced advocate of compulsion) was appointed Director of Recruitment in October with the task of carrying out a canvass of the country's manpower. On the basis of the newly completed National Register, every man between eighteen and forty-one was personally asked to attest – to undertake to enlist when called for – subject to the pledge that

Women porters at Marylebone

A woman guard on the Metropolitan Railway

A woman bus conductor

The Ladies' Fire Brigade

attested men would be divided into the single and the married, each of these groups being sub-divided into twenty-three classes according to age. These would be called up as required, starting with the younger single men and leaving the married men until all the unmarried had been called. Certain reserved or 'starred' occupations under the Register were exempt – munitions-making, coal mining, railway work, the merchant service, public utility services and some branches of agriculture. The canvass was accompanied by a great campaign to encourage attestments, headed by a special appeal from the King himself addressed to 'My People'. But despite all the calls and invocations, when the scheme closed in December, it had to be admitted that it was a failure. Out of over two million single men who had not enlisted before its commencement, Lord Derby reported that owing to exemptions for various reasons only 343,000 had effectively attested. Now, as the Government recognised, there was nothing for it but compulsion.

Meanwhile, with public sentiment swinging strongly towards conscription, it had become embarrassing for any fit-looking young man to be seen not wearing khaki. There had been social pressure on men to 'join up' ever since the early volunteering days of 1914, when the popular romantic novelist, Baroness Orczy, had sent a jingoistic appeal to the *Daily Mail*, addressed to the 'Women and Girls of England'. 'Your hour has come!' she exhorted them. 'Together we have laughed and cried over that dauntless Englishman the Scarlet Pimpernel and thrilled with enthusiasm over the brave doings of his League. Now we shall form ourselves into an Active Service League, its sole object: influencing sweethearts, brothers, sons and friends to recruit. Pledge: I hereby pledge myself most solemnly in the name of my King and Country, to persuade every man I know to offer his services to his country, and I also pledge myself never to be seen in public with any man who being in every way free and fit has refused to respond to his country's call.' Twenty thousand women joined the League, receiving special badges, and the King himself acknowledged the movement.

By mid-1915 the lost illusions about the short duration of the war, and the lengthening casualty lists, had intensified this attitude. It was increasingly felt that unenlisted men were dodging their clear-cut duty and leaving all the sacrifice to their brothers in khaki: they were not 'doing their bit'. And it was now that the 'white feather' activity began, said to have been originated by an admiral in Folkestone who urged young women to present men in civilian dress with white feathers. As the idea caught on, any young man not in khaki – who may well have been rejected as medically unfit or have neglected to wear the armlet issued to him to show that he had enlisted or was in a 'starred' occupation – was liable to be dubbed by irresponsible females with the 'Order of the White Feather'. Typical of the treatment accorded to the man still in 'civvies' was an advertisement appearing in *The Times* in July: 'Jack, F. G. – If you are not in khaki by the 20th I shall cut you dead – Ethel M.' War widows and mothers who had lost sons would stop young civilians in the streets and demand why they were not doing their duty. Young women formed leagues pledging themselves not to marry young men who had not joined up. Males of service age were publicly insulted, like the two young men in a London tram who, as an observer noted, were assailed by three girls with the words: 'Why don't you fellows enlist? Your King and Country want you. We don't.' Thereupon one girl stuck a white feather in one of the men's button-holes.[7]

But if they were chivvying and hounding the men, British women were themselves now rallying to the call of duty in ever-increasing numbers. For them too there was now to be a vital part in the industrial revolution that was overtaking Britain. This year, besides taking on a host of civilian jobs normally done by men, they were to be absorbed in their thousands into Lloyd George's war factories. At the start of 1915, when most available paid war work had gone to the unemployed wage-earners, there had been some frustration among ordinary housewives. There was little they could do but help with money-raising efforts like flag-days, attend sewing teas, pack parcels for prisoners, look after Belgian refugees, or make sandbags. But their chance came in March, when the Board of Trade issued an appeal to all women willing to take 'paid employment of any kind' in trade, commerce or agriculture to enter their names on a Register of Women for War Service at any employment exchange. The appeal added: 'Any woman who by working helps to release and equip a man for fighting does national war services.'[8]

The response was immediate. Of the 124,000 women who signed up, many soon found themselves in Government offices, working in the Censor's department and the Census of Production, Post Office sorting departments and the greatly expanded War Office. Others undertook War Office remount work and replaced men as cooks in military camps and convalescent hospitals. Outside Government employment, hundreds took jobs in the clothing, tailoring and leather trades, as gardeners and agricultural hands, laboratory assistants making the synthetic drugs for which there was a greatly enhanced demand, tram and bus conductors, bank clerks, ticket-collectors on the tubes and railways, plumbers' assistants, milk and newspaper deliverers, gas-meter readers. Others again took to driving cars and delivery vans, became lift attendants in the big stores and even servants in the leading London clubs – an innovation pioneered by the staid Athenaeum, where members were surprised one day to see two trim parlourmaids serving tea and coffee in place of the traditional waiters. In the nursing field women replaced RAMC orderlies, and there was a significant increase in female medical and dental students. As the year went on, there were in fact few occupations – a considerable number of which had been the exclusive province of men – into which women did not penetrate. Their determination to share in the war-effort was shown in mid-July when, in pouring rain, a procession of 30,000 women paraded London carrying banners which proclaimed: 'We demand the right to serve.'

Though women were already employed in munition-making in the spring – on Good Friday an observer noted them working energetically at Woolwich Arsenal alongside the men – their large-scale entry into munitions came only after the creation of the Ministry of Munitions. At first the bulk of them were recruited from other industries and so were inured to factory conditions. While mostly engaged in automatic and semi-automatic processes, in some cases they were allotted the whole operation of shell-making from start to finish, involving some twenty-one separate tasks. It was soon found too that women, with their more sensitive touch, excelled in fuse-making. Such was the patriotic appeal of munition work that it even attracted women from the sheltered upper classes, becoming, as Mrs Pankhurst put it, the 'latest society craze'. The Hillman Motor Company opened a factory for instructing ladies 'with a few hours of leisure', and Vickers trained a group of 'leisured' women at Erith for the week-end relief of normal workers. The *Manchester Guardian* told of a titled lady, a 'munitionette', who gave a dinner party to celebrate her first month of work. Among her guests were a duchess, the wife of a Cabinet Minister and a working-class woman colleague called Mabel. The table was covered with oil-cloth and the plainest meal was served. The butler had been sent to the theatre 'to get him out of the way'.[9]

It is surprising that this woman still enjoyed the luxury of a butler, unless he was too elderly for any kind of war employment. Soon, at any rate, the public appeal for economy in manpower (and womanpower) would severely reduce the number of domestic and other servants. It was estimated that during the whole war no less than 400,000 women were to leave domestic service (and many, having tasted the joys of a freer life, would never go back). But the wholesale entry of women into war work did not go unopposed. Inevitably, after their age-long subjection as the inferior and weaker sex, they were met with prejudice and opposition. Trade unionists objected that they would reduce the standard of men's wages, some workers even going so far as to threaten to strike. And in the early spring of 1915 farmers, though gravely concerned at the shortage of agricultural labour, were loth to take on women employees. But with some 80,000 skilled and 300,000 unskilled workers needed in munition work and tens of thousands more required on the farms and elsewhere, the old-time prejudices had to be buried. The dearth of munition hands was such that before long girls of fourteen were accepted for unskilled jobs, though those under eighteen were barred from night work.[10]

But inequalities still persisted. Despite agreement with the Unions that men and women should be paid equally for piece-work, the women found themselves generally receiving less than men. In the national shell factories, while the top weekly wage for men was £4 6s. 6d., that for women was £2 4s. 6d. – a difference admittedly often accounted for by the more skilled jobs done by men. By the end of 1915 the munitions plants were employing three women to one man, but still at one Croydon factory the women who had replaced men earning up to £3 weekly received 12s. 6d.[11] In other work, among private firms, conditions were sometimes deplorable. A bad example was that of a food-preserving company at Limehouse where, for 10s. a week with 2d. an hour overtime, women worked in a dank and steaming basement workshop dealing with food that was often vile-smelling and decomposing. The firm was said to be the purveyor of turtle soup to the Royal household.[12]

Conditions were also primitive in some of Lloyd George's new factories. The workshops and living accommodation, quickly run-up in sometimes virgin country, were often devoid of proper facilities. By the end of 1915 the health of women was being affected not only by overwork but by having to plod considerable distances to and from their work over rough muddy tracks in all weathers. Sometimes it was impossible to get a drink of water during night-shifts, and meals were eaten among the dust and fumes of the workshop. Conditions were hardly better for some workers living at home. A committee on the health of workers told of exhausted operatives struggling for places on overcrowded transport and spending long hours in travelling. Family life was 'impossible', the committee reported: while mothers and older children were busy making munitions, the younger ones suffered neglect at home. (Referring to male munition workers, the committee recorded that in their lodgings the beds were never empty and the rooms never aired, this being prevented by their turn-and-turn-about use by the day and night shifts.)

But the new working women of Britain bore themselves stoutly and for the most part cheerfully through all their discomforts. While they were certainly sustained by a strong patriotic sense, there was another reason for their ready acceptance. Scores of thousands of them were for the first time tasting the joys of emancipation. However hard and irksome, the daily stint in the war-plants and offices, and the multifarious other tasks they were undertaking, spelt for them a new exciting freedom, an escape from pointless leisured existence or dull domestic routine. And they embraced this liberty eagerly, shedding the old inhibitions and restraints with a joyful abandon. Many used language that would have horrified their mothers. Smoking, the use of cosmetics, and drinking in public houses became common. There was a transformation in women's clothes as short skirts and brassières steadily ousted the long dresses and camisoles of 1914; and soon the 'land girls' were to shock the strait-laced by wearing trousers off duty.

The great feminine take-over was now visibly changing the normal balance of sexes in Britain's working life. In London, for instance, this could be seen in the underground trains where often, in the rush hours, every seat in a carriage would be filled by women and girls while the men were relegated to strap-hanging. In any case the men of military age were growing fewer every week. One kind of male had already vanished from the scene – among the first to volunteer. 'From the streets and haunts of fashion,' recorded one contemporary chronicle,[13] 'soon disappeared the "nut". The "nut" was the finest flower of male fashion. He was an elegant idler, strenuous only in getting "the last ounce" out of his motor-car. He smoked incessant cigarettes. He cultivated a manner almost effeminate. He made harmonies of neckties and symphonies of socks. Gold was too strenuous for him, and most things "too much fag". His chief attitude to life was to be "fed-up" with everything that imposed any strain, physical, moral, or mental. To social observers he was quite a perplexing portent, for his advent and presence, an apparently decadent type of masculinism, synchronised with the advent of a strenuous feminism, so that the easiest explanation of both seemed to be that each phenomenon explained the other ... And then with the war the "nut" vanished and the Young Briton leapt to life. The call of his race was answered in his blood, and his fripperies dropped from him. He now lies under many a white cross in the fair land of France ...'

The eclipse of the 'nut' symbolised the ending of an era. It was a sign of the new times that, at the traditional Sunday Parade in Hyde Park in March 1915, in place of the throngs of top-hatted, frock-coated young men who had strolled there a year before, limped a few wounded blue-clad soldiers. But signs were abundant everywhere. Perhaps as a sedative for tensed nerves, cigarette-smoking became widespread among troops and civilians. There was a universal knitting craze: to comfort the troops in the trenches, miles of khaki wool were transformed into waistcoats, helmets, scarves, mittens, body belts. 'We knitted', a writer recorded, 'at theatres, in trains and trams, in parks and parlours, in the intervals of eating in restaurants, or serving in canteens. Men knitted, children knitted.'[14] At the annual Daffodil Show at the Horticultural Hall, Westminster, in April, there was a new specimen, 'a bold, well-balanced flower, a tall grower' – with the name of 'Lord Kitchener'. On a darker note, a coal shortage at the beginning of the year had precipitated hoardings in cellars, with steep price rises and profiteering. And in the East End of London and elsewhere, soaring rents were causing distress and even strikes, and evictions were rife, the trouble being greatest in munition-making areas where housing was gravely deficient. In Glasgow 15,000 people demonstrated against a 20% increase, while on Tyneside indignant workers were paying

18s. weekly for a half-share in a bed which was occupied by two other tenants as soon as they had vacated it.

One product of the times was the weakening of customary moral taboos and increased sexual laxity – the result of the new freedom being enjoyed by women and the feeling that life, for the fighting man at least, might be short. 'The effect of the war on lower-class morals is amazing,' noted the outraged Lord Sandhurst in April. 'The whole country seems morally infected. I have heard from many sources in town and country that the women, middle-aged as well as young, pursue the men, and indeed I have observed a good deal of it myself.'[15] There was much talk of the scandal of 'war babies'. One Member of Parliament boldly but unavailingly proposed that 'natural' children of soldiers should be adopted as children of the State.[16] Instead, it remained the rule that, in respect of soldiers about to be drafted overseas, no affiliation order could be applied for by the women who were to bear their children.

Another matter for concern was the rise in drunkenness. This was largely due to the suddenly increased affluence of war workers, and in a more general sense to the febrile 'eat-drink-and-be-merry' attitude to life engendered by the war. Excessive drinking had soon begun to affect war production, and by the start of 1915 had become enough of a problem to worry the Government seriously and provoke temperance reformers to demand total prohibition. In the words of Lloyd George it was (together with what he enigmatically called 'professional rigidity') 'our most dangerous foe'.[17] It resulted in heavy absenteeism, especially after weekends, and Lloyd George cited an instance of over-indulgence in which a large group of workers prolonged a bank holiday into an entire week. In March 1915 the Shipbuilding Employers' Federation reported, as one of hundreds of cases, the example of urgent repairs to a battleship being delayed for a whole day by the absence of the riveters 'through drink and conviviality'.

It was not only men who were over-indulging. Women too were taking to drink in growing numbers, both the war workers who enjoyed the new freedom of frequenting the public-houses and quaffing their beer and porter alongside their male colleagues, and the housewives, unsettled at the disruption of home life through the absence of husbands and fathers. Scandalised critics claimed that some of these women were squandering their separation allowances on drink and neglecting the welfare of their children, and suggested that all wives of servicemen should be subject to police supervision, and even that all women should be barred from public-houses. But while the Government had no intention of introducing any sort of prohibition, it was realised that steps must be taken to curb the abuse. At the end of February Lloyd George delivered a resounding speech at Bangor, in which he declared: 'Drink is doing more damage in the War than all the German submarines put together ... We have got great powers to deal with drink, and we mean to use them.'[18]

This signalled the start of a powerful anti-drink campaign in the press. On Easter Monday King George himself, in a pronouncement known as 'The King's Pledge', added his support to the movement. 'The King will be prepared to set the example', it was stated, 'by giving up all alcoholic liquor himself, and issuing orders against its consumption in the Royal Household, so that no difference shall be made, so far as His Majesty is concerned, between the treatment of rich and poor in this question.' Prominent men, including Lord Kitchener, followed the King's lead, and recipes for barley water and other non-intoxicating drinks appeared in the papers; but the campaign was not highly successful. Even the House of Commons refused to dispense with its own alcoholic refreshment. In June the Government moved further, to establish a Central Control Board with wide powers for regulating drink in military and munition-making areas, restricting the hours of public-house opening and prohibiting the sale and supply of intoxicants, the custom of treating (this last being claimed as a potent cause of drunkenness). But even these measures could be side-stepped by thirsty workers. In the restricted Clyde area some operatives, armed with their Friday-night pay-packets, would take a tram to areas where the drink flowed unlimited. But with the fuller implementing of the Board's powers, by the end of the year Britain's drinking facilities were severely curtailed. The stringent 'No Treating' order of October forbade treating of civilians in hotels, restaurants, public-houses and clubs unless the drink was consumed with a meal. A month later the purchase of spirits was forbidden except between noon and 12.30 p.m. from Monday to Friday. Public-houses were open from noon to 12.30 p.m. and 6.30 p.m. to 9.30 p.m. A further deterrent – though acting more harshly on the poor than the rich – was the sharply rising price of drink, imposed by increased duties. It was the poorer drinkers, moreover, who were harder hit by the practice of diluting the beer.

But amid all the wartime trials and tribulations affecting the Home Front, there were still reminders of Britain's invincible normality. In the spring it was fervently debated whether or not the Derby and Ascot race meetings should be banned as a war measure, and it was decided that such events should be continued as contributing valuably to national morale. In July the country was distracted and intrigued by one of those sensational domestic dramas so dear to British hearts – the notorious 'Brides in the Bath' case, in which George Smith was tried and sentenced to death for murdering, by drowning in their baths, three unfortunate women with whom he had gone through a form of marriage in order to dispose of them and secure their small savings. That autumn, as noted in the diary of Lord Bertie of Thame, the British Ambassador to France, Viscount Harcourt held a big partridge shoot in which 1,800 birds were 'bagged' in four days. 'I don't like that sort of thing in these times,' recorded Lord Bertie. 'Here (in France) there is no shooting at all.'[19] Three weeks later, while on a visit to London, Lord Bertie noted: 'Carlton restaurant cram-full. No signs of war within, except for some few men in khaki and a few limping. All the rest as in piping times of peace, low gowns (very low), nearly all the men in evening swallow-tail coats and most of them wearing white waistcoats.'[20]

To crown all, in May, in the formal dignity of the High Court, the Lord Chief Justice, Mr Justice Avory and Mr Justice Low had solemnly decided that a winkle was a fish.[21]

Whatever aims and motives activated this 45-million-strong nation in which entrenched peacetime ways persisted so strangely amid the wartime atmosphere, anti-German hatred was hardly the strongest. 'The English are fighting for their honour, for the defence of their existence, and the security of the British Empire,' wrote a French observer, 'but they do not know as we do the passionate wrath and bitterness of hate.'[22] There was a simmering resentment against the 24,000 enemy aliens who remained uninterned, and an occasional individual outburst against citizens of German extraction. In December 1914 a Leicester businessman had attacked those two eminent industrial magnates, Sir John Brunner and Sir Alfred Mond, as 'German swine', and been promptly and successfully sued by them.[23] But in general overt anti-Germanism was rare. Yet the capacity for hatred was always there, not far below the phlegmatic British surface; and it was suddenly aroused early in May by what seemed an appalling act of German brutality – the torpedoing off the Irish coast of the British liner *Lusitania,* en route for Liverpool, with the loss of over 1,000 lives, many of them American.

A surge of shocked anger ran through the country, venting itself on the German aliens who were still at large (19,000 were already interned). The mood was fanned by the press, which raged against the barbarous enemy. In London's Smithfield market furious butchers turned out their German colleagues, and German merchants and brokers were expelled from the Baltic Exchange and Stock Exchange. Hundreds of top-hatted stockbrokers marched through the City to the Houses of Parliament to urge the Prime Minister to intern all Germans. There were violent scenes in the East End, where German shops were attacked and looted, and squads of 'specials' with drawn batons fought to restore order. In one manifestation of resentment, German pianos were thrown into the street and commandeered by the crowd to accompany the singing of patriotic songs. Popular feeling was such that the Government was forced to take drastic action. On the 14th May Mr Asquith announced in the House that all male enemy aliens still free would, with certain exceptions, be interned or, if over military age, repatriated along with women and children; while naturalised Germans, being British subjects, would remain free and unmolested.

The *Lusitania* outrage moved King George himself to wrath. On the 13th it was announced that, by royal command, the names of the German Emperor, the Emperor of Austria and other German royalties – including the Duke of Cumberland, another cousin to the King – were to be struck off the Roll of Knights of the Garter.

If the sinking of a great British liner in nearby waters brought the war abruptly closer to all Britons, they were now to feel its impact right in their streets and homes – in the form of enemy attack from the air. Germany was launching the first of her Zeppelin raids, to rain down bombs and spread destruction and (it was hoped) terror among the British enemy. The Zeppelin campaign had started in April with a few light forays over East Anglia, causing little damage. On the 10th May the assault was stepped up by a heavier raid on the Southend area, the first of a series of intermittent attacks on East Anglia and the South-East that lasted until mid-October. Slow and unwieldy, the long silvery aircraft stole over the North Sea in the night hours, a weapon whose effectiveness was, at the best, more psychological than military. From the ground below, pencilled searchlights would probe the sky for them and onlookers roused from sleep would peer up at them, caught momentarily in the beams, more in curiosity than fear. London itself escaped the serious attentions of the 'Zepps' until September when, on the nights of the 7th and 8th, two heavy raids struck at the heart of the capital around St Paul's Cathedral, leaving a wreckage of gutted and smouldering warehouses and a casualty-toll of 38 killed and 124 wounded. For British civilians in London and elsewhere, as they heard the crash of bombs and anti-aircraft guns and surveyed the ruins of their homes, there was the realisation that they were no longer immune from war. Now they too, like their soldiers, were in the firing line.

Nevertheless, the new and harsher experience of the people at home did not seem to bring them nearer in spirit to the men in the trenches. A gulf separated them, a gulf that could never really be bridged having regard to the total disparity of danger, hardship and sacrifice as between soldiers and civilians. Yet amid the relative comfort and security of the Home Front and despite its essential remoteness from the brutish actuality of war, civilians were beginning to show a belligerence towards the enemy fiercer than that of the soldiers. But it was a mood stirred by what was happening to themselves rather than by a realisation of what the troops were undergoing. It was almost as if they were fighting their own war, while letting this interfere as little as possible with their normal everyday life. Soldiers on leave sensed a lack of general interest in the wider conflict. The young subaltern Robert Graves in London in September, at the time of the Zeppelin raids, was surprised at 'the general indifference to, and ignorance of, the war', and found people mainly interested in 'business as usual' or pre-occupied with their personal Zeppelin experiences. On one occasion he started telling some friends his own story of front-line bombing, and when they realised he was talking about France 'the look of interest faded from their faces as though I had taken them in with a stupid catch'.[24] This was symptomatic of a division between combatants and non-combatants that would widen as the war continued.

But the impressions of a serving soldier like Graves, coming as he did from the horrific world of the battlefield and steeped in experiences which were unimaginable to the civilian, were perhaps not entirely valid. Behind the self-centred attitude and seeming 'business as usual' preoccupations of the Home Front, especially evident amid the luxury and workaday bustle of the metropolis, lay Britain's serious, solid and ever-increasing war-effort (an effort which, it is true, could never be claimed to be whole-hearted so long as military conscription remained unadopted). The Zeppelin raids, and such events as the sinking of the *Lusitania* – and the shooting of the heroic Nurse Edith Cavell by the Germans in Belgium in October for aiding the escape of Allied prisoners – were valuable in that they stoked the fires of civilian anger and stirred Home Front workers, however different their viewpoint from that of the troops, into fresh exertions to prosecute the war. In this they were encouraged not only by the belligerent outpourings of press propaganda, but by the virtually unanimous voice of the Church.

The Bishop of London spoke for churchmen when, in an address delivered in May, he referred to the lack of ammunition and added that though vengeance was God's, He carried it out through the agency of man. But while the Church remained in no doubt about the righteousness of Britain's struggle, a controversy arose as to the precise place to be taken in it by her clergy. Should priests, it was asked, enlist as fighting men? The question came to a head in the autumn, after thousands of clergy of all denominations had received Lord Derby's circular asking them to attest. As they were in an 'unstarred' occupation, there seemed no official objection to this. But the Archbishop of Canterbury then intervened, re-affirming the pronouncement he had made in August 1914 on behalf of his fellow-prelates, that ordination was not consonant with combatant service in the field. Notwithstanding, many patriotic younger clergy remained dissatisfied; and 1,000 curates of military age petitioned the Bishop of London asking permission from the heads of the Established Church to enlist as combatants. Their request was unavailing; and for those clergy who wished to don khaki and serve their country, there remained, as before, the task, hardly less hazardous than fighting itself, of ministering to the troops amid the shells and bullets of the battlefield.

Pronouncements like the Bishop of London's in May suited the 'war-to-the-end' advocates rather more than that of Dr Edward Lyttelton, Headmaster of Eton, made in a sermon in

London shortly before. Taking a line unusual for churchmen at that time, Dr Lyttelton preached on the text: 'Love your enemies.' 'If we are going to act as a Christian nation,' he said, 'we are bound to apply true Christian charity on a scale to which we have never risen before.'[25] In more belligerent quarters this was taken as giving too much comfort to the pacifist-minded. It gave rise to a powerful reaction, and feeling flared up again when a letter appeared in *The Times* in August, asserting that the pro-German statements of Dr Lyttelton – and of the writer George Bernard Shaw – were being repeated around Berlin for the encouragement of the enemy. This evoked a reply from Dr Lyttelton. 'I believe the German spirit, as now manifest,' he said, 'to be an utterly dangerous and abominable thing, and that the hope for peace and honour among mankind rests, so far as I can see, in a decisive victory of the Allies; and that I have often said ever since the war and will continue to say it to the end.'[26] With this unexceptionable declaration the matter was buried.

In the stirring-up of patriotic ardour and anti-German sentiment, no individual was more prominent, now and throughout the war, than that colourful adventurer, Horatio Bottomley. Through the columns of his weekly, *John Bull*, and other papers, and in rousing speeches up and down the country, he rallied the nation's fighting spirit, especially among the working and lower middle-classes, stimulated recruiting and generally encouraged the war-effort in a way that made him – despite his sometimes highly unorthodox methods – the Government's most valuable unofficial propagandist. A demagogue with unequalled powers of firing huge audiences to fervour, he was said by one writer to be the most influential man in Britain after Kitchener. After addressing a packed and vastly successful meeting at the Albert Hall, he offered his services to Mr Asquith, the Prime Minister, as Chief Recruiting Officer. The Premier politely declined the proposal, telling Bottomley that he could work more effectively in a private capacity. Bottomley's continuing ambitions to join the Government were in fact never realised, which was probably just as well, for his wide-ranging talents needed more latitude than would have been provided by the formal confines of Whitehall.

But amid the nation-wide support for the war, there was a small current of opposition – by pacifists, conscientious objectors and anti-conscription advocates – that as the year progressed and conscription seemed increasingly certain, was becoming more and more vocal. One group, the No-Conscription Fellowship, had been formed the previous autumn, stating its belief that 'there is one interference with individual judgment that no State in the world has any right to enforce – i.e. to tamper with the unfettered free right of every man to decide for himself the issue of life and death. We contend that the individual conscience alone must decide whether a man will sacrifice his own life, or inflict death upon other people.'[27] In the spring of 1915, with membership confined to men of military age, it began to be organised as a national body; and in the autumn, after the termination of the Derby Scheme, it held a national convention at which its chairman, Clifford Allen, declared: 'We have created a society of a unique character.'

Among the No-Conscription Fellowship's leading members was the philosopher and mathematician, 43-year-old Bertrand Russell. As the war progressed, Russell was to offer a constant challenge to authority as a vigorous advocate of pacifism and conscientious objection. He was to be fined for issuing a pamphlet protesting at a two-year prison sentence imposed on a conscientious objector, deprived of his Cambridge college lectureship, refused a passport to the United States where he had been offered a post at Harvard University, and in 1918 sentenced to six months' imprisonment for contributing a pacifist article to the news-sheet *Tribunal*. It was the brilliantly intellectual Bertrand Russell who, more than any other individual, represented British anti-war opinion in these years.

Another movement was the Union of Democratic Control, championed by such pacifist figures as Ramsay MacDonald, Pethick-Lawrence, Arthur Ponsonby, C. P. Trevelyan and E. D. Morel. With popular pro-war sentiment running high, at the end of November the Union took a considerable risk in staging a public meeting in favour of 'Peace' in the Memorial Hall, Farringdon Street. Predictably the gathering was disrupted by demonstrators, among whom were colonial troops who, it was said, had gained admission by forged tickets. Stink bombs were thrown, the platform was stormed, banners were torn from the walls, and the promoters had to hide in cellars or escape by back doors. Outside the hall was a large crowd of anti-peace demonstrators which, on the motion of its leader, Cecil Chesterton, unanimously passed a resolution declaring: 'That Peace shall not be made until Prussia is utterly and completely crushed.'[28] It was asserted in the press that such Peace meetings were organised by German agents. 'Utter Rout of the Pro-Germans', claimed the *Daily Express*. Such were the hazards of deviating from the general uncompromising 'war-to-the-end' attitude that permeated Britain after sixteen months of struggle.

Chapter 4

FRANCE

'If only the civilians can hold out'

INCREASINGLY involved and immersed in war as civilian Britain now was, her commitment during 1915 was still markedly less than that of France. In France, over and above all else, even including the presence of an invading army on French soil, there was the universal impact of conscription, which drew virtually every fit man between the ages of eighteen and forty-seven, regardless of social position or class, into the fighting forces and kept ever in the forefront the human tragedy of the war. Hardly a household remained unaffected by this wholesale summons to arms. 'Business men, industrialists, professors, farmers, employees, priests of every faith, have come forward and endured the rough life of the bivouacs in winter,' recorded a contemporary. And (thanks not least to the uncertainties engendered by the rigid censorship) the fate of these men was an ever-present anxiety to their families at home. 'Each day the wives, mothers and fathers await the postman who will bring them news of the absent one,' added this writer. 'Where is he, what is he doing, what sufferings is he undergoing? Is he ill or wounded? Is he dead? How many have opened with trembling hand the fatal letter which begins: "Be proud of ... who has just died like a brave man"?'[1] The extent of the call on fighting manpower was such that by mid-1915 a total of 5,444,000 men had been drafted. And already by the end of 1914 the toll of casualties (killed, missing and wounded) had reached 855,000.[2]

Added to this was the handicap of lost industrial resources. After the battle of the Marne and the stabilisation of the front

France was waging war deprived of 6% of her territory and 14% of her industrial work-force. But her real loss was greater than this, for with altogether ten departments affected by war, nearly 12% of her soil and some 21% of her manufacturing labour were out of commission.[3] The losses were particularly severe in coal-mining, metallurgy, glass-working, textile, sugar, industrial alcohol production – just those industries most vital to her war effort. Together with the exacting manpower demands for the army, these deficiencies posed grave industrial and labour problems. Right at the start of the war the Government had endeavoured to meet labour difficulties by granting temporary exemptions from the army and extended leaves, organising employment through official agencies, and by utilising the unemployed, refugees and foreign and colonial workers, factory work, including night-shifts and overtime, was intensified; women were employed everywhere and disabled soldiers were trained in war work. The initial paralysis had thus been partly overcome, so that by July 1915 75% of pre-war establishments were back at work. But with the ever-growing need for war production, the difficulties were still mounting. And now Viviani's Ministry, realising that the war would bring no quick decision but would be hard and long, began to concentrate on making the most efficient and economical use of France's manpower by balancing her military and industrial needs. This meant, primarily, bringing men out of the army to increase munitions production. So, under the direction of the energetic Albert Thomas, newly-appointed Under Secretary for Armaments, 300,000 skilled workers were released for the arms factories and coal mines – a number soon to be increased to 500,000.

Throughout 1915 the efforts by Government agencies and employers' associations to recruit war-workers intensified. The combing-out of operatives who had been drafted to the army was handled by a special Labour Bureau and the Ministry of Agriculture set up a labour service to borrow soldiers for urgent farm work. But the massive drive for munitions was producing one anomaly: the striking contrast between the pay of temporarily-recalled soldiers, and demobilised troops and civilians performing the same work. In the huge Decauville plant the former were receiving 8 sous (4d.) an hour, hardly more than starvation wages. Moreover the men, unlike soldiers at the front, received no family allowance. So hard did they find these conditions that a number of them applied to return to the front. At a cartridge factory at Vincennes, the writer Henry Bordeaux, serving as a staff officer, was to remark soon after on temporary soldier-operatives working for 25 centimes a day and living in barracks, while at an adjoining State factory demobilised troops were earning up to 15 francs a day and living at home. 'There are families of workers earning 50 or 60 francs a day and they are junketing on this money,' Bordeaux added. 'We are in process of building ourselves a difficult society.'[4]

Around Paris large factories had begun to arise late in 1914, and many existing plants like the Renault works at Billancourt had quickly switched to war work, producing shells, guns in place of cars, war planes instead of civil aircraft. Small iron workers' shops had obtained lathes and executed urgent orders with the aid of State loans. Other factories, new and adapted, were busy throughout the provinces. To encourage production, President Poincaré set about visiting the munitions centres. In June he inspected State factories at Tarbes, Toulouse and elsewhere. Impressed with the workers' output, he handed out medals of bronze, silver and even gold. At the great Creusot arsenal (Seine-et-Oise), which was turning out, among other things, 11,000 shells daily, he was gratified at the 'tremendous activity'.[5] But in other spheres he found a disturbing lack of drive. In February he had complained bitterly to the diarist Michel Corday at the 'aggressive complacency and tyrannical reaction' of the General Staff and War Departments for their slackness in producing a vital explosive component, phenol, which had previously been supplied by Germany. 'They are making 15 tons where they ought to be making 120,' he lamented. 'One might fancy these people have got all eternity in front of them.'[6]

But while the war industries boomed, less essential industries – starved of workers – were declining and wilting. A typical casualty was the wine business. At Charente, one vineyard which normally produced 300 barrels annually was reduced to 50, the cause being lack of labour to treat the mildew on the vines. On the other hand, an unexpected beneficiary from war was the town of Angoulême, whose chief industry, paper-making, might have anticipated being hard-hit by the appreciable reduction in the size of newspapers (largely caused by the censorship and the contraction of space devoted to advertising). But instead, Angoulême was prospering through a vastly increased output to provide for the enormous consumption of paper by the military authorities – that familiar feature of French bureaucracy, *la paperasserie*.

As the nation settled to the struggle, in the life of Paris war seemed, in the words of one resident, to have become 'a permanent factor'. The capital saw a vast influx of middle-aged workers not only French but Belgian, Italian and Spanish, and before the end of the year the pre-war population had almost doubled. On the outskirts collections of new hutments were proliferating into small townships, humming with the machines that were turning out war material. The official war communiqué was now a feature of daily existence and countless households had their war maps, carefully staked out with little flags to show the progress of the fighting. From January onwards people were flocking to the War Museum at the Invalides to see the display of captured German banners and other enemy trophies.[7] Interest in war themes was to continue throughout the year with exhibitions at various re-opened museums – the works of Henri Regnault, killed in the Franco-Prussian War, tapestries from beleaguered Reims, *objets d'art* from Belgium, paintings by artists with the armies. There was a vogue for special 'Days', dedicated to war orphans, to those who had suffered in the war, and so on. In July the ashes of Rouget de l'Isle, famous author of the Marseillaise, were transferred with great pomp from the Arc de Triomphe to the Invalides. Accompanying all this was a revival of religious feeling, as shown by the kneeling throngs in the city's churches.

In the sombre days of January Paris had shown few outward signs of gaiety. Mourning was ever more common, and the economy campaign was dictating a simpler, less extravagant style in women's dress (though some less patriotic dressmakers were offering full instead of clinging skirts and large hats instead of the new smaller ones). Absinthe was now banned by Parliament for the duration. Cafés and restaurants closed at 10.30 p.m. and the trams and Métro shut down early. And with stricter orders for lighting, as an air-raid precaution, the city at night was unwontedly gloomy. So deserted were the streets that it was possible to walk through them around 11 p.m. and hardly meet a pedestrian, while the lighting was so poor that street names were not discernible. Yet behind the darkened curtains night-life was continuing, with theatres, cinemas, concert-halls, night-clubs and brasseries crowded until the curfew hour. 'Café de Paris cram-full,' noted Lord Bertie in February. 'A good many demi-mondaines . . . For the moment, *the* place to go.'[8] But to critical observers there was something disreputable about the pleasure-seekers in these more fashionable haunts. 'At Ciro's and Columbin's at tea-time', commented the diarist Michel Corday sourly, 'there is a decadent crowd of people, a sort of bloom on our decay.'[9]

Corday was quick to remark the contrasts and anomalies created by the war. With cynical eye he observed the smartly-uniformed officers at the War Ministry, 'wallowing in the commandeered limousines of millionaires', who, but for the war, would have known nothing of such privileges.[10] He noted too that same phenomenon that was beginning to be observable in Britain – the growing civilian indifference to the plight of disabled soldiers. An officer who had lost an eye at the Marne told him how friends became disinterested when he described how he had been wounded. Another officer, with both legs amputated, declared: 'Yes, just at this moment I am a hero. In a year I shall be a mere cripple.'[11]

But this attitude was probably untypical. More representative was the general spirit of concern for the fighting man and his welfare that showed itself in the scores of hospitals, work-rooms and depots busy providing comforts and necessities for combatants and their families, that had sprung up all over Paris. Amid the teeming daily life of the capital, no one could easily forget the nearness of war. Even the removal of Paris from the Zone of the Armies in the spring made little difference to its war-girt atmosphere. It was still subject to many military regulations: a pass, for instance, was necessary in order to leave the city, and early morning market carts entering from the country were searched.[12] Moreover, as a reminder of the enemy's presence, late in March Parisians had their first Zeppelin raid. This caused more excitement than panic, and no casualties were reported. Many people slept through it, while others, hearing the fire-engines, thought it was a fire. One woman, looking skywards, said anxiously: 'They're going to drop some bombs.' 'Well,' said an old workman standing near, 'you wouldn't want them to drop flowers.'[13] An eye-witness of the raid was President Poincaré, who was roused from sleep in the Elysée Palace by a telephone warning. From his bedroom window he saw the city suddenly plunged in darkness, while the searchlights on the Eiffel Tower and Arc de Triomphe pierced the clear sky. He made out 'a gigantic golden shape in the sky,' and 'the glowing shells passing above it, like a shower of meteorites'.[14] Pursued by searchlights, the Zeppelin turned northwards and disappeared.

Yet with returning summer, Paris could still present a deceptive peacetime look. Its restaurants crowded with chattering diners, the women in the Avenue du Bois 'talking clothes and hats',[15] the flowery beauty of the Luxembourg Gardens where children played, mothers sat sewing and old men gravely played croquet, all belied the hard reality. In strange contrast was the picture (described in letters to an English peer from a Paris friend) of Paris in late June as a 'desert' and the Bois de Boulogne empty, with women cab drivers and tram and bus conductors everywhere replacing men and the fashionable Hotel Crillon almost entirely staffed by old men and boys, its corridors filled with German war trophies.[16] The author Arnold Bennett, just then visiting Paris, gave his own laconic impression: 'View from hotel ... Young men and women playing silly ball game in dust ... No buses. Concierges sitting out at night on pavements ... Number of young men for various reasons left ... Lack of chicory and salt. Sound of guns in distance. Variety of uniforms. Bad puttees. Women's heavy mourning.'[17] The mourning theme was taken up by another Englishman, who noted that women had widely adopted the black straw mourning hat, trimmed with black and adorned with bunches of stone-white grapes. The effect was even worse, he said, when jet-black grapes were substituted for white. One sad effect of war that this writer noted was the disappearance of the famous bookstalls along the *quais*.[18]

If stern critics like Corday found Paris too indifferent to the war, other places farther afield seemed a world away from the struggle. At Evian spa, the Royal Hotel was preparing for the season with this prospectus: 'Evian being situated in the neutral zone, this situation prevents it receiving wounded soldiers, and the summer season there will preserve all its usual charm.'[19] At Monte Carlo, gambling was, as always, the chief interest. 'God and Père Joffre, and what he stands for, and death, and all those real things,' deplored an observer, '... what dreams they are beside this fantastic affair of numbers and a little white ball.'[20] Yet even the distant Riviera bore its signs of mourning. At Nice the entrance halls of the local newspaper offices were filled with the perfume of the little bouquets of spring flowers placed by relatives around the photographs of their menfolk killed in the war.

Yet sometimes the show of business as usual could be a mark of stubborn courage almost under the enemy guns. Nancy, ancient capital of Lorraine, 220 miles east of Paris, swarmed with life and movement despite its closeness to the front and frequent air-raids. Visiting it in February, Henry Bordeaux remarked admiringly that one could fancy oneself on the Paris boulevards as they used to be. Four months later the Bishop of Nancy issued a pastoral letter praising the 'noble example' of the women of Lorraine who, he said, were staying on in their ruined homes and in the absence of husbands and sons were cultivating the fields in preparation for future harvests.[21] But, the bishop was constrained to add, there were some women who seemed to be thinking too much of the misfortune of their country and their families. Perhaps this was excusable, for in front-line regions like Lorraine the women of the countryside, so often carrying on single-handed, were bearing a heavy burden. Apart from them, the only workers left on the land were men above military age and the very young.

In another war area, near Verdun, children of fifteen were seen wearing themselves out working in the fields. By now, indeed, the war was seriously affecting the whole of rural France. Farming communities were becoming depopulated through shortage of younger men, many of whom had already been killed or wounded. At remote Vimines, in the Savoy, as Bordeaux learnt from his wife, two farmers had given up owing to the deaths of their sons while, of the three sons of another, one was dead, another missing and the third wounded. Soon after, an Englishman visiting Champrosay, near Paris, saw only old men, women and children. In this entire commune, 55 out of a population of 1,500 had been killed, and almost everyone wore mourning. These, he said, were the average statistics for all French villages and were 'pointed to as showing how much greater has been France's sacrifice compared with that of England'.[22]

It spoke much for the country women with sons and husbands at the front that they were more cheerful than those without. Bordeaux' wife spoke of one woman with a young baby, whose husband had been in the trenches for over six months and had come through without a scratch. 'It is the prayers of the little ones that protect him,' said Mme Bordeaux. 'Yes,' answered the woman, 'I make this little thing pray too.' The baby was eight months old, born after her husband's mobilisation.[23]

But there was another aspect of the wartime sufferings of

French women that was causing concern in the spring of 1915: the question of those unfortunates who had become pregnant after being raped by German soldiers. There were said to be as many as 60,000 such women. Much exercised about the ethics of the problem, people were asking: should human life be respected or should abortion be allowed? The matter had several times been discussed by the Cabinet, but ministers had refused to consider abortion, deciding instead to extend the number of foundling hospitals. Corday's sardonic comment on this was: 'So they respect human life in poor little foetuses whose existence will be nothing more than one long hardship. But they do not respect human life in the form of youths of 20.'[24]

For the great majority of France's women, as for those of Britain, 1915 was a year of revolution and liberation. Flocking from accustomed feminine occupations and sheltered homes into the free-and-easy and often rough atmosphere of wartime employment, they too threw aside the traditional restraints of their sex and embraced a new freedom and independence. As in Britain, the transformation was not only social but economic, for thousands of them quitted low-paid jobs as domestics, clothing-workers and the like to receive much higher wages in the munition factories. And while they replaced men in a host of commercial, public service and other more ordinary occupations, it was in the vastly expanded munition factories that their contribution was most significant. Already by mid-1915 there were 30,000 women employed in private arms plants in Paris and elsewhere, making shells, rifle parts, bombs, explosives, cartridges, aeroplane parts and fuses. They were also engaged in turning, counter-sinking and boring. A further 14,000 were working in State factories, chiefly on checking. By October the total number had risen to 75,000.[25]

In general, women were assigned tasks of a limited kind, not needing a long apprenticeship. They were found to be good at operations calling for dexterity and more assiduous and sober than men – though they exhibited, it was claimed, the feminine defect of talkativeness. For this reason they were placed far apart, so that they had to shout to make themselves heard. This attracted the forewoman, who promptly imposed a fine. But were these women factory hands being exploited? In May a leading figure in the feminist body *La Ligue du Droit des Femmes* asked whether they were not working longer hours than men, alleging that in some cases the women were starting at 8 a.m. and the men at 9 a.m., and in others, while the men left at 6 p.m., the women continued until 7 p.m. But in other spheres efforts were being made to promote their welfare by the provision of crèches, nursing rooms and nurseries where the mothers could look after and leave their children.

As the war continued this new working status was to affect not least the wives of soldiers – and indeed the husbands themselves. Such wives, receiving 1 fr. 25 centimes a day for themselves and 50 centimes for each child, and earning additional money for war work, enjoyed a financial and personal independence previously unknown. When their husbands returned on leave they were liable to find them changed by their new life and perhaps not so dedicated to the home. This could all too easily widen the gulf between soldiers and those in the rear that was to become a universal feature of the war. And Frenchwomen's wartime emancipation was producing that other inevitable result: the loosening of accepted moral standards and increased sexual freedom. Corday noted in May that Parisian women of all classes were leading what he called fast lives. The popular phrase, he commented, was: 'Must have a man about the house.'[26] At the same time he reported a fresh outbreak of syphilis. In September Henry Bordeaux referred to growing evidence that the wives of servicemen were not preserving their 'dignity and fidelity'. He attributed this to a decline of normal 'collective influences and a lack of priests and spiritual life'.[27]

A further wartime casualty was sensitiveness to the ordeals of the men in the trenches. For civilians who over the lengthening months had been fed with terse communiqués impersonally reporting 'battles' and 'advances', and optimistic handouts, custom was beginning to dull the real meaning of what their troops were experiencing and enduring. As described by the subaltern Robert Graves, the same thing was happening in Britain (where indeed more freedom of reporting was allowed). There was the Frenchwoman on a suburban railway station who, during the September fighting, was overheard to say happily, after reading the day's communiqué: 'We have advanced 400 yards!' and then change the conversation.[28] Linked with this attitude was a belligerence – again, the parallel was seen in Britain – that dismissed the idea of peace as a calamity, something not to be considered in view of the sacrifices already made. That the front-line *poilus* thought otherwise was shown by a sergeant's story that when one man shouted the well-known battle-cry '*On les aura!*' (We shall get them!), his comrades would echo sarcastically: 'Yes, frozen feet!' or 'Yes, lice!' In August another sidelight on the growing gap between front and rear was given in the cartoon, in a comic journal, showing a soldier in the trenches, with his feet in mud and bullets flying around, saying with an air of concern: 'If only the civilians can hold out.'[29]

The intransigent civilian mood was encouraged by the press which, through fear of the censorship and in an effort to pander to the lower instincts of its readers, was putting out a stream of 'hate' material. 'This incessant inculcation of hatred', noted Corday, 'will remain one of the outstanding phenomena of our national life during the war. The Press will prove to have been ... one of its chief instigators.'[30] In March another observer was happy to note that French public opinion was awaking to the necessity of treating the German Emperor and his family in the only way they deserved, namely by hanging them. In an article entitled '*La Haine Sacrée*' (Sacred Hate), a writer declared: 'Shooting would be too good for them.'[31] To instil the fighting spirit (presumably into soldiers), in April postcards appeared inscribed: 'The Ten Commandments of the Soldier – Thou shalt always kill . . .', and 'The Greeting of the Bayonet – Hail to thee Rosalie [trench slang for bayonet], thou fount of charms.'[32] French anger was powerfully provoked in May by the sinking of the *Lusitania*, which gave rise the feeling that a people capable of approving such a crime must be exterminated.

While anti-German feeling ran strong, pro-British sentiment was not as warm as it might have been. The first enthusiasm for the BEF in 1914 had given way to doubts about the extent of Britain's war-effort. Scepticism had been aroused by the fraternisation of British with German troops at Christmas 1914, and many Frenchmen, not appreciating that Britain was without conscription, were puzzled at the paucity of British troops in France. Another cause of unease was the industrial trouble occurring in Wales in July, to which the conciliatory attitude of Lloyd George, Minister of Munitions, was adversely compared with the current desperate resistance of the Russians at Warsaw. All this was largely the fault of French propaganda, which failed to explain how Britain was contributing to the war. This lack of rapprochement was in some degree mutual, for in Britain too there was an inadequate realisation of what France was doing. Neither Britain nor France, in fact, was being brought to see the other's viewpoint. 'Britain', a contemporary neatly suggested, 'has never understood the effects of 1870 or what it is like to be invaded; France what it is like *not* to be invaded.'[33]

With conscription an accepted fact of French national life for over forty years, France was spared the anxious doubts and questionings that the issue of its adoption was causing in Britain during 1915. She was thus spared too such demonstrations as the invidious 'white feather' crusade that Britain experienced, though she had her own minor problem of the *embusqués* – the shirkers who managed to find themselves safe civilian jobs. And in so far as conscription admitted of no exemption on moral grounds, conscientious objection – already a controversial matter in Britain and soon, with the introduction of conscription, to become more so – was ruled out. But like Britain, amid the general and mostly whole-hearted support for the war, France had her small anti-war and pacifist factions.

Before 1914 the French Government had recognised the potential danger of subversionist activity in the event of war and prepared to detain a large number of known agitators, many of them aliens; but on the outbreak had decided to leave them free. In the euphoric atmosphere of August 1914 this may have seemed a sound decision, but in the light of later events, with France increasingly strained, war-weary and open to pacifist influences, it was to appear less wise. Already in 1915 reports of defeatist activity among troops and civilian workers were reaching M. Malvy, Minister of the Interior, but Malvy was taking no action to stop it. Suppression, he believed, might defeat its own end by antagonising the workers, many of them strongly left-wing. A specific anti-war group, meeting secretly in the war's early months under the leadership of a man named Monatte, had been associated with the revolutionary journal *Vie Ouvrière*. One member was the trade unionist Merrheim, secretary of the *Fédération des Métaux*, who in May 1915 flouted the censor by publishing in his union journal an open denunciation of the war. Four months later French pacifists were encouraged by a declaration condemning the war issued by the International Socialist Conference which had met at Zimmerwald in Switzerland, attended by French and German delegates. The *Vie Ouvrière*, which had been shut down in August 1914, thereupon revived itself to the extent of circulating anti-war pamphlets to subscribers. But at the most, at this stage, such activities had a minimal effect on the general war-effort.

Unlike conscription, a problem that affected France in 1915 as well as Britain (though perhaps less significantly) was drink. At the start of the war the military authorities had attacked that time-honoured French institution the bistro, and also wine-sellers, café proprietors and purveyors of all kinds of spirits, as being a threat to the war-effort. Hours of opening were rigorously fixed, soldiers were prohibited from buying wine and spirits except at certain times and women forbidden to do so altogether. Notwithstanding, by April 1915 the growth of the drink habit was causing some concern. Women as well as men were taking increasingly to spirits, notably the female munition-workers who, with good wages in their pockets and their new sense of freedom, were following their male companions' example. Mothers, it was said, were even giving their young children *canards* or lumps of sugar dipped in Calvados, and in the working-class districts they were rumoured to be lulling their babies to sleep by lacing their feeding bottles with brandy. Whether or not as a result, it was ordered that women (and youths under eighteen) should be served with only the weakest alcoholic drink. This meant that women were denied the enjoyment of that pleasantly cooling drink for a hot day, a lemon squash with a dash of Angostura. What was called the 'demoralisation' of the worker followed, it was charged, from the opening of indoor bars in the large towns – these being foreign to the French character, to which the traditional terrace café was far more congenial. Serious or otherwise, the drink question took on a touch of the ludicrous with a new military rule of July, which forbade the serving of soldiers in uniform with any alcoholic liquor in cafés except beer or wine. This produced the sight of an officer sitting in front of a civilian and drinking the civilian's cognac while the latter reached over from time to time to refresh himself with the officer's beer.[34]

But one drink of which Parisians were seeing little was champagne. The war was having a disastrous effect on the champagne trade. The previous December a famous café that had normally sold some hundred and sixty bottles a day had not sold twenty over the whole month. However, this was a small privation when set against the general abundance of the Frenchman's table in 1915. As regards food, thus far the sole result of the war was seen in rising prices, some pressure on reserve stocks and a threat to imports on account of shipping shortage and the depredations of German submarines. There was some risk to flour supplies owing to the requisition of grain by the army, and lack of flour-milling staff and transport.

Moreover, the year's sugar crop was below average. In December the Council of Ministers held a long discussion on *la vie chère* (the high cost of living), in which it was proposed to ask Britain for deliveries of frozen meat, and subsidise the co-operative butcheries in Paris to reduce meat prices. Malvy was so concerned at the rising prices that he expressed fears of trouble in the capital.[35] But whatever the difficulties, the fine traditions of French gastronomy could still be maintained – even within range of the German guns. That month the Bishop of Nancy entertained Henry Bordeaux to a dinner comprising the choicest dishes of Bordeaux' home locality of Savoy. They sat down to sweetbreads, pigeons on rice, roast chicken in gravy with artichokes, a salad mixed by the bishop himself, seasoned with wine, a special gateau and a millefeuille. This was washed down with a wine from Thiaucourt which would soon no longer be obtainable as the Germans had destroyed the vine-stocks, and a vintage Montmélian wine.

President Poincaré – reserved, conscientious, sensitive to the ordeals of the troops and attentive to the national war-effort – frequently visited both the front and the munitions centres in the rear. With his peaked cap, knickerbockers and leggings, the shortish, bearded President failed to cut an impressive figure, and earned the troops' nickname, 'the chauffeur'. Henry Bordeaux affirmed that the troops did not take him seriously, adding that Poincaré could not assume the weight of all France's sufferings and would do better to remain at the Elysée performing his task of directing the nation's affairs. Poincaré may well have undertaken his tours partly in order to get away from the cares of his presidential desk, for by virtue of his office he was in constant touch with Ministers and closely involved in day-to-day governmental matters – and these, during 1915, were proceeding far from smoothly under the premiership of René Viviani. Beset by criticisms over its conduct of the war in both the West and the Balkans, the position of the Government was becoming increasingly uncertain. In June Viviani confided in Poincaré that he was finding it impossible to continue governing, declaring he was 'worn out, despondent, disgusted'.[36] He repeated his plaint at a Council of Ministers two months later, and finally resigned with his colleagues in October, to be succeeded by the Socialist Aristide Briand who aimed, with his broad coalition Ministry, to strengthen the *Union Sacrée* that had been somewhat shaken by the events of 1915.

These same events had by the end of the year had their effect on the nation's morale. With the continued failure of the Allied offensives of 1915 to achieve any breakthrough, hope and optimism were steadily being eroded by realisation of the stalemate, so appallingly costly in casualties, that was settling on the war. And yet, amid the generally subdued mood of Frenchmen, there was – in Paris at least – a strange streak of gaiety, a brittle euphoria, that contrasted sharply with the gravity of the times. A grand performance of the Russian ballet at the Opera House was arranged for the end of December, in anticipation of which a fashionable Paris costumier was exhibiting jewelled gowns priced at up to 3,500 francs. The performance itself was an affair of glittering splendour, playing to a packed house and lasting five hours. 'Never in ante-bellum days,' recorded the American, J. G. Coolidge, who was present, 'have I seen anything more magnificent. The general feeling is that it was a mistake.'[37] On the other hand, perhaps such a brilliant spectacle was seen as a morale-raiser. But the paradox of extravagance or high spending on the Home Front while the ill-paid fighting men huddled in the mud of the trenches now seemed an inescapable fact of the war. It was evident among not only the rich but all classes. A popular store in the Rue de Rennes was said to have sold a million more articles in 1915 than in 1913, largely scent and fancy underwear. The same phenomenon was seen in Britain. In December Lord Sandhurst was disturbed to note that in the north of England the high wages were being spent 'in pianos, the latest kind of motor-bike, and brass bedsteads – the trade can't make them quickly enough.'[38] Such free spending on inessentials had, however, to be seen alongside that other and more patriotic form of outlay which Frenchmen, Britons and Germans alike were contributing towards the cost of the war—the huge national War Loans to which citizens rich and poor were subscribing. Already since 1914 they had invested hundreds of millions of pounds in Government-floated loans, and would continue year by year to take up further issues in answer to vigorously mounted Government appeals in all three countries, to help finance the vast and steadily mounting war expenditure.

Chapter 5

GERMANY

'Gott strafe England'

THANKS largely to the foresight and organising ability of Walter Rathenau, Germany had by the spring of 1915 overcome her initial munitions shortage and converted her vast chemical industry and highly progressive engineering industries to the large-scale production of war material. And her machine-tool industry, second only to that of the United States, was enabling her to equip numerous new munitions plants. In founding the War Raw Materials Department in August 1914, Rathenau had compiled an inventory of the nation's resources, collecting information from some 1,000 firms which normally received Government contracts. To muster the nation's raw materials by some method short of State socialism – a measure too far-reaching and experimental to be undertaken in wartime – Rathenau created bodies known as War Industries Companies (such as the War Metal Company, the War Chemicals Company and so on), drawing their personnel from business and professional men and working under Government supervision. Their function was to commandeer the needed materials and transfer them to the manufacturers as directed. In April Rathenau handed the whole organisation over to the Prussian Minister of War. It was now a smoothly working department employing five hundred officials, with its various subsidiary companies staffed by some thousands. Rathenau was able to report that the nation's supplies were secure, 'that the blockade had been defeated and that a scarcity of essential materials no longer threatened the fate of the war'.[1]

But if Germany's war-production had moved into top gear quicker than that of the Allies and seemed fully capable of matching theirs, industrially she was already fighting what was bound in the end to be a losing battle. For at the outset of the war the German leaders had allowed only for a lightning campaign. They had made no real preparations for a prolonged struggle against an adversary who was potentially equally strong and wielded in addition the powerful weapon of blockade. Even though Germany's war-effort now looked every bit as formidable as that of the Allies, henceforth she would be faced with the task of providing for all her war needs almost entirely without external assistance, while Britain and France would be able to call on the aid of the world's greatest industrial power, the United States. To carry on the war for any length of time, the nation whose peacetime share of the world's trade had been exceeded only by that of Britain would be forced increasingly to rely on her own resources. But of all this, of the privations and difficulties to come, there was little sign amid the belching war-factories and vigorous, teeming activity of Germany in this first springtime of the conflict.

Though their first high enthusiasm for the war had faded by the end of 1914, Germans had no doubts about their ultimate victory. If, as the months of 1915 passed, nothing spectacular occurred to bring this nearer, by August – after a year of war – they could proudly contemplate the glittering successes gained by their armies. They saw nearly all Belgium and 15,000 square miles of France occupied, most of Russian Poland conquered, large parts of Russia's Baltic provinces in German hands, and German military power intact. Moreover their navy was stronger than in 1914 and was sinking thousands of tons of British merchant shipping. Perhaps they forgot that German Southwest Africa and most of their colonial empire had been lost. And at this stage they had every faith in Germany's self-sufficiency, isolated as she was in Central Europe. They believed too that time favoured them at least as much as their enemies. Above all they were confident that their armies could not be dislodged from the territories they held and to this extent had already, militarily at least, 'won' the war.

But these successes had been attained only by an immense expenditure and deployment of Germany's able-bodied manhood. In Germany, as in France, there was hardly a family that had not contributed a father, son or husband to the fighting forces. And with casualties of dead, wounded or missing running at some three million after twelve months' hostilities, a vast number of homes had felt the direct impact of war. But while, in Germany too, the younger men were beginning to be noticeably scarce in the towns and countryside, Germany had a deeper reservoir of manpower than France. Some six million men were now under arms, consisting of the nation's trained soldiers between the ages of twenty and thirty-nine, a proportion of trained men aged thirty-nine to forty-five, and well over a million volunteers including men both over and under military age. Behind these stood a substantial untapped reserve of able-bodied men liable to call-up when required, and now working in the war industries. No question had yet arisen of lifting the age for compulsory service above forty-five (as was done in Austria-Hungary early in 1915).[2] And supplementing the male manpower in civilian work were – besides prisoners of war – up to 500,000 women, the ladies of leisure, the girls and housewives, the organisation of whose employment or re-employment on a voluntary basis had started in the first days of the war. Thousands were in the munitions industries, while there were few less essential kinds of job in which they were not replacing men.

Among the women of the three belligerent nations German women were the most domesticated and least feminist-minded. At the same time they were generally robust and accustomed to hard work. Treated by men as the inferior sex, they accepted this position and looked on them as masters whose commands they readily obeyed. If a husband and wife were out shopping, the wife probably carried the parcels. In entering a restaurant or other public place, it was customary for the wife dutifully to follow her spouse. When leaving, the husband would be helped on with his coat before the wife. The typical German housewife was docile, thrifty, devoted to her husband and home. Men of the official classes would consider a woman with progressive, feminist views as they regarded 'a Social Democrat, something hardly to be endured'. Middle-class girls enjoyed a good broad education with plenty of opportunity for sport They rode, skated and made sturdy swimmers and hockey-players. From their mothers they learned the skills of domestic science. As for working-class girls, according to an observer they had many worthy qualities, being 'ambitious, persistent and earnest'. And 'instead of flirting or turkey trotting at night, they make a practice of going to the Turnvereins, to exercise in the gymnasiums there'.[3] These varied characteristics were to account for the conscientiousness and tenacity with which Germany's women at home supported their menfolk in the fighting line.

Meanwhile life in Berlin and other cities was taking on an increasingly wartime aspect. Everywhere, in shops, offices and private houses, war maps were displayed, showing eager citizens the progress of operations. Berlin's hotels and public places were adorned with posters as numerous as the recruiting appeals appearing in Britain, among the most conspicuous being the large yellow placards urging Berliners to take their gold to the Reichsbank. Though a few ramshackle taxis were still plying to and from the Berlin railway stations, private car had almost vanished from the streets. Car-owners who could not reach their businesses in any other way had at first been allowed to use them, but had soon had to find other means of travel. Even bicycles were forbidden except for business pur poses and for children travelling to school. A familiar sight now in the capital was the crowd of anxious Berliners poring over the casualty lists posted outside the building at the corner of the Wilhelmstrasse and Dorotheenstrasse. Pathetic scenes were witnessed there as relatives read the names of dead or wounded menfolk. On a less warlike note, theatres, concert-halls and cinemas were well attended, and would continue to be through out the war. With a fine disregard for current enmities, Shakespeare's plays were being performed as usual, and French and Italian concert music played. 'Films', in the words of one writer, 'were intensely patriotic and more or less fanciful.'[4] Even more liberal, British and French daily papers were freely available in Berlin's smarter hotels and the cafés on the Unter den Linden, as well as in the provinces. *The Times*, it was said, was most popular. A feature of the period was the fresh wave of spy fever that swept Berlin in June. It 'seems as if every second person at least is on the verge of lunacy and that this venomous attitude towards your neighbour is a new form of war-pestilence', commented Princess Blücher, who added that she knew of dozens of cases of informers spreading false and malicious stories.[5] German officialdom seemed to be endorsing the spy-hunt mania by its tightened security measures against aliens entering Germany. In July the wife of an American newspaper correspondent was forced, at the frontier, to strip to the skin and take down her hair in order to be searched.

This attitude was in line with the sustained spirit of 'hate', chiefly directed against the British. A potent weapon for expressing this hate was seen to be the Zeppelin. As early as the autumn of 1914 children had been singing a song whose words went: 'Fly Zeppelin! Fly to England! England shall be destroyed with fire!' Now postcards were being sold all over Germany showing the Zeppelins bombing enemy towns. Newspaper cartoons showed Britain being raided. One, entitled 'Zeppelinitis', portrayed Nelson descending from his column in Trafalgar Square to take cover in the Underground. It was sub-titled: 'The End of England's Sea-Power.' There was a great demand for caricatures of the British at home. Among the favourites was one called 'Family Life in England'. It depicted a group of women, and children aged from two upwards, seated round a table and working away with knives and other tools to turn ordinary bullets into dum-dum bullets.[6] Wild calumnies circulated, like that which alleged that King George was offering £1 to anyone who would bring him a

German.[7] The sinking of the *Lusitania* in mid-May was greeted with a surge of exultation. The Germans gloated over the achievement of one small submarine and boasted that England, faced with such a threat to her life-lines, must soon give in. But Princess Blücher noted that some of the loudest approvers of the sinking were soon having second thoughts about it, though less on humanitarian grounds than on account of its political unwisdom.[8] The hate burned on throughout the year, to be further fanned at Christmas by the Allies' curt rejection of peace feelers put out by the Chancellor, Bethmann-Hollweg. England, with her arrogance and inhumanity – it was now said – was responsible for the vast and continued bloodshed. And now the hatred was projected against America too. Americans in Berlin found themselves cold-shouldered by Germans, who blamed their country for supplying the Allies with the means of continuing the war and thus avoiding defeat. One vociferous anti-American likened America 'to a great greedy vulture, feeding on the carrion of the battlefields of Europe, and growing ever grosser and more complacent as the masses of its gory food increased'.[9] The reverse side of this coin of hatred was an intensified appeal to patriotic feelings through the image of the iron cross. The shops were full of articles – postcards, cigarette-cases, pipes, pocket-books, mugs, walking-sticks, handkerchiefs, brooches, rings, even pairs of garters – marked with this emblem of German military valour.

The hatred campaign was sometimes so far-fetched as to appear ridiculous. Not only did Germans greet each other with the standard '*Gott strafe England*' but they answered it with an automatic '*Er strafe es*' (May he punish it). This was even an accepted opening to telephone conversations. And in cafés it was not unusual for some wild-eyed patron to jump on to a table and declaim Lissauer's 'Hymn of Hate'. But if such sentiments were prevalent among ordinary people, the more thoughtful Germans were not so rabid. Many to whom the writer De Beaufort talked expressed a disappointment that Germany and Britain were at war. Some even confessed to an admiration for their enemy. One lady said to him, 'You must admit that when an Englishmen is a gentleman he is the greatest gentleman in the world.'[10]

But amid the general 'hate' and belligerence, another mood was stirring. While the Socialists were voicing their opposition to the war and demands for peace in the Reichstag, for the first time signs of unrest appeared among the public. In June some five hundred women gathered in front of the Reichstag in a somewhat vague demonstration against the failure of von Bulow, the German Ambassador in Rome, to prevent Italy from entering the war against the Central Powers (Italy had declared war on Austria-Hungary on the 23rd May). They also complained that the whipped cream was not as good as before the war, grumbled at the high price of food and called for the return of their men from the trenches.[11] The assembly was promptly dispersed by the police and no word of it appeared in the newspapers. In November there was trouble in the great industrial centre of Leipzig, following which the local Socialist newspaper, the *Volkzeitung*, was suppressed. In November too, on the occasion of an important Reichstag speech by Bethmann-Hollweg, on the question of peace, a few hundred women marched down the Unter den Linden in Berlin chanting 'Peace, Peace'. The parade was broken up by the police with drawn swords, a number of arrests made, and the ringleaders sentenced to short terms of imprisonment. The event had been expected to cause considerable trouble, and as a precaution the authorities had closed the gates of the Unter den Linden. As a result there was little disorder; but again the press was silent.[12] In December Berlin saw a further peace demonstration. Witnessing this was James Gerard, the American Ambassador, who was told by a demonstrator that the people were tired of a useless war and of going short of meat. As before, there were no press reports.[13] The vein of war-weariness running through these manifestations may not have been widely representative, but it was significant. Equally so was the discontent, expressed in Berlin and Leipzig alike, at the increasing cost and scarcity of food.

Germany's basic food predicament in wartime was shown by the fact that in peacetime only 80% of her needs were covered by home production.[14] In other words, to feed 20% of her population she relied on imported foodstuffs. When these imports were cut off by the war, she had to increase her domestic production accordingly, or suffer severe shortage. But in peacetime the Germans were hearty eaters, enjoying perhaps six larger or smaller meals a day. For early breakfast they would take coffee and rolls, following this with a more substantial meal at 9 a.m. After a good lunch they would partake of afternoon tea or coffee and cakes, and dine solidly at about 7 p.m., possibly rounding off the day's eating with a late supper. One authority has estimated that as much as 35% of this intake was unnecessary. Moreover, there was conspicuous waste, notably of bread. Before the war it was apparently customary, when the wallpaper needed cleaning, to buy a dozen hot loaves, cut them in half lengthwise and rub them over the paper.[15] But all this had changed with the coming of war. The Government had then mounted a widespread campaign to encourage economy and simple living. 'Eat Less' slogans were posted everywhere, meetings and exhibitions were held, and the message of frugality was spread by clergy, schoolmasters and others. There was a drive against waste, and special garbage pails had to be kept for food remains. In a new-found spirit of sacrifice and patriotism, the public had responded, readily accepting the adulterated 'War Bread' introduced in October. With steeply rising prices rather than scarcity the immediate problem, the Government had decreed a series of maximum-price regulations. But the new asceticism was not evident everywhere. In October a large restaurant in Berlin's Leipzigerstrasse was offering a generous menu of hors-d'œuvres, soup, fish, entrée, roasts, cold meats, salads, vegetables, sweets, together with unrestricted bread. The only injunction towards moderation was a prominent notice on each table asking patrons not to eat two dishes if one was enough.[16]

The first real indication of stringencies to come was bread rationing, introduced in January 1915. About the same time, in a powerful appeal for economy, a notice headed *Ten Food Commandments* was produced for display in railway carriages, stations, shops and even domestic kitchens.[17] It ran as follows:

'Germany is Standing against a World of Enemies who would Destroy Her.

'1. ... They wish to starve us out like a besieged fortress. They will fail in that because we have enough breadstuffs in the country to feed our population until the next harvest, but nothing must be wasted.

'2. Breadstuffs must not be used as fodder.

'3. Therefore, be economical with bread in order that the hopes of our foes may be confounded.

'4. Respect the daily bread, then you will have it always, however long the war may last.

'5. Teach these maxims also to your children.

'6. Do not despise even a single piece of bread because it is no longer fresh.

'7. Do not cut off a slice more than you need to eat. Think always of our soldiers in the field who, often in some far-off, exposed position, would rejoice to have the bread which you waste.

'8. Eat War Bread. It is recognisable by the letter K. It satisfies and nourishes as thoroughly as any other kind ...

'9. Whoever first peels potatoes before cooking them, wastes much. Therefore, cook potatoes with the jackets on ...

'10. Do not throw away leavings of potatoes, meat, vegetables and so on, which you cannot use, but collect them as fodder for cattle ...'

Even though these injunctions were precautionary rather than indications of any immediate shortage, they were of a severity that would be paralleled in Britain only in the worst days of 1917, when the massive shipping losses caused by the German U-boats threatened the country with starvation.

In June the Imperial Grain Office was formed, to control the purchase and distribution of grain. This benefited the public by keeping the bread queue within manageable limits and assured every citizen of his daily ration at a reasonable price. But it was only the forerunner of many similar controls. As other foods started to grow scarce, further Imperial Offices were to be set up to regulate potatoes, sugar, meat, fats, spirits, vegetables and fruit. To help with the adequate feeding of the population, People's Kitchens and workers' canteens were established this year in Germany's larger cities. They were well managed, comfortable and popular. But despite the price-fixing measures, food prices continued to rise. In May, the general level was reported to be 65% above that of July 1914, as compared with an increase of 35% or less in Britain.[18] Meanwhile, great efforts were being made to increase agricultural production. Every available piece of ground was being ploughed and sown. 'The whole Empire', says one account, 'was converted into a vast field.'[19] Nevertheless, the autumn bread grain harvest, at ten and a half million tons, was some four million tons below the hoped-for yield.[20] Rather than sell at the fixed price, the producers hoarded their grain or sold it through underground channels. The Government's reply was to raise the maximum price, with the almost inevitable result of provoking discontent and even rioting.

By spring 1915 the food even at one of Berlin's best hotels seemed to be deteriorating. In March an American dentist, lunching with a friend at the famous Adlon, took his own bread with him to supplement what he called 'a very poor meal'.[21] In July there were reports of growing dissatisfaction among ordinary people, especially at the soaring prices. As to actual shortages, the most acute lack was of butter. That same month there was a serious riot in Chemnitz, Saxony, when a butter store was stormed. In December a butter shortage caused angry women to storm shops and markets in Berlin. While the poorer people went short, illicit supplies were going to the rich. The manager of one of Berlin's largest hotels was imprisoned for forcing the staff to give him their butter allowance and selling it to the hotel guests. Milk was another scarce commodity that autumn, the result, it was said, of too many calves being killed in the spring and also of the lack of sufficient feeding for the cows. The situation was beginning to cause complaints and recriminations all round. The townspeople blamed the farmers for withholding supplies, the consumer blamed the middleman, and everybody blamed the Government and that hated figure, the food profiteer. But, despite the difficulties, Germany was as yet feeling no marked pinch. The very greatly increased exports of foodstuffs from the United States to neutral countries in 1915, as compared with 1913, indicated a source of supply to Germany untouched by the blockade.[22] And more than one observer was discounting any question of Germany being gravely short of food at this time. 'It cannot be pretended that the British blockade made any visible impression on food conditions,' commented one writer.[23] And James Gerard, the American Ambassador, remarked in June: 'Germany has plenty of food.' In November Gerard went further. 'Efforts to starve Germany will not succeed,' he noted. 'We shall be on meat and butter cards, but that is only a precaution. The people are still well in hand. Constant rumours of peace keep them in hand.'[24]

But with the autumn came signs of another kind of shortage, bringing home to Germans the army's vast ammunition needs. In October a circular was sent to every house in Silesia and Austria, ordering an inventory to be made of all copper, brass and similar metals contained in chandeliers, on roofs and elsewhere. Householders could be seen listing their possessions, while speculating sadly when they would have to tear them down for melting into tools of war. Soon after, a big copper collection took place in Berlin. Cartloads of old pots and kettles, candlesticks, door-knobs and chandeliers were a common sight being driven through the streets to the collecting offices, to be weighed and paid for. Individuals would make their way there with some treasured item, anxious to get the good money the Government was said to be offering. The demand was apparently fairly urgent, for James Gerard observed workmen on a new building near the American consulate stripping the copper roof.

If Germany was not starving in 1915, the less privileged Germans could well feel resentful at the plenty that was still being enjoyed by the rich. Princess Blücher, resident at Berlin's fashionable Esplanade hotel, had reason to note this, not without a twinge of conscience. 'A man looking in at the Esplanade the other night,' she noted in December, 'his face pressed against the glass of the door, showed an expression of hatred and disgust at the elegant public within at their supper, in which there were few signs of the frugality expected in such times as these.' This incident had seemed to confirm her growing concern at the inequality of sacrifice brought about by war, as between the rich and other citizens. A month before, she had asked herself uneasily what some ordinary mother would think on seeing the display of wealth and luxury at the Esplanade. 'Will she not say,' the Princess queried, ' "Is this what we are sacrificing everything for"?'[25] But by the end of 1915 inequality of sacrifice was becoming an issue that extended beyond the mere matter of food and good living. Its implications were reaching into the whole of Germany's wartime life.

In the exalted mood prevailing in August 1914, Germans had been ready for every sacrifice. They believed in a Deity who, in return for such a supreme effort, would bless their arms and bring them speedy victory. In this spirit they had banished all pre-war differences and presented a united front, bent on fighting a war whose success would bring them their due reward. But when the hoped-for quick victory had not materialised, the people's fervent initial faith had declined. And as the months of 1915 passed with little sign of an end to the struggle, the justification of the war through religion was suffering a painful reverse. Germany's Deity seemed to have deserted her despite her enormous exertions. While every German remained proud of the magnificent achievements of the army, there was a latent sense of frustration that these were bringing to the Home Front nothing but the promise of increasing difficulties and disappointments. In particular, Germans were realising that the notion of equal sacrifice, so eagerly embraced at the start of the war, was proving illusory. While worthy and deserving people were afflicted by loss and ill-fortune, the undeserving were flourishing. This could be seen in any town. The writer Mendelssohn-Bartholdy depicts a situation as it might appear among families in a typical street.[26] In the first house there would be a schoolmaster and his family of five sons and one daughter. Two sons had been killed and one was missing. The daughter had become a pacifist. The mother was reduced by her troubles to semi-invalidism, while the father's school was failing as a result of the war. The second family consisted of a self-important father in charge of a large depot. Only two years junior to his neighbour, he had five sons, all too young for the army. In the next two houses there were two widows, the first one very comfortably maintained by a son living abroad, the second – outstandingly kind and generous – in a state of penury because her income, payable from funds in Britain, had been stopped owing to the war. Nearby were two bookshops. One was closed because its owner, a delicate man of literary tastes, had enlisted. The other, specialising in political pamphlets and trashy comic papers and haunted by dubious characters of military age, was thriving. Such was the inequality of sacrifice whose examples, becoming all too common, were beginning to spread disillusion among Germans.

The realisation of these inequalities was affecting not only the civilians but the men at the front. Returning home on leave, they noted the differing impact the war was having as between one family and another. This helped further to weaken the fine initial spirit of national unity in which Germany had gone to war. Whereas soldiers and civilians had at first been 'in it together', now the sacrifice looked less fairly spread. For this and other reasons was arising the inevitable gulf between the fighting man and the Home Front, perhaps more marked in Germany than in Britain or France. The German troops were more cut off from home because they were fighting on enemy territory, had little leave and were subject to rigorous censorship of letters to and from their families. Such separation had a two-way effect, isolating the Home Front equally from the troops. Intensifying the gulf was that universal factor, the different picture of the war as actually experienced by the troops and as presented to the civilians by distorted newspaper reports. Soldiers on leave were beginning to be disgusted (like those in Britain and France) with the spirit of hate prevailing at home. In May a young officer on leave in Berlin told a friend that he was longing to get back to the front so as to have a little peace and quiet and escape the venomous hatred and vindictiveness against the enemy and the incessant talk of cruelties and reprisals. 'Out there we all do our duty,' he said. 'We obey the orders and do what we are told, and have no time to think or feel all this horrible hatred and revenge.'[27] But for the Germans, both troops and civilians alike, there appeared to be a special grievance that provoked disunity and mutual misunderstanding – the Etappe.[28] This was the semi-military, semi-civilian organisation that administered occupied and neutral territory and included hospitals, rest cantonments, newspaper correspondents' headquarters and so on. It was the target for heated abuse from the fighting men as a safe billet for non-combatants, and civilians saw it as a refuge from the privations of the Home Front, where shirkers lived on the fat of the land. While some abuses may have occurred within the Etappe, most of the tales of extravagance and malpractice originated through rumour – itself stimulated by the strictness of the censorship.

By the end of 1915 it was becoming clear to what an extent Germany had relied, from the point of view of morale, on a short war. At home the ordinary man was murmuring un-easily at the comforts still enjoyed by the privileged and the profiteers, and at the front the soldiers were beginning to resent their treatment as mere cannon-fodder.[29] But if the heroic spirit of 1914 had evaporated, the nation still had a deep fund of discipline and endurance on which to draw. One truth about the total war in which Germany was engaged had, however, emerged, as it had emerged among the other belligerents: the basic inability of the Home Front to identify itself fully with the ordeals and experiences of the fighting men. Just as, in Paris, Proust's fictional Verdurins could deplore the tragedies of war while comfortably pursuing their daily lives, so many good Germans carried on patriotically yet entirely untouched by the war's realities. Mendelssohn-Bartholdy cites, as such, 'a clubroom of respectabilities' composed of militia officers and presidents of patriotic associations serving as commandants of prison camps, railway depots, hospitals and so on; or the staff of some trade union secretariat, or Protestant elders preaching Christ instead of the High Command's latest order against the exercise of charitable feelings towards wounded prisoners. The great majority, Mendelssohn-Bartholdy suggests, refused to acknowledge that in war they had come to face 'a gruesomely naked truth', in the sight of which men wearing their regulation, respectable clothes had become a ridiculous incongruity. 'They remained immune to the war to the last.'[30]

This immunity was partly the direct fault of the German censorship. At the time, and for months afterwards, the battle of the Marne was studiously kept from the public, with the result that distorted accounts of it leaked out through unofficial channels. Orders, however, were given to all German officials in July to say that the war would last a long time – at least a year and a half. But such was the clumsiness of the censorship, in its regional variations and inconsistencies, that what was suppressed in one district might be fully published in another. There was the case of an article appearing in a Munich journal in 1915 on the subject of retaliation against prisoners of war. The article was published with blank spaces in place of every sentence condemning a German retaliation measure. A few weeks before, the material had been put out unmutilated in a public lecture in a large town that was the seat of a Prussian *Generalkommando*. Officers of the staff had been present and nobody had objected. And soon afterwards it had been printed in full in a book which had passed the censor in Württemberg. The three districts concerned were contiguous.[31] But while home censorship's left hand did not always know what its right hand was doing, the rules governing neutral correspondents, including those from the United States, and their dispatches overseas, were being tightened. Late in 1915 these correspondents were called to the War Press Bureau in

Berlin and told that the German Government wanted their agreement regarding their future wartime activities. They were asked to pledge themselves: to stay in Germany for the duration unless they had special permission to leave; to guarantee that their dispatches would be published in the United States precisely as sent from Germany after editing and passing by the German censorship; to supply their own headlines and guarantee that these would be printed unchanged. After vainly protesting at these virtual decrees, the correspondents signed.[32]

As in Britain and France, the upheaval of war was now causing a loosening of moral standards, to the dismay of the higher-principled. A letter taken from a German prisoner in December asked what had become of the resurrected ideals and moral ennoblement boasted by the 'jingoists'. Never had the writer seen so many 'cocottes' at Munich. Dances *sans voiles* were all the vogue there, and Munich's largest hotel had instituted a tea-room for the exclusive use of officers and cocottes. More significant still was the 'truly scandalous' conduct of a large number of officers' wives. 'So much for the ennobling effects of the war in Germany,' concluded the writer.[33]

Meanwhile more orthodox entertainment was flourishing, in a general atmosphere in which earnestness was the national watchword. With dancing officially banned, the theatres were presenting plays of serious or patriotic tone, and classical ballet was this winter drawing crowds. But Christmas, when it came, was no time for celebration. Many people had thought that they would never see a second wartime Christmas. From a resident's description, Berlin had for weeks been wrapped in an 'impenetrable veil of sadness', with white-faced, black-clad women moving sadly through the streets, some bowed 'under a burden too heavy to be borne'. Devout Roman Catholics sought consolation at Midnight Mass. A typical chapel was filled with wounded soldiers, nurses, nuns and pale, sorrowing women, praying for the dying and dead, and for themselves that they might never again 'spend such a Christmas of anguish and suspense'.[34] The shops made half-hearted attempts at

Christmas sales, which were promptly forbidden. Seasonal fare fell short of its traditional plenty. One neutral resident, unable to find – or possibly pay the inflated price for – a turkey, clubbed together with four friends and made do with pickled ox-tongue.

Part Three

1916: THE FULL STRAIN

Chapter 6

THE GENERAL SCENE

No end in sight

WITH Russia badly weakened, the Germans decided this year to focus their main operations in the West. In February, in the hope of delivering a decisive blow at the French, they mounted a massive assault against Verdun, on France's North-Eastern Front. The thinking behind this was that, to defend their historic and much-prized citadel of Verdun, the French would if necessary throw in all their forces and so exhaust themselves to the point of defeat. But after violent and costly fighting that lasted into July, the French stood firm and Verdun remained uncaptured. At the start of that month the British launched their great offensive on the Somme. The battle raged throughout the summer, but again with no breakthrough achieved and at huge cost in casualties. Meanwhile, in the East, the summer saw a heavy Russian offensive that, while initially successful, ended with the Russian gains retaken in a determined German counter-offensive. At the end of August, Rumania declared war against Austria-Hungary and Italy against Germany. At sea, at the end of May the Battle of Jutland took place. Though inconclusive, it was claimed as a success by both sides. Despite the vast efforts of the belligerents, victory this year remained as elusive as ever.

As the church bells of Britain, France and Germany rang in the year 1916, they heralded a year of dour, dogged and unrelenting struggle. After seventeen months of war, increasingly costly in human, material and financial terms, no one could now see the end. All that the belligerents could do was fight on, digging even deeper into their resources, organising themselves even more rigorously, making even greater exertions than in 1915. Each side was still confident of victory and had as yet no thought of giving in. The faint peace-calls heard in each country during 1915 counted for nothing against the prevailing popular mood of 'war-to-the-end'. Likewise Pope Benedict's message of the previous Easter to the President of the United States asking that his country should work unceasingly for peace, and the President's own speech of May offering mediation whenever it was asked, had gone unheeded in Europe. But in their common determination to continue the war, all three belligerents were now increasingly faced with the problem of how to continue it to a successful conclusion.

The attrition strategy – nibbling attacks or larger offensives against powerfully defended trench positions – was achieving no result beyond a huge wastage of men and expenditure of ammunition. The chief battleground of the Western Front was becoming a stark wilderness of mud and destruction, with the opposing sides hardly moving. Yet the military chiefs had found no effective alternative method of fighting the war. All that could be said of the attrition formula was, as General Joffre had put it in 1915, 'it is the final battalions that bring victory'.[1] But who would possess the final battalions? Even if the belligerents could go on feeding and financing themselves (prophets who in 1914 had foretold early financial collapse had long since been proved wrong), and ensuring adequate war materials, an acute difficulty now confronting them all was growing manpower shortage. The enormous demands of the fighting forces, matched by those of the Home Front for the war factories and munitions plants, would in 1916 stretch their available manpower to the utmost. For the civilians in the rear, regimented and regulated still further by the vast State-run war-machines, 'total war' would take on a yet grimmer meaning.

Chapter 7

BRITAIN

Conscription at last

In Britain the war had already wrought changes that would have seemed inconceivable eighteen months before. The trend towards State control (especially in social matters) noticeable before August 1914 had multiplied a hundredfold. With all the country's main industrial, transport and other interests – railways, shipping, coal, iron, wool, sugar, food, agriculture, munitions – virtually taken over, Government departments and sub-departments had proliferated, centrally and locally. Now almost the entire life of the people was regulated by Whitehall. Multifarious laws and rules under the capacious umbrella of DORA, telling citizens what they could and could not do, had intruded into the national scene in an unprecedented way. Old freedoms had disappeared, established customs and practices which normally would have taken decades to change or modify had been swept away with a well-nigh revolutionary speed. Women, performing scores of tasks which were hitherto the province of men, were emerging to take an entirely new place in society. On the working front the trade unions, in a wartime alliance with Government and industry, had foregone cherished privileges and accepted, albeit temporarily, dilution of labour. War-workers were prospering as never before, and in their new-found affluence were, despite the steep rise in prices, spending lavishly on what to them had previously been luxuries – good clothes, furniture, motor-bicycles, jewellery, entertainment. The booming war industries had produced that sinister wartime figure, the 'profiteer'. Taxation had reached unequalled heights to help pay war costs that were running at £5 million a day. But amid the general transformation total war was imposing on Britain, the most significant was the innovation that was introduced at the beginning of 1916 – military conscription.

Conscription had been increasingly foreshadowed in the later months of 1915, after the failure of the Derby Scheme to produce the requisite number of volunteers. Now, on the 5th January, with Mr Asquith's introduction of the Military Service Bill, it became an established fact. Under the exigencies of war, Britain was at last committed to the principle of compulsion – a principle that had hitherto been so alien to British ideas. It was significant of the times that even the Labour Party, in a conference at Bristol, while declaring against conscription (as had the trade unions), decided not to oppose the Act.

The first Military Service Act (another would follow shortly) provided for the call-up of single men and childless widowers aged eighteen to forty, at the same time exempting clergymen, employees in munitions or other essential war work, sole supporters of dependents, the physically unfit, and approved conscientious objectors. Regarding these last, it authorised the appointment of tribunals to examine exemption claims. But conscription, now that it had come, did not proceed entirely smoothly. The local military authorities, implementing the Act over-rigorously, started summoning for medical examination men already exempted under the Derby Scheme, and attesting men previously pronounced unfit. They refused, it was claimed, appeals for exemption from men with obvious physical defects, thus breaking ministerial pledges.[1] Meanwhile the War Office was expressing anxiety that the system was failing to produce sufficient men. Other trouble arose through an apparent unfairness in call-up as between married and single men. The call-up, in March, of married men who had attested under the Derby Scheme provoked strong protests on the ground that large numbers of unattested bachelors – many of whom had hastily entered war factories since National Registration – were evading service. Groups of married men held mass meetings, and a National Union of Attested Married Men was formed which lobbied Members of Parliament and

Government leaders, calling for equality of sacrifice. In view of the strength of feeling the Premier undertook to study the possibility of releasing those who had been improperly called-up. Finally, after a secret House of Commons session at the end of April, Mr Asquith took the only possible step, and in mid-May introduced a second Military Service Bill, which made all men between eighteen and forty-one, married and single, liable to conscription (the single to be called before the married).

Within nine days the Bill was on the statute book, taking the conscription principle to the ultimate limit. Relative to her population, Britain's contribution to the real fighting of the war would now at last be on a par with that of France and Germany. As one historian has remarked, she now had 'a law which seemed an absolute reversal of every tradition for which she had stood in the past'.[2] Even more expressively, another commentator called the measure 'the greatest revolution in our social system since the institution of feudalism under William the Conqueror', adding that 'the nation had reverted in the great crisis of its fate to the method of Saxon and Norman times, when the King had a right to take for the purpose of national defence every man, ship and available chattel in his dominion'.[3] Accepting the gravity of the war situation and already conditioned by the exigencies of DORA and the rest, the public bowed to this last and most drastic erosion of ancient liberties, though in the industrial field there was some discontent at what seemed the too determined 'hunting-down' of men for the colours.

The tribunals set up under the Act, one in each borough, started operating in March. These, consisting of members of the local authority, were soon clogged with exemption claims. Most came from employers seeking immunity for their employees on the ground of indispensability. Many others were put by men with domestic responsibilities – those who were the sole support of widowed mothers and so on. According to one account, exemptions were freely granted despite the objections of military representatives at the tribunals. Lord Derby, as Director of Recruiting, was highly dissatisfied and demanded that the starred occupations (numbering one hundred and sixty) be combed out for eligible recruits.[4] But while some reports remarked on the leniency of the tribunals, others complained of their severity, especially in dealing with conscientious objectors.

Predictably, conscientious objection now became a burning issue. The coming of conscription had left objectors who were eligible for service with no alternative but to stand up and declare and defend their beliefs before the tribunals. Majority public opinion, as might be expected, was strongly against them. To the ordinary citizen, whose kinsmen had already donned or were now about to don khaki to 'do their share', the men who demurred – on whatever pretext – were skulkers and cowards. Women, especially, took pride in the number of relatives who were serving at the front, while they regarded a conscientious objector or 'conchie' connection as a disgrace. The common feeling was graphically reflected in a contemporary account which – ignoring the genuine convictions of the many sincere objectors – reported that one objectors' organisation, among many set up throughout the country, had 'arranged a mock tribunal for coaching "curs" in all the arts of pious humbug to escape the drill sergeant'. It spoke of the 'extraordinary number of able-bodied young men belonging to the new school of religious hypocrites'. 'Young agnostics', it added, 'became suddenly converted to a new form of Quakerism that did not require any belief in God, but only a belief that the man who would not fight would steal the job of the man who did.'[5] It went on to assail, particularly, the Society of Friends (a body with profound pacifist beliefs) which, it alleged, had totally disregarded Christ's teaching on wealth, and while itself becoming one of the richest communities in Britain, had escaped the ultimate duties attaching to its wealth by exaggerating the doctrine of non-resistance.

With Britain committing herself ever more totally to war, the problem of the conscientious objectors was admittedly a difficult one; but the treatment accorded to many of them makes a sorry story. Amid the general atmosphere of hostility and contempt, they faced the tribunals at an initial disadvantage. These bodies were notably inconsistent in their handling of claimants – not surprisingly, since such claims had never been judged before. Some refused absolute exemption on any pretext, though the act authorised this in the case of Quakers and others who could show that, as pacifists, they had opposed militarism before the war. Some tribunals, it was said, only questioned the applicant as to whether he took exercise, what he did on Sundays or even whether he washed. Objectors turned down by the tribunals were deemed to be in the army. If they failed to report for service they were arrested as deserters and handed over to the military, to be court-martialled and imprisoned, in many cases suffering harsh treatment. Those who refused to wear khaki and accept military training, records Mrs Pankhurst, were bullied and terrorised and kept in handcuffs.[6] Some were thrown into dark punishment cells and given bread and water, being forcibly fed if they went on hungerstrike. Others were even threatened with shooting. As Mrs Pankhurst notes, in May the well-known pacifist Professor Gilbert Murray learnt that a group of objectors had been sent to France to be shot. He hurried to question Lord Derby, who confirmed that they were likely to be shot, and then saw the Prime Minister, who promised to notify the Commander-in-Chief, Sir Douglas Haig, that no executions must be carried out without the Cabinet's knowledge. In May, likewise, a slight relaxation in the treatment of conscripted c.o.s was conceded by an Army Order, which decreed that they would not be kept in military custody but transferred to civil prisons. But their victimisation continued, as shown by a statement made in Parliament six months later that men suffering from organic ailments like heart trouble were housed at a Woolwich hospital with venereal disease patients, with defective sanitation and no protection from infection.

A basic defect of the Act was that it failed to define the precise meaning of 'conscientious' and left to the individual tribunals to place their own, often unsympathetic, interpretation on the applicant's claim. The appeal tribunals, to which rejected applicants had recourse, were hardly more accommodating. Unsuccessful objectors who were also physically unfit were particularly unfortunate. They were liable to be drafted, despite appeal, into the special newly-formed Non-Combatant Corps for objectors (whose duties comprised trench-digging, erection of barbed-wire entanglements, removal of mines, stretcher-bearing and any other work short of actual fighting), and when their health broke down a pension was refused them on the ground that their disability was not caused by war service. One writer, summing up the whole unhappy 'c.o.' situation, commented: 'When war mentality takes hold of a land, reasoned justice departs to the winds.'[7]

But the cause of the objectors did not go unsupported or unorganised. Local c.o. groups sprang up all over the country, and a National Council against Conscription was formed, incorporating the existing No Conscription Fellowship which now issued an appeal: 'Freedom of conscience must not be sacrificed to military necessity. Men's deepest religious and moral convictions must not be swept aside. We believe in human brotherhood.'[8] Another pronouncement came from the left-wing pacifist Philip Snowden, who protested in a pamphlet 'British Prussianism, the Scandal of the Tribunals', that many local tribunals refused to receive evidence which claimants were permitted to bring forward. But these were only isolated voices crying in a hostile wilderness. In April an anti-conscription demonstration sponsored by the East London Federation of Suffragettes was held in Trafalgar Square, to be broken up by colonial troops and civilians amid rowdy scenes. And in May a centenary celebration meeting of the London Peace Society, planned to be held in the Memorial Hall, Farringdon Street, had to be cancelled as permission to use the hall was withdrawn. Such pacifist meetings as did manage to take place generally ended in disorder.

The refusal of exemption to many of the leading objectors, like Clifford Allen, chairman of the No Conscription Fellowship, and Fenner Brockway, editor of the journal *Labour Leader*, was a measure of the unyielding attitude of the tribunals. And even churchmen (though not surprisingly, in view of the Church's outspoken support for the war) voiced their opposition to the movement. In July a writer in the Anglican quarterly *The Optimist* asserted that the objector who in the name of conscience refused to fight was really supporting an immoral German militarism, and should be exiled from the community whose authority he was defying. Soon after, an archdeacon, preaching a sermon on 'British Citizens and their Responsibility to God', declared: 'The most specious of modern false prophets are those who come forward at local tribunals: they look not for Divine guidance in the struggle in which our nation is engaged, but at the recorded Divine commands in days gone by. The Christian soldier may be thoroughly chivalrous and in the course of his duty kill many men whom he does not hate. It is the spirit of hate that Christ would have us exorcise.'[9] In academic circles, too, the pacifist-objector received scant sympathy. In July the Council of Trinity College, Cambridge, removed Bertrand Russell – who had recently been fined £100 for making statements calculated to prejudice recruiting – from his lectureship in Logic and Mathematics, ostensibly as a consequence of his conviction under DORA.

Though conscription was generally accepted as a harsh necessity – and it meant an even more profound upheaval and fresh anxieties in Britain's emptying homes – among the war workers it caused some disquiet. The vigorous comb-out for the army reached into the factories, and there was evidence that conscription was used as a lever to enforce industrial compulsion. Trade unionists who fostered discontent or promoted strikes were made liable for call-up when they would otherwise have been exempt. But apart from the conscription trouble, there was a chronic and simmering unrest among the workers that was causing the Government constant worry. This was largely a product of the war itself (though industrial militancy had through various causes been increasing sharply since 1911). As Lloyd George explains, there were sundry reasons for the wartime discontents – the long hours and hard conditions of work, the shifting of workers from their homes to often inadequate accommodation, their sense (despite their high wages) that they were working to enrich their employers, their subjection to new disciplines and loss of prized rights and privileges.[10] All these factors were contributing to an uneasy mood which erupted in such strikes as those of 30,000 jute workers at Dundee, 15,000 Liverpool dockers and 20,000 Glasgow munitions workers, all in late March. The situation for the Government was complicated by the fact that any conscription of the workers on the military pattern was impracticable. As regards the spirit of the mass of war workers, on the evidence of Lord Sandhurst, this – in one plant at least – was better among the older than the younger men. Visiting Cammel Lairds at Liverpool the previous December, he had noted concerning the 12,000 employees: 'Some, the greater proportion by far, heroes who do their utmost and put in all they know, but the younger generation seem to care nothing except for earning and spending money; very many work just enough to ensure what they call luxury – they seem to care nothing for the war and the country, and prefer football to war news, declaring nothing shall make them serve. I was struck by the number of youths in the Works.'[11]

And yet, for all the seeming shortcomings of the war workers, in August Lloyd George was to report to the Commons a spectacular increase in armaments output: the annual (1914–15) production of 18-pounder shells now turned out in three weeks, of medium shells in eleven days, of heavy shells in four days: output of high explosives sixty-six times as great as early in 1915; a fourteenfold increase in machine-gun output and a sixfold increase in heavy gun output over 1914–15. Moreover, though the year was to show a notable extension of dilution and female employment, the trade disputes for 1916, numbering 581 and affecting 284,000 workers, were to prove the lowest for nine years.[12]

The coming of conscription inevitably intensified the demand on the services of women. Now more than ever they would be

Boy Scouts help with the harvest

Allotments at Dulwich

Pulling beet at Blackmoor Farm, Selborne

A group of land-girls

needed to fill the growing gaps left by the call-up of men from factory, office, shop, farm and public service. And as they assumed yet new tasks and poured in increasing numbers into jobs they had already taken over, the feminine revolution that had started in 1915 proceeded a step further. By August, the total number of women replacing men in various forms of civil employment was 766,000. This was in addition to at least 340,000 women employed in munitions and other War Office establishments. But, in the realm of women, the first Government move of 1916 was to obtain land workers. In February there was a call for 400,000 women to carry on the country's agricultural work. A scheme was introduced for recruiting and training through Women's County Agricultural Committees and, as a tangible sign of their patriotic service, volunteers were issued with armlets. Then in March, the Home Office and Board of Trade asked employers generally to organise their work so as to replace enlisted men with women. Meanwhile determined efforts were being made to improve working conditions in the factories. Women welfare officers and inspectors were appointed to secure proper tea-breaks, improve protective clothing, report breaches of factory regulations and so on. In addition, extensive housing schemes were being carried out. All this was an example of reforms being swiftly produced by war exigencies that otherwise might have been deferred for years.

There was certainly much need for supervision and improvement. The very needs of war had introduced new hardships, hazards and health risks into industry, and notably for women. Mrs Pankhurst cites conditions in a London aircraft works, where women laboured from 8 a.m. to 6.30 p.m. and sometimes later for 15s. weekly, painting wings with varnish which gave off toxic fumes. Tired and under-nourished, they were a prey to industrial poisoning. It was common for six out of some thirty women to be lying ill, even unconscious, outside the workshop. In the munitions plants the explosives with which the shells were filled were highly harmful to the handlers. TNT caused eczema, and its fumes produced symptoms like those of pneumonia and jaundice. They turned the skins of the fillers a bright mustard yellow, to earn for these unfortunates the name of 'yellow girls'. The TNT women, says Mrs Pankhurst, were as far as possible kept out of sight in the factories; and restaurant owners ordered their managers not to serve them. There was the case of a woman banned from an Oxford Street café because she was wearing a khaki-coloured raincoat – being mistaken for a munitions worker, as the firm later admitted when apologising.[13] How unsightly were these ill-fated workers was recorded by an observer who met a group on a Midlands railway station: 'A short local train came in and disgorged a couple of hundred de-humanised females, Amazonian beings bereft of reason or feeling, judging by the set of their faces, bereft of all charm of appearance, clothed anyhow, skin stained a yellow-brown even to the roots of their dishevelled hair, by the awful stuff they handled.'[14]

For many women working hours (though shortened later) were grievously long, amounting to nearly twelve hours daily. On top of this, some had to endure long hours travelling to and from work, in great discomfort. An example was quoted of a girl rising at 3.45 a.m. and getting to bed at 11 p.m., having to spend five hours travelling and waiting about. It was feared that such waiting was a factor in drawing workers into the public houses to drink. Moreover, in some areas there was a grave accommodation shortage. This led to the setting-up in 1916 of an official Lodgings Committee, charged with registering and inspecting premises.

Despite women's widespread response to the call, some – as suggested by articles about 'slackers' in the press of mid-1916 – were still hanging back. At any rate there were still substantial vacancies in war work. In August thousands of aircraft workers were being called for. But the general impression in London was of women at work everywhere. They were seen driving cars and drays, collecting tickets on the underground, working lifts at hotels and offices. Some big hotels boasted a woman hall-porter – 'an Amazon in blue or mauve coat, gold-braided peaked cap and high top boots'.[15] On the trams and buses there were young 'conductorettes' in smart blue uniforms, hats with brims turned up at one side, skirts to their knees and leather leggings. There were women police, and behind the scenes innumerable clerks, cooks and cleaners, at military hospitals as well as civil establishments. Many women were in the bakery and other trades, and 25,000 had been absorbed into the Post Office. So the great recruitment went on. But at the same time, a wealthy fashionable few seemed untouched by the war revolution. In September, as reported in *The Queen*, a society woman at the Dahlia Show wore a tiger skin thrown over the shoulders of her soft grey frock; and another paraded in a frock of claret-coloured silk, ruched with taffeta.

London, indeed, was full of strangely contrasting scenes of peace and war. An observer has described it at this time on a typical late spring afternoon. The streets were crowded with well-dressed if not exactly gaily-dressed people. It was the 10s. day at the Royal Horticultural Show. In Leicester Square an exhibition of portraits of contemporary 'intellectuals' was drawing a good attendance, and the theatres, music-halls and cinemas were filling up. People were even coming away because there was no more room. 'All was as usual on a May day in London,' notes the writer. But behind the peacetime normality and the indifference were grim reminders of the war. The newspaper posters were carrying the stark headline: 'The Charnel House of Verdun.' And from Charing Cross was coming the familiar daily procession of ambulances. A young mother held up her child to see them, exclaiming: 'Let girlie see the wounded soldiers! Oh, look! There are whole brakes full of them.'[16]

For Britons in general the war was becoming a way of life. After two years, its impact was everywhere noticeable. Apart from the ever-lengthening casualty lists, the mourning, the familiar sight of blue-clad wounded soldiers, there was the host of small things. If individually unimportant, together they were changing the pattern of civilian living. Matches, for instances, were becoming scarce; newspapers were shrinking;

travelling, with trains cancelled, restaurant-cars abolished, stations closed and the wartime buns and sandwiches of the railway buffet earning a name for nastiness, was becoming increasingly uncomfortable. Though people were still taking holidays, old posters advertising 'Lovely Lucerne' and 'Gay Boulogne' struck an ironic note on shabby station walls. There was a call for economy in dress, and smart clothes, along with evening dress in theatres, were now 'bad form'. Errand boys were disappearing, and professional men were carrying home their household groceries. Suburban housewives were cleaning their own doorsteps. Cars were being laid up; whisky was weaker and more expensive; and owing to the call-up the postal service was less efficient. As a sign of full employment, tramps had vanished from the countryside, and it was said that there were now no poor in England except the 'new poor' – writers, musicians and so on. To signalise the new prosperity, eating out was popular: the large London cafés were nightly crowded with customers seeking a little glitter and relaxation after a day's work amid the city's wartime drabness.

While theatres and music-halls, now subject to amusement tax, continued to draw big audiences eager for distraction, in the sphere of reading people were discarding light fiction in favour of more serious works on the war and similar themes. But, ostensibly in the name of economy, the Home Office now decreed the closing of museums and picture galleries, regardless of the itinerant crowds of servicemen and others who might have been glad of these amenities. Critics of the closure contrasted it with the proliferation of London's night clubs, of which were said to be a hundred and fifty in Soho. Here toothbrush-moustached young subalterns danced with their 'flapper' girl-friends to the new jazz which had just crossed the Atlantic. Meanwhile, the 'pub' had begun to decline, due to the regulation of hours for serving liquor. War was proving a great equaliser, mixing the social classes (as in the munitions factories) and breaking down old etiquettes – on the trams and buses, for instance, in which junior officers who in 1914 would not have dreamed of using such plebeian transport were now everyday travellers, cheerfully handing their fares to the 'conductorettes'. It was also transforming fashion by removing commonplace materials from civilian use. Women ceased wearing tight stays as the necessary steel was commandeered by the Air Board, and the machines for making the eyelets were likewise requisitioned. City men had to abandon their top hats because, owing to the commandeering of hay and straw they could no longer maintain the horses which drew their cabs to the City, and their tall hats would have come to grief in the buses and tubes.

Amid the all-embracing restrictions of DORA – and these were now more multifarious than ever – civilians were subject to strange small prohibitions whose purpose was not easily seen. In February the chiming and striking of London's public clocks was banned between sunset and sunrise, and some months later it was forbidden to whistle for cabs between 10 p.m. and 7 a.m. More useful was the famous daylight saving order introduced in May at the suggestion of the London master-builder, William Willet. When Willet had earlier proposed his scheme for advancing Greenwich time by one hour in summer he had been regarded as a crank, but now the value of his 'summer-time' plan was seen – the idea was even taken up in Germany. With the clocks thus put forward, the need for artificial lighting was reduced and vital war work could continue for an extra hour in daylight. Additional time for healthful recreation was also available. Meanwhile, as the great battles of 1916 raged across the Channel, at Verdun and later on the Somme, the war impinged deeper than before into the public consciousness. It was reported in May that the Christian name 'Verdun' was frequently being given at British baptisms: a recognition of the fearful and prolonged struggle being waged by the French around that beleaguered citadel.[17] And at the beginning of July the rumbling of the guns was heard in the peaceful English countryside to bring home to Britons – and among them Lloyd George, who apparently heard them at his house at Walton Heath – the reality of the great British offensive just opened on the Somme.

This year the August Bank Holiday was suspended by Royal Proclamation. Most workers gave up the break without complaint, though at Hull 4,500 dockers refused to work except at holiday rates. In London, according to a diarist, 'everybody was working'. The capital, he noted, now showed inescapable signs of war's impact. The Life Guards in Whitehall had abandoned their scarlet and plumes for plain khaki. Big Ben was silent, its dials darkened at night. In St James's Park the five-acre lake had gone, its bed being filled with temporary buildings. In the streets the civilians looked notably drab, the men's trousers being baggy and frayed. Oxford Street, its shop fronts dingy from lack of paint, had few shoppers. Hyde Park's flowerbeds were bare of blooms for the war's duration. The traffic in Piccadilly was restricted to a few cars, the odd hansom cab and even a couple of Victorian 'growlers'. The only sign of pre-war life was in the theatres. These were booming, with *Peg o' My Heart* at the Globe, *A Little Bit of Fluff* at the Criterion, *Chu Chin Chow* at His Majesty's, and *Daddy Long Legs* at the Duke of York's.[18]

But the theatres too were being invaded by the general permissiveness that was a feature of the times. In the autumn General Sir Horace Smith-Dorrien protested to the press about the demoralising tone of certain public performances, complaining of the 'vulgar and suggestive gags' being used on the stage. Was it patriotic, he asked, to lead young people to regard vulgar pictures, low posters and suggestive performances as part of the daily life of an Empire that had risen to its present leading position? But the loosening standards were natural reactions to the strains and anxieties of wartime life, as were the sundry fads and crazes that now became current. Pet dogs were popular, especially with well-to-do women, there was a vogue for the hotel *thé dansant*, at which, for 2s. 6d., patrons could escape the drabness of home or work and take tea in a plushy lounge and dance the fashionable tango, or just listen to the music and watch the scene; and there was the horrid practice of 'gobbling chocolates and sweets in theatres' by well-fed and prosperous-looking people who, as a letter-writer to the *Daily Mail* accused, were thus depriving the fighting troops of what should have gone to them.[19] Yet along with these 'pleasure-as-usual' preoccupations was that bellicose streak, already mentioned, that serving officers like Robert Graves continued to find odd. Outstanding in its pugnacity was a letter featured in the *Morning Post*, from a 'Little Mother', replying to 'A Common Soldier' who had written appealing for peace. 'To the man who calls himself "a common soldier",' it ran, 'may I say that we women ... will tolerate no such cry as "Peace! Peace!" where there is no peace. The corn that will wave over land watered by the blood of our brave lads shall testify to the future that their blood was not spilt in vain ... They have all done their share, and we, as women, will do ours without murmuring and without complaint. There is only one temperature for the women of the British race, and that is white heat ...'[20] So popular was this letter that it was reprinted in pamphlet form, selling 75,000 copies in less than a week.

'England looked strange to us soldiers,' commented Graves, when on home leave in the autumn. 'We could not understand the war-madness that ran wild everywhere, looking for a pseudo-military outlet. The civilians talked a foreign language; and it was newspaper language. I found serious conversation with my parents all but impossible.'[21] One thing that startled Graves was the mounting vogue of spiritualism, resorted to by mothers trying to get in touch with their dead sons, and wives with husbands. He himself spent an uncomfortable night in the house of a bereaved lady, where in the small hours his sleep was broken by weird rappings, shrieks and laughter. This searching into the beyond, suggests one writer, was a substitute for a religious faith dimmed as a result of the war.[22] Spiritualist seances became fashionable, and along with mediums, palmists, fortune-tellers and crystal-gazers were much sought after. There were many little rooms around Bond Street and Oxford Street to which seekers after consolation could repair for soothsaying and thought-reading sessions. The new craze was obviously open to fraud. Dozens of mountebanks were prosecuted, but to little effect. In December, it was revealed at the trial of a self-styled psychic called Almira Brockway that in one month she had collected £115 for interviews in which she professed to make contact with spirits of departed people. The wave of superstition created a big demand for charms and mascots. There was the popular 'bow-wow' bulldog, crouched in a threatening posture, selling for 10s. 6d. in gold. There was the pocket copy of the New Testament – a best-seller among troops at the front for its supposed efficacy as a protective talisman. More disquieting, people were taking to drugs, notably cocaine, the possession of which was made an offence punishable by a £100 fine and six months' imprisonment.

A basic cause of the spiritualist boom was the steeply rising tide of casualties. The great Somme offensive, in which the British killed on the first day numbered over 19,000, brought bereavement to a myriad new homes. For the overwhelming majority of the bereaved, reading the terse official telegram, there would be the consolation that the son or husband had died fighting for his country. But for a tiny handful there would be a more brutal notification leaving no room for comfort, and underlining an official callousness that seemed to belong to another age. In April a humble East End Jewish family received an official letter informing them that their son had been court-martialled and shot for desertion. Behind this shattering communication lay a pitiful story. In September 1914 the eighteen-year-old lad had enlisted without his parents' knowledge and after some months' front-line service, in which he had been wounded, had broken down, to be arrested, tried, convicted and shot. His parents had known nothing even of his arrest. It was not until Sylvia Pankhurst had learnt of this case and campaigned in burning indignation with the authorities that the practice was changed, and relatives were henceforth informed that the man in question had 'died of wounds'.[23]

Looking back from an age of instant news, by radio and television, it is strange to consider that the sole source of information in World War I was the newspaper. And under the censorship of that time, a contemporary writer has pointed

out, the newspaper was far from reliable.[24] The appearance of
an item in the press was no guarantee of its truth, and at the
same time many matters of importance might remain un-
mentioned. What the press most effectively did was to reflect
the opinions, moods and gossip of the day. It was guilty,
however, of circulating wild and unfounded rumours about
the enemy which led to misplaced popular optimism, or, at
the least, of failing to kill such rumours as spread around by
word of mouth. There were many such – as that large numbers
of discouraged German troops were surrendering, or that they
had suffered huge losses. There was one story that in recent
raids on the enemy lines the trenches were found to be full of
stuffed figures, or even corpses, armed with dummy rifles. But
the wildest rumours related to food shortages. There were
tales of violent food riots in Berlin, Munich and Dresden. The
streets were full of 'living skeletons', frantic women were
storming the shops in search of food, and mobs had been
mown down by machine guns because they demanded 'Peace
and Food'. Generally originating from 'neutral' sources, all
were eagerly and too credulously received in Britain.

Unduly glamorising the conduct of the troops in action
was a common fault of the press (as Robert Graves and others
were lamenting). In October an officer from Ypres told
Arnold Bennett that newspaper correspondents' accounts of
'men eager to go over the parapet made him laugh. They were
never eager.'[25] The generally sanguine tone of the press had
worried the Press Bureau as early as March 1915, when it had
asked papers to be less optimistic. But sometimes they trans-
gressed by being over-alarmist. In November 1915 the *Globe*
was suppressed under DORA for alleging – despite official
denials – that owing to Cabinet disagreements over the conduct
of the war, Kitchener had left the War Office. This was charged
to be a false statement tending to depress His Majesty's subjects
and give comfort to the enemy. (The *Globe* was later in trouble
again for libellously claiming that Mrs Asquith had sent food
to German prisoner-of-war officers.) Admittedly the Bureau
had a difficult task keeping a middle course, but at times it

could be comically pedantic. Dealing with a front-line report that included the quotation of Kipling's line 'The Captains and the Kings depart', a censor erased the words 'and the Kings'. When questioned in Parliament about this, the Home Secretary (Sir John Simon) replied that as the censor knew there were no kings present at the time, he thought it wrong to say they had departed.[26]

For the British in 1916 the most cheering anti-German propaganda lay in the reports of the enemy's near-starvation. These contrasted comfortably with conditions in Britain, where as yet there was no real food shortage. For most of the year the only sign of scarcity was in the rising prices. By November the prices of essential commodities had increased by 75% over those of July 1914, and working-class living costs by 60%. But if, with wages rising steeply too, the pinch was hardly being felt, the question of food supply was – for a nation so largely provisioned from abroad – now causing some concern. There had been controls of various kinds since the start of the war, beginning with the establishment of the Committee on Food Supplies. The Board of Trade had dealt with milk supplies, and sugar had been handled by a Royal Sugar Commission. Late in 1915 the increasingly difficult shipping problem had necessitated the creation of a Ship Requisitioning Committee; and in October 1916, to stop the growing speculation in wheat, a Royal Commission on Wheat Supplies was set up. Finally in December, as a measure of the mounting seriousness of the problem, a Ministry of Food was formed, and a Food Controller appointed.

Apart from having to pay more, the public was able to eat almost as in peacetime. There was no rationing, and in the earlier months little sign of stringency beyond a few appeals like that of a group of leading public men, in May, for a weekly meatless day. Later, indications of shortage and future privations began to appear. In November citizens had their first taste of 'war bread' – an economy forced by the dangerously increasing activities of German submarines. That month it was reported that London possessed only two days' wheat stocks, there being no ships in the Atlantic to bring wheat to England.[27] At the same time another more determined public appeal to reduce meat consumption was made. The civil population, it was said, was consuming daily £500,000-worth of meat; and if all would forgo meat for one day a week, demands on shipping would be greatly lessened. Meanwhile *The Times* was reporting gross extravagance in luxuries. In one big London store a staff of six confectionery assistants were kept busy serving customers (mostly women) from a stock of some seventy varieties of sweetmeats. Soon after, the Sugar Commission reduced supplies to confectionery makers. Poorer people suffered some hardship through the bad potato harvest caused by a wet autumn, and now for the first time a few queues appeared. Even at one London club the high standard of fare (and service) was apparently declining. Dining at Brooks's in August, Lord Bertie of Thame complained 'food was beastly and the wine-glasses the thickness of a seltzer water bottle'.[28]

It was now that Britain's growing food difficulties produced a historic innovation: the birth of the allotment system. Christmas time saw the issue by the Government of an Order facilitating the acquisition of land for small holdings and market gardens. In consequence the Board of Agriculture was authorised to take possession of various unoccupied lands for growing food. ' "Idle land for food" is today's slogan,' reported a writer. 'It is likely that Boxing Day 1916 will be mentioned in years to come as marking the start of a movement for turning the urban classes of the community on to the vacant lands for the raising of food.'[29] In those last chilly days of the year, groups of people could be seen in the quiet suburban districts of Greenwich, Tooting, Clapham, Dulwich and Wimbledon, right around to Hampstead, busily digging and forking the soil in the great cause of cultivating vegetables for feeding Britain at war. Every bit of spare land was being turned to use, undeveloped building sites, front and back gardens of empty houses, corners of the parks and commons, golf courses, tennis courts. It was a movement that in the next year would grow to huge proportions, popular, practical and immensely productive.

Meanwhile, if sufficiently fed, the country was growing accustomed to wartime restrictions in drink. The controls imposed in 1915, and especially the 'No Treating' order, had considerably decreased consumption. Greater temperance had been encouraged by such bodies as the YMCA, YWCA, the Salvation Army and Church Army, whose 'dry' canteens, established in the large industrial and munition-making centres, had drawn many workers away from the public houses. Those who still drank beer or spirits found them weaker and more expensive – if available at all. In May, brandy became unobtainable without a doctor's prescription,[30] and during 1916 the Ministry of Munitions took over most of the whisky distilleries for the manufacture of alcohol for provisions. But despite all the regulations and limitations, including the so-called 'Beauty Sleep' order which prohibited restauranteurs from serving officers with drink after 10 p.m., the illicit sale of alcohol in shady night clubs flourished. In the scores of 'dives' that sprang up in Soho, late revellers could drink spirit served in coffee cups and champagne masquerading as innocent lemonade. Nevertheless, all in all, the anti-drink measures would by the end of the war have reduced the nation's consumption of alcohol by more than half as compared with 1914.[31]

In its efforts to contend with all the problems of running the war, the Asquith Coalition Government had during 1916 been experiencing increasing difficulties. Late in 1915 an Inner War Cabinet, or War Committee of the Cabinet, consisting of five ministers, had been formed to expedite vital decisions and action on war matters. But even so, as the months passed the feeling grew that the war was not being conducted vigorously enough. There was criticism in Parliament and the press and public discontent. Many of the Government measures – the closure of museums and galleries, the economy campaign, the introduction of summer-time – seemed too mild for the urgency of the times, while graver issues like the growing German submarine threat, the manpower position, and the efficacy of the blockade on Germany, were being left unsettled. Meanwhile, abroad, the costly indecisiveness of the Somme offensive, the unbroken strength of the enemy and the setbacks in the Balkans made a generally uninspiring war picture.[32] Amid growing dissatisfaction the Asquith Coalition carried on until late autumn when, after the disappointing outcome of the Paris Conference in November,[33] its days were clearly numbered. On the 5th December Asquith resigned, a sadly discredited leader, to be replaced as Prime Minister two days later by Lloyd George, who headed a new Coalition. The change immediately inspired the country with fresh hopes of a more energetic prosecution of the war.

Of all the matters facing the new Government, the most pressing was manpower. Foreseeing yet heavier demands on this precious asset in 1917, one of its first acts was to announce the establishment of a system of national service under which yet more men and women were to be registered and recruited for war industry. Vitally necessary in itself, this was also a counter-move to what was happening that same month in an equally hard-pressed Germany: the passing of a sweeping measure, sponsored by Field Marshal Hindenburg himself, mustering all men still available into essential service. Germany's comb-out had already been more drastic than Britain's, but Britain's anxiety about the working of her recently introduced military conscription had been shown in September by a concerted search for 'shirkers'. Thousands of men in London and other cities had suddenly been rounded up by military police in raids on theatres, cinemas, football fields, parks and other public places and called on to produce papers. Those unable to satisfy the police were marched off, to the gibes of the crowd. According to a writer, 'the excited imagination of a war-fevered public was to blame for this ill-judged measure'.[34] The military authorities had apparently received complaints about the numbers of 'skulkers' at large. But the fears proved unfounded, for few evaders were netted.

This first year of total military effort was for Britain a year of grievous loss in the realm of military leadership. Early in June Lord Kitchener, Secretary of State for War, was drowned while sailing in the cruiser *Hampshire* on a mission to Russia. The *Hampshire* had struck a German mine near the Orkneys and sunk with nearly all hands. The news of Kitchener's death caused nation-wide shock and consternation. The sorrowing public could hardly believe that this revered figure, the soldier with the pointing finger whose bold-moustached features were immortalised on the 1914 recruiting posters, was really dead. (It was even rumoured at first that the announcement was put out to mislead the Germans.) In Whitehall silent crowds stood outside the War Office, whose windows were shuttered by drawn blinds. Flags flew at half-mast over public buildings and hotels. For British morale this was the sharpest blow in a year of disappointments and deferred hopes. It reinforced the general mood which by the end of 1916 was settling into a weary resignation, far from the buoyant optimism of two years earlier. Victory was still certain, ran the common feeling, but in view of the failure of the bloody Somme offensive to break the lengthening deadlock, how, when, and at what cost would it finally be achieved?

Paradoxically, the chastened mood did not prevent people, and especially those to whom the war had brought a new-found prosperity, from trying to enjoy life. A writer to *The Times* complained of the lavish spending of young women munition-workers and their sweethearts, who were eagerly buying up cheap jewellery and furs. But on the whole this year's Christmas season brought little joy. In London the weather was dank and foggy. A diarist noted the subdued spirit of a Christmas service at Hampstead, with many worshippers in mourning.[35] In the streets and tubes almost everyone looked sad and depressed. Hotels and restaurants were allowed no extension of hours, and staged no elaborate festivities. The only concession to Christmas was the waiving of a recent economy order so as to allow a larger meal at lunchtime. Another London observer found most cheer in Whitehall, where the lighted windows signified unremitting work.[36] Here and there the gloom was relieved by merrymaking soldiers and their girls, and by speeding taxis with white satin streamers, bearing wartime newly-weds. The town was full of troops travelling on leave – seeming oddly alien amid the civilian scene. 'They looked more like strange beings from another world,' wrote MacDonagh, 'full equipped as they were, and stained with the mud of the trenches.'[37]

The diarist MacDonagh summed up this 'festive' season thus mournfully: 'Third Christmas of the war and the gloomiest. To wish each other "Merry Christmas" is a mockery. Of such is the prevailing gloom . . . We recall our fondest hope and belief last year that this Christmas we should eat our dinner in peace.'[38]

So the old year passed, uneventfully save for the recital of prayers for victory in the churches. The news was uninspiring and the press, with no stomach for peace without total victory, was roundly denouncing the Peace Notes recently emanating from President Wilson and the German Government. With some acuteness the usually frivolous *Tatler* assessed the impact of 1916 on the Home Front: 'Another year of Armageddon behind us . . . But how very nearly three years of it *have* changed the face of the world . . . The rich become poor, the poor rich; scallywags and office-boys suddenly popped into realms of wealth; obscure *commerçants* from the wild North metamorphosed into Whitehall Nuts . . . Social climbers on the top rung at last, photographed and paragraphed and fairly going it as Hospital Benefactors.'[39]

Chapter 8

FRANCE

'An outstanding effort is called for'

For France, 1916 was the year when the war started to bite hard and deep. It was the year of Verdun. The drawn-out struggle around this historic citadel that had traditionally guarded the path of the invader from the East was more than just one more battle: it was a dogged effort to preserve what was for Frenchmen a supreme symbol of national pride and honour. To hold Verdun, France was prepared to throw in all her resources, as demonstrated by the toll of casualties that, according to General Pétain, in three months from February to May amounted to over 150,000, including 23,000 dead. The Verdun campaign left an indelible mark on the French Army, and increased the incipient war-weariness of the civilian population. Throughout the spring this showed itself mostly in 'a spirit of resignation, with almost no complaints', as Michel Corday noted;[1] and even in July, when the fight for Verdun was still unresolved, the general mood remained steady. This was largely due to the war-induced conditions of prosperity and the fighting tone of the press, which was stubbornly proclaiming 'War to the bitter end'. But the nation's deeper feeling was expressed by President Poincaré, who wrote in May: 'If Verdun should one day be taken, what a disaster! If it is saved, how shall we ever be able to forget at what a cost?'[2]

A writer living in Paris recalled the city's mood at the start of the German offensive, and later.[3] At first Parisians felt they were re-living the days of August 1914. There was the same overwhelming onrush of the enemy, the same headlong retreat of the defenders. When the advance was halted, people were afraid to believe it. They went to bed in suspense, and rose at dawn to queue at the newsagents, waiting for the newspapers. And when the French still held, 'maps grew soft and pliable with much handling'. Civilians pored endlessly over them, studying the heights, contours and positions of the woods. Anxiety returned when Verdun was imminently threatened again and one commander replaced another. Yet the chief feeling was that even if Verdun did fall, Parisians would not despair. During the hardest fighting Frenchmen asked themselves what their British allies were doing. They seemed to be sitting inactively on their own front, and this was very short compared with the French line. As the battle dragged on, Parisians settled into a state almost of apathy, unable even to enthuse more than briefly over the generals, Pétain and Castelnau, who had saved Verdun. At the time of the citadel's greatest peril, the chief thought of Frenchmen was that any sort of compromise peace with the Germans had become impossible: they would rather die than yield. The only quarter where courage was flagging, reports the writer, was Parliament: there were deputies in the Chamber who believed that France had nothing more to hope for, and that any continuation of the fighting would cripple her irretrievably and put her at the enemy's mercy.

If this was a minority view, Verdun was nevertheless causing much concern in the Chamber, to the embarrassment of the Briand Government which, since entering office the previous November, had been facing increasing criticism on various counts. One cause of disquiet had been the independent, autocratic attitude assumed by the Commander-in-Chief, General Joffre, who in his oversized GHQ was running military affairs virtually without reference to the Government. The issue had come to a head on the matter of Verdun's defences which, it was claimed, Joffre had failed to prepare against the coming assault. Amid mounting parliamentary complaints and challenges, Briand was in June finally compelled to grant a secret session of the Chamber. From this he emerged in a stronger position, having undertaken to limit the powers of GHQ and uphold parliamentary rights. His leadership was further reinforced by a persuasive speech at a secret session of the Senate, held in July. He was helped too by a slackening of the fighting at Verdun and the opening of the British offensive on the Somme; and amid a general easing of tension his Government recovered its ascendancy sufficiently to carry on (though remodelled in December) until the end of the year and beyond. The vulnerability and steady rise and fall of wartime governments in both France and Britain seemed a weakness – or was it a strength? – inherent in the democratic system.

While the Verdun struggle raged, eating up vast masses of war material, it was vital to maintain and increase the arms output. To this end the influential Albert Thomas, Under-Secretary for Armaments, addressed a powerful call to the workers at Le Creusot in mid-April. It was of the kind that, in Britain, only the silver-tongued Lloyd George could have made. 'The spirit of war is the spirit of sacrifice and self-denial,' Thomas declared. 'It is the subordination of all individual interests to the common interest, the consent to social discipline and organisation, the willingness to dedicate all one's strength for the safety of one's country.'[4] As a more general morale-booster, on France's National Fête-day, 14th July, a great inter-Allied march took place through Paris. Watched by cheering crowds eighteen-deep on the boulevards, contingents of French, British, Belgians and Russians paraded past, and the President, in his familiar chauffeur-like uniform, presented decorations to the relatives of five hundred dead Frenchmen. But while such demonstrations could raise spirits in volatile Paris, another mood was reflected in the provinces. A woman correspondent of *The Times*, travelling through France in mid-1916, reported a discouraging scene.[5] From Brittany to Provence, the impression she received was one of 'stagnation'. The women and old men working on the land were labouring on almost automatically with no enthusiasm. The bourgeoisie or middle classes seemed to have disappeared behind closed shutters, intent on saving their sous. The women in the munitions factories were, according to local officials, 'intoxicated' with the money they earned, and were spending it recklessly, in a way unknown before. With few exceptions, life in provincial France seemed to have come to a halt with the mobilisation order of August 1914. Even the war factories appeared only half-alive. It was noticeable too what a gulf separated the northerners from the people in the south. The northern refugees in Provence were unhappy in the southern sunshine and homesick for their own grey skies. And the Provençals talked to them of *'votre guerre'* (your war), disowning the struggle as no concern of theirs.

In these respects, Paris was obviously not France. Like London and Berlin, it had an unquenchable life of its own. Alongside its plain evidences of war – the widespread mourning, the ubiquitous *mutilés*, the emergency restrictions – flourished extravagances and frivolities that seemed inseparable from a wartime capital. Such things could afford a retreat from war's realities, help to banish underlying fears and anxieties, or just pander to the whims of insensitive civilians with money to spend. One observer noted, at the start of the year, the self-centred attitude of Parisians, who disliked having their peacetime lives disrupted. Another commented on the outlandish fashion fads and undiminished quest for pleasure. Small boys were being dressed up as soldiers, and little girls decked out in 'horizon-blue' policemen's caps and cloaks. A new vogue of short flared skirts, high heels, peaked hats and low-cut blouses was making women look like 'shop-girls out on the spree'.[6] At one hairdresser's it was impossible to get an appointment for a week, owing to bookings for coiffures for a fancy-dress ball.[7] Restaurants and theatres were filled nightly. All this despite the 40% rise in the cost of living, and was made possible by increased wages and, notably, the high profits earned by war contractors – a new class acquiring a social prestige hitherto enjoyed by public officials.

The paradox showed more starkly during the dark days of Verdun. The lavish spending, the fine cars and over-dressed women in the Bois, the literary men masquerading in uniform at the Press Bureau, the back-biting gossip of sheltered non-combatants while the bitter struggle raged a few score miles to the east – all, as Bordeaux lamented, gave the impression that the war was forgotten. But at the beginning of July the war was suddenly brought nearer by the rumbling of the Somme guns, that same ominous sound that was heard across the Channel in England. But the strange ambivalent life of Paris continued. 'Today there are only men in anguish or men celebrating,' recorded Bordeaux that autumn, observing, fresh from the front, the crowded gaiety of a smart restaurant.[8] Amid the high spending jewellers in particular were doing well, for many of the 'new rich' were salting away their profits in jewellery to escape taxes. But at least the war-workers were sharing in the good living. At a Versailles restaurant Michel Corday noted a party enjoying a meal of expensive dishes and wines. 'They exhaled a clinging odour of chemicals,' he observed.[9] Less commendable was the luxurious summer holiday-making that was taking place at resorts like Deauville. During August such places were crammed, and the parade of wealth was reminiscent of peacetime. At Deauville one army contractor was said to have paid £17,000 for a single pearl.

In general these wartime frivolities were little more than the froth on a nation regimented and harnessed like Britain and Germany, and like them striving to marshal all its resources for fighting the war. There were bound to be abuses and evasions in even the best-organised country. But the now vast output of war material, sufficient to feed the voracious needs of Verdun, was an index of France's effort. The number of war-workers in Paris, 61,000 in January 1915, had by April 1916 grown to 144,000. In all France during the same period, the figure had multiplied threefold.[10] But the extent of France's contribution could be measured above all by the impoverishment of her manpower. The rural areas, especially, were becoming denuded of men, increasing numbers of whom would never come back. At a typical small commune in the Savoy, thirty-eight of the seven hundred and fifty inhabitants were already dead by August 1916.[11] Of the retired older men who had returned to the land to replace their sons, several had recently died, worn out by overwork. The women too were becoming exhausted and dispirited. In the towns, and even Paris itself, fit young civilians were now a rarity. Months earlier, Henry Bordeaux had deplored the disappearance of the men, remarking sardonically: 'all the shirkers and the bandy-legged, the one-eyed and the goitrous will continue to flourish along with the fifty-year-olds'.[12] In 1915 French losses had exceeded 1,400,000, including 50% of the army's regular officers, and in five months of the Verdun battle the casualties were 363,000. To make good these inroads, 200,000 youths of the 1917 class (those who would be twenty in 1917) were called up in January 1916, and more would inexorably follow.

In these conditions the call for women was intensified. The woman war-worker, both as a substitute for the called-up male and a performer of new tasks specifically created by the war, was already an accepted part of the French scene. To appreciate her contribution in the latter field one had only to visit, for example, the great Renault factory near Paris, where early in 1916 thousands of mob-capped and aproned women were at the benches making and testing shells and fuses. It was a form of emancipation that disturbed sensitive observers. Frenchmen in any case, far more than British or Germans, disliked seeing their womenfolk in any sort of 'unfeminine' role. To Michel Corday it was painful to see the long rows of girls at their lathes, making tiny machines all designed for killing.[13] But as the comb-out of men continued, the women took on yet more male jobs. In July, in order to recover temporarily-released soldiers for the army, it was forbidden to employ men for certain specified tasks that could be performed by women. The category of jobs was extended in November, so that henceforth few men were employed in the arms factories except for work too heavy for women. As the feminine 'take-over' increased, steps were taken to improve welfare conditions. In April a Committee on Female Labour was appointed, which set up more crèches and saw to the care of pregnant women.[14] Night work was strictly controlled, so that girls under eighteen were forbidden to work at night, those between eighteen and twenty-one only temporarily and in exceptional circumstances, and no women could labour at night for more than ten hours.[15] Inspectors were charged with enforcing these rules. Industrialists who had been chary of adopting female labour now accepted it more willingly. Women, it was found, went home to rest and sleep, while the men tended to spend leisure time at the bars and cabarets. The output of female labour compared with that of men was reckoned at 80%, but women's level of achievement was sometimes higher than men's on account of their patience, dexterity and greater equanimity.

It is not surprising if in the general climate of the times and the abnormal conditions of life, the marriage bond was put under strain. With their soldier-husbands away and often not heard from for long periods, wives were too easily led to form liaisons with other men. This was an effect of war observable in every belligerent country, and already noted by French commentators in 1916. Now Corday remarked on it again, asserting that war would 'unmask the frailty of marriage'.[16] He claimed that 80% of women were delighted to be free of their husbands, while half of these had actually taken lovers. It was a tragedy that was running through the lower classes, he said – but in fairness to these hard-working women, there is no evidence that they were any more unfaithful or promiscuous than their better-placed sisters.

Whatever their other trials and difficulties, the French were still, through most of 1916, hardly affected by food shortage. While Germany was already under heavy strain and having to resort to all kinds of unpalatable and improbable food substitutes, France, like Britain, was as yet feeling no real pinch. Indeed, throughout the war, those Frenchmen who 'knew the ropes' would scarcely lack for anything. According to one writer, the only real trouble Parisians experienced arose from the fact that nobody could be persuaded to obey the spirit of any of the elaborate regulations drawn up for the general benefit of the community.[17] Though Food Ministry succeeded Food Ministry and system followed system, the fact remained that on meatless days (when they came in 1917) meat could always be obtained, and sugar could be had even after it was officially unavailable. In the spring of 1916 the food in Paris was, in the words of a visiting Englishwoman, 'quite excellent'.[18] There was no noticeable scarcity, the only limitation being that dinner at restaurants was restricted to two courses. A companion of hers – and this was at the height of the struggle for Verdun – was annoyed because, when dining in Paris, he had to go without a tempting *mousse* of duck, having already consumed *filet de bœuf* and *langouste*.

Nevertheless, behind the façade of near-plenty, problems were beginning to appear. In May, to save the expense of imported wheat, national bread was introduced. 'Here we are with a "national bread!" ' wrote a Parisienne, Louise Delétang, who apparently found it highly appetising. 'They are giving us a less white bread, less refined, but as good and more nourishing. One is tempted to kiss it before devouring it!'[19] The sugar factories and beet distilleries were affected by a dearth of skilled men to repair the machinery to deal with the 1916 crop, which meant a delay in getting in the yield. And the refineries were suffering from the lack of cargoes from the West Indies, the result of shipping shortage. Brewing was being hampered by malt scarcity and transport difficulties. Output from the wine distilleries was restricted by the high prices of basic and other materials – sugar, packing-cases and bottles. Champagne and other sparkling wine production was likewise hard hit, lack of skilled labour being an additional factor. Cheese and butter output, on the other hand, continued to be satisfactory, with women and children replacing men in the factories, though at the end of the year less was seen of the popular Roquefort cheese, owing to the requisition of sheep. Preserved butter was meanwhile being increasingly produced to reinforce supplies of the fresh commodity.

With little lacking, Frenchmen were still prone to wastefulness, as in the piping days of peace. Conscious of this failing, in June the daily paper *Le Matin* arranged a luncheon party – referred to by wits as 'Delights of the Dustbin' – with the aim of demonstrating how much eatable food was wasted in preparing meals by the throwing away of cabbage leaves, fish-heads and so on.[20] There was sense in the project, for by autumn there were signs that France's food position was not impregnable. In Paris grocers' shops people were queuing to obtain scarce sugar, butter was being sold only by the quarter-pound, while oranges had disappeared from the fruiterers'. Moreover the year's harvest had proved poor. Wheat, rye, pulse and potato yields were 35% below normal. In late November President Poincaré noted with anxiety that the lengthening of the war was slowly creating grave difficulties for the feeding of the population, adding that the Government was contemplating serious restrictive measures.[21] Soon after, at a meeting of the War Council, a number of severe-seeming provisions were agreed: the adoption of a standard national bread and banning of long baton rolls (so dear to Frenchmen); complete banning of ices, sweets and chocolate sweets, only slab chocolate being permitted. Though these regulations were not applied at once, the President and his wife as far as possible gave immediate effect to them in the Elysée Palace, regardless of the eminence of their guests.

In various directions signs now appeared that life for Parisians would henceforth be less comfortable. Already in May, as the diarist Louise Delétang reported, fabrics like serge and gabardine had doubled in price in the *grands magasins* compared with pre-war, and footwear was '*inabordable*' (unobtainable).[22] However, the relaxing of a few regulations, like the return of buses to the boulevards in June and the re-opening of other closed routes soon after, and, in November itself, the resumption of ordinary opera performances (though without boxes and with evening dress prohibited), seemed to suggest easier times. But in November citizens were suddenly startled by new restrictive measures. It was announced that under an Economic Council shortly to be set up, meatless days would be ordered. Further, that in order to conserve lighting, no shops would be lit by electricity or gas after 6 p.m., except places where food and drink were sold, and chemists' and barbers' shops. Restaurants were to close at 9.30 p.m. instead of 10 p.m., and theatres, music-halls and cinemas were to shut on one night in the week and their lighting reduced by 50%.[23] Notices now appeared on the walls appealing for economy in the use of coal. Despite the continued liveliness of Paris, the Sunday evening crowds on the boulevards, the packed restaurants and theatres, the unprecendented 'guzzling and the passion for luxury' (as noted by Corday, who attributed these extravagances to the highly-paid lower classes'),[24] it was clear that at last, after more than two years of war, the capital was having to tighten its belt.

Corday was probably too censorious of the so-called lavishness of the wage-earners. Many of these were war-workers labouring hard and long, who were making the most of their leisure with good money in their pockets. (In fact, prices were rising fast enough to nullify much of the benefit of their high wages.) Seen against the massive war-effort and the tensions and anxieties of the times, the strenuous search for distraction was part of the picture of a nation at war. But, along with the toil, the effort and the pleasure-seeking, ran a strange indifference to the war itself. In October the diarist Henry Bordeaux observed a 'Paris glittering, avid for pleasure', and witnessed a revue at the Théâtre Michel, in which an army priest married a pregnant woman and a comedienne in brief skirts sang a song about fecundity. 'Is it here one would go to seek guidance?' he asked.[25] He told too of a newspaper photographer sent to take pictures of the crowds buying war loan at the big banks and finding no one to photograph. On the other hand, the man found a long queue outside the Ministry of Pensions waiting to draw pensions. 'One feels in Paris a lassitude or forgetfulness of the war,' he commented.[26]

Yet this apparent 'lassitude' did not preclude a strong streak of anti-German hatred and bellicosity. Typical of the 'hate' mood was the satisfied remark of a certain actress, who had taken up nursing, that recently there had been no trench truces and that the French were shooting Germans who tried to fraternise. In January a newspaper organised an exhibition of German vandalism. Another paper declared that those who had been pacifists before the war were leading France headlong towards the renunciation of all her glories. For much of this attitude the censorship was responsible – notifying one journal in January, for instance, that all discussion of peace was forbidden. Three months later, during the Verdun battle, the censors erased an entire article in the paper *Excelsior* entitled 'Let us Prepare for Peace'.[27] Yet at least, as the devastating struggle for Verdun continued, the pugnacious 'Fight On' tone of the press helped to steel public opinion against any faltering. But much of the widespread apathy was due to a growing mistrust of what appeared in the papers. This in turn was due to the repressive hand of censorship, which kept the public in virtual ignorance of what was really happening at the front. In September 1915, alone in the French press, Joffre's Order of the Day for the French offensive in Champagne ('The general offensive has started . . . It will continue day and night. Remember the Marne. Conquer or die . . .') had been suppressed.[28] A year later – in contrast to British practice – still no French journalist was allowed near the fighting line. Even if a special correspondent managed to get a report back from the front, the censor's watchful eye would water down to trivialities anything he wrote.

Views expressing approval of the war could be certain of the censor's blessing. In January *Le Petit Parisien* published an article by the historian Lavisse setting out his reason for fighting on. All the Frenchmen who had died, he said, could not be allowed to have sacrificed themselves in vain; the French had a right to vengeance, and this war, which had been thrust upon them, could provide a revenge for the defeat of 1870; Frenchmen could not live without honour and glory, and it was their duty to free the world from tyranny. To counter these highly orthodox patriotic sentiments, the pacifist-minded few had of course no public platform. They mostly relied on their voices being heard at syndicalist meetings, where speakers – some of them anarchists – fervently argued that the war was not one of aggression on Germany's part, and that the workers were sacrificing their lives for a handful of people at the top. But the issue was strong enough to split the ranks of a large trade union, the General Confederation of Labour, in which a minority led by Merrheim declared its opposition to the war, against a war-supporting majority headed by Jouhaux. Meanwhile there was a growing trickle of peace propaganda in the semi-clandestine press. By mid-year Government concern was being aroused by the pacifist activities of a small sheet, *Le Bonnet Rouge*, whose suspension was ordered on account of its provocative articles, written by a certain Almereyda and others. The suppression was, however, cancelled by the Minister of the Interior, Malvy, after Almereyda had promised to cease his pacifist campaigning. (More was to be heard of *Le Bonnet Rouge* in 1917, as Frenchmen were affected by increasing war-weariness.) But on the mass of the French people neither the officially-inspired war-mindedness of the press nor the views of the peace-mongers had much effect. Their mood, after twenty-four months of war, was somewhere between the two extremes: resignedly, and without enthusiasm, they were prepared to carry on. But among her fellow-Parisiennes the writer Louise Delétang detected ominous signs of strain. 'It's time this bloodthirsty war was over!' she commented in August. 'The women have become thin, worn out by this distressing anxiety, the constant expectation of disaster.'[29] And President Poincaré sensed a disturbing undercurrent. 'There is everywhere, in the Parisian population and in the Chambers, a vague malaise,' he noted in November. 'The "defeatists" are gaining ground every day . . . Suspicious miasmas float in the air.'[30]

In view of the uninspiring Home Front situation, there was some truth behind the cartoon in which the *poilu*, depicted amid the dangers of the trenches, was saying sardonically: 'If only the civilians can hold out.' This was one illustration of the gulf between soldier and civilian that was steadily widening as the war continued. Each, immersed in his so totally different existence, was becoming more and more of a stranger to the other. Across the Channel, in London, the diarist MacDonagh was noting the phenomenon when he saw troops on Christmas leave as 'strange beings from another world'. Princess Blücher was observing the same thing in Germany. In France, too, Henry Bordeaux (like Robert Graves in England) was continually expressing the serving soldier's sense of alienation from the Home Front, stressing, perhaps too obsessively, the pleasure-seeking and high spending that was only a superficial part of the French wartime scene. Basically, the gap was inevitable. It stemmed partly from the fact that life on the Home Front, though profoundly transformed by the switch to war production, was bound to go on much as usual. It was also due to the inability of civilians to grasp the horrors of battle through their own remoteness from physical danger. The only taste of real war that Parisians experienced in 1916 was a Zeppelin raid in January in which twenty-four people were killed. There was, too, the growing preoccupation of people at home with their own affairs – the anxieties, the restrictions, the growing drabness, the hard and unaccustomed war work.

Apart from all this was the distorted picture of the war presented by the press. 'The papers still mention "French soldiers" as if they were a special caste,' complained Corday in March. 'Do they forget that they are talking about ordinary peasants torn from the land, and that the young soldiers called up since the war were given only a few months' training? . . . The French soldier is merely a peasant in a steel helmet.'[31] Especially infuriating to the troops themselves was the over-romanticised, optimistic press treatment of military operations, the glamorising of French soldiers as heroes, the denigrating of the Germans as brutes and cowards. Men returning home on leave were dismayed and depressed to find the civilians, fed with such *bourrage de crâne* (eyewash), holding totally false ideas of what the front was really like, and unbelieving or indifferent when they were told the truth. There were many other things that distressed the soldier: the huge discrepancy between the daily pay of war-workers (10 to 15 francs) and their own (25 centimes); the lavish living of the profiteering contractors; the crowded cafés and theatres; the sudden prosperity and changed attitude of their munition-making wives (there was the *poilu* returning from a year in the trenches who, on seeing his wife decked out in some extravagant wartime mode, exclaimed: 'Hello, I'd forgotten this was carnival time').[32] Such things were making the soldiers feel like exiles from the nation's life and strangers in their own land. It was one of the war's ironies that these millions of conscripts felt closer to their brother soldiers than to the people at home for whom they were fighting.

But sometimes the papers themselves did service by publicising the soldier's viewpoint. In December *Le Petit Parisien* printed this heartfelt appeal from a fighting man: 'We ask of the Home Front neither gratitude, lyrical effusions nor fine literature, but action and an effort comparable with ours. There should not be a France at war and a France at peace (i.e. a civilian France), but a single France. We do not want the communication to be severed . . . Each should wear his hair-shirt . . . Those who have not suffered physically, who have not received the sacrament of suffering, have not the right to speak . . . First the mud and the frozen feet, the rats, the fleas, the rotten straw, the watch among the corpses; afterwards, we shall see. [We need] a higher direction that should make itself felt everywhere; the weak and mediocre should be removed, the incompetent dismissed; sanctions should be instituted; and lastly, all top positions should be occupied by men of courage . . . An outstanding effort is called for.'[33]

Chapter 9

GERMANY

'They have the habit of obeying'

FOR Germany, 1916 was the year of peak effort, the year before decline set in, forced by the immense and irreplaceable drain being imposed on her resources. The great battle of Verdun, launched by her in order to bleed France to death, had on her an effect almost as disastrous as it had on France. Her losses up to the end of June were 337,000 compared with French casualties of 363,000; and even by paying this fearsome price she failed to take the citadel or break the French beyond recovery. As if this effort were not enough, Verdun was closely followed by the battle of the Somme, with its further huge casualties. And all the time the Home Front, toiling to supply the vast demands of the army, was being steadily weakened by the tightening blockade. In view of the pressures Germany was enduring through this year, the nation's morale remained on the whole fairly steady. Certainly at the start of the year there was still a general belief in ultimate victory. In February Colonel House (the envoy sent to Europe by President Wilson to study the possibility of American mediation for peace) reported to Lloyd George on his return from Germany that the Germans were confident of victory and proudly pointing to the conquest of an area larger than the whole German Empire. He added that he saw no marked indication of privation or strain.[1] A visitor to Berlin in March found the people tired of the war and still bitter against England, 'but everyone was calm and resolute, resolved to fight to the bitter end, and no one had any doubt who would win'.[2] It was to this dour determined mood that the Chancellor appealed when he spoke to the nation in April. The German people, he declared,

148

possessed a 'perfectly gigantic moral reserve. We went out to battle,' he continued, 'for the protection of our unity and freedom – the whole nation united like one man. It is this united and free Germany that our enemies desire to destroy.' Though, as the year progressed, the dogged spirit was wavering in the face of a growing weariness and longing for peace, in September the American newspaper correspondent, Edward Bullitt, still found the Germans 'amazingly solid' against giving in. He revealed the secret of their endurance when he said: 'They have the habit, as have no other people, of obeying.'[3]

But if the masses laboured on in a mood of muted resignation, widening cracks in the façade of political and industrial unity now showed that the *Burgfrieden*, or civil truce, proclaimed in 1914, was over. Determined voices were now speaking out against the war. Strikes – previously very few – increased, and there was an open split in the already restive Socialist ranks. The previous December over a third of the one hundred and eleven Social Democrats had declared their opposition to the Government. More serious trouble arose in March, when the Reichstag debated an emergency budget. After the Socialist Haase had belaboured the Government for its mismanagement of war affairs, seventeen Social Democrats voted against the budget. These opposers straightway met and formed a new parliamentary party, the Social Democratic Labour Fellowship. Spurred by this secession, a few like-minded trade union leaders joined the rebels. The Government, in a move to counter the spread of revolutionary feeling, banned the more extremist public meetings, seized certain printing presses, and temporarily suspended outspoken left-wing papers. Then on the 1st May, during the Labour Day demonstrations in Berlin, Karl Liebknecht – the radical young barrister Member of the Reichstag who had been a thorn in the Government's side both before and since 1914 as a violent anti-war crusader – was arrested for incitement to public disturbance. He was borne off by the police shouting 'Down with the war! Down with the Government!', and his pockets were found full of revolutionary leaflets. Liebknecht was tried and convicted of treason, and sentenced to four-and-a-half years' penal servitude. That he was not shot may have been due to the Government's fear of inflaming public opinion too dangerously. The strength of popular anti-war sentiment was shown by the mass peace meeting at Frankfurt on the 1st October, at which 30,000 workers passed a resolution demanding peace on the basis of the status quo.[4]

Though they might be calling for peace, the workers were still strong in their determination not to see Germany beaten. But now they were beginning to feel a heavy strain. Despite the rapid rise of wages in the war industries (which was drawing so many agricultural workers away from the land that measures had to be taken to stop the drift), the war workers were far from enjoying prosperity. Owing to the rise in prices, their average daily real wages fell by nearly 22% between March 1914 and September 1916, while the real wages of workers in the civilian industries dropped by 42% in the same period.[5] This loss of purchasing power, together with growing food scarcity, was causing great discontent. But, as against this, the shortage of labour strengthened the workers' position when it came to making their grievances felt, whether political or in the matter of living standards. The sudden upsurge of industrial troubles in 1916 was largely due to these factors. Among the most serious was the three-day strike of 55,000 Berlin workers in June – a protest, organised by a small group of radical shop stewards, against the sentencing of Liebknecht. Equally significant were the Ruhr coal mines strikes that occurred in August, whose immediate cause was food shortage and the failure of wages to keep up with prices. In view of Germany's rigidly military regime the general policy of the Ministry of War in countering the strikes was less harshly repressive than might have been thought. It was seen in a directive issued in July to the Deputy Commanding Generals of districts, ordering them to act cautiously so as to avoid creating martyrs. Strike leaders were to be arrested and either tried for treason or sent into the army, while the workers were to be ordered to return

Zeppelin raid on Shoreditch

Funeral of air-raid victims at Folkestone

'White feather' flag hoisted in the East End

Anti-German riots in the East End

to work, and threatened with punishment if they refused.[6]

A further great call-up of men for the army had preceded the Verdun campaign. There was now hardly an able-bodied male under forty-five not in uniform or employed in munitions, the mines or transport work. This caused a redoubled demand for the services of women. As in Britain and France, they were pouring into the war industries and every other kind of job to supplement and replace the men. A visitor to Berlin in March reported 'no men anywhere, women are doing everything'.[7] In Essen the great Krupp plant, which used no women before the war, now employed 12,000. Though women were not subject to mobilisation, in Berlin there was a very efficient women's department of the Central Labour Exchange for finding them work. Directed by the formidably energetic Dr Klausner, masculine-looking with her short hair and 'villainously dressed', it had been placing thousands of women in skilled, semi-skilled and unskilled jobs since the start of the war. By now there was little that German women workers were not doing. They were driving mail and delivery vans, delivering the post, toiling on the land, working in open mines (but not underground), operating electric cranes in iron foundries, ticket-collecting on the railways, running tramcars and acting as subway conductors. They paved streets, dug ditches, laid pipes. They were even employed on construction work on the Berlin underground railway, labouring with picks and shovels like navvies. Employers in the munitions factories, iron industries and mines were finding them intelligent but less able than men to stand noise and heat and – rather obviously – to lift heavy weights. Though there were many types of work from which women had been banned before the war, they were now performing a number of tasks – equally unfeminine – from which no one had even thought of excluding them. And one important pre-war restriction which had been removed concerned hours and conditions: women could now work a twelve-hour day and an eight-hour night shift. For child-bearing they were allowed two weeks' absence before the birth and four weeks after, receiving two-thirds of their normal wages. With typical German thoroughness, a network of women's welfare services had been set up. There were war kitchens, day nurseries, kindergartens, leagues of housewives; and women themselves had the opportunity to serve in Red Cross and refugee centres and institutions for wounded soldiers. The largest women's organisation was the National Women's Service League (*Nationale Frauendienst*), whose object was to aid soldiers' wives or widows, and their families, and to help ensure that they had adequate food. Closely linked with this was a body, with branches all over Berlin, for distributing war relief.

By now, war was creating in Germany a feminine revolution at least as spectacular as that in Britain or France. The old domestic picture of the *hausfrau* placidly passing the time gossiping with friends to the accompaniment of clicking knitting-needles was no longer typical. She knitted still when she had time, though now for strict reasons of economy rather than out of womanly habit. But by the end of 1916 even knitting – a ubiquitous practice at the start of the war in shops, trams, trains, theatres and (it was said) churches – was vanishing from the German scene owing to the commandeering of wool for army clothing needs. But many other changes were occurring. With their husbands at the front, and spending their days at work, women were becoming more self-reliant, less apt to look on the peacetime breadwinner with the former awe. They were having to cope with problems of daily living – food queues, scarcities and high prices – and make decisions in a way that they had never done before. (And they were standing up to the rough-and-tumble of their wartime jobs with commendable spirit. Women tram conductors, it was reported, had a way of subduing unruly passengers with a thrust of the long hatpin they wore in their caps.) All this was breeding the beginnings of a sense of independence. And though there was no organised campaign for women's suffrage in Germany, the National Council of Women of Germany, with its 600,000 members, was showing signs of interest in the women's vote. But there were those, like the Baroness von Bissing, head of a women's organisation, who feared that German women would grow too attached to their new life and not want to return to their old domestic existence. The Baroness had another care: to educate women and girls out of strange superstitions. She had 'to make them understand that they will not have crippled children if their husband or lover comes back from war lacking an arm or leg'.[8]

Manpower strained towards the limit, a growing shortage of many materials and of food: as the battle of Verdun raged throughout the spring and early summer, this was the dominant picture of civilian Germany. For the ordinary citizen, faced with an all-round deterioration in living conditions, the most immediately felt deprivation was in the matter of food. He could somehow carry on in patched, threadbare or ersatz clothes, but without proper nourishment he could neither maintain the strength to work nor keep warm when winter coal ran short. Morale, too, was bound to suffer. The most persuasive propaganda, even the news of military successes (or reverses suffered by the enemy) could avail little when the stomach remained unsatisfied. It was now, in 1916, that the basic weakness of Germany's food situation started to be seriously felt. At least three factors were combining to bring this about. There was the falling-off of food imports from neutrals like Holland, Denmark and Switzerland, which were beginning to fear for their own supplies. There was the dearth of agricultural labour, despite the army's efforts to spare workers for the land during 1915. And there was the recent poor potato crop, aggravated by the farmers' holding back of stocks in order to secure higher prices. This hit the industrial areas particularly hard, to the extent that production began to suffer, causing many firms to resort to buying on the black market. One industrialist was quoted as saying: 'We have been robbing the strength of our workers and officials for two years, and it can't go on for ever ... Now the workers are so far at the limit of their strength that it is really to be taken seriously when they say "We cannot work more than nine hours".'[9]

Bread had already been rationed since the previous February. Now, a year later, the Reichstag decreed rationing for meat, potatoes, milk, sugar, butter and soap. Only green vegetables and fruit remained exempt, along with poultry and game. But despite this, shortages continued, aggravated by faulty distribution and hoarding by speculators who sought to charge higher prices than those officially fixed. Pork disappeared, there was a run on sugar, and meat became so scarce that in April the Berlin butchers were closed for five days. James Gerard, while acknowledging that the position was getting 'very serious', forecast that before the Germans were starved out, they would starve the Belgians, Russians, Poles and their two million prisoners of war. Soon after, he reported that the country people, gravely short of food in some districts, were faring worse than the townsmen, the policy being to keep the latter as content as possible.[10] But some country-dwellers appeared to be doing better than the townsfolk, for it was said that they were jeering at the townsmen, who were restricted to artificial honey, while they themselves were spreading their bread with plentiful butter surmounted with a thick slice of ham. In March a Berlin lady was confined to bed with what she called 'Ersatz' illness, caused by the chemicals in her diet – a hint of the widespread adulteration that was soon to condemn Germans to consuming a vast range of substitute foods. Despite the multifarious decrees, rules and regulations – or perhaps because of them – waste was being caused by mal-distribution. There were reports of large quantities of butter and potatoes held up in depots, and getting spoiled, while consumers clamoured for them. Queues lengthened at the food shops. Women were getting up in the middle of the night and settling outside the shops on camp stools, knitting and gossiping. One woman was said to have taken her sewing-machine with her. 'We can hardly complain of starvation,' wrote Princess Blücher in May, 'but the whole population is being under-fed, which of course in the long run means deterioration of physical and mental forces in all classes.'[11]

Meanwhile, the public, if not starved, was getting restive

and impatient. There were food disturbances in several towns. In March angry crowds in Cologne roused the mayor twice in one night and forced him to open the food market. They also tried to storm a sitting of the town council. In Bonn, queues waiting for lard rations started to riot when favoured customers, driving up in their carriages, were given immediate service. Policemen who moved in to quell the trouble were nearly lynched. In July a mob of women in Düsseldorf demonstrated outside the Town Hall for more meat and potatoes. When the mayor offered them beans and peas, they replied by smashing all the windows. Shortly before, a crowd had besieged Berlin's Hotel Esplanade and looted the bread supplies, in the belief that the guests here were living in the lap of luxury, whereas they were receiving the same ration as all other citizens, that is, 1,500 grammes of bread a week and 400 grammes of flour. But, to bear out accounts that some country-dwellers did better than townsmen, there was the example of Krieblowitz, in Prussia, the country home of the Blücher family. Here, in September, there was venison, game, milk, butter, flour, bread, vegetables and fruit in abundance.[12]

An impression of Berlin's food difficulties during this summer comes from Mrs Bullitt, the wife of the American newspaper correspondent.[13] On one day in early June she was glad to get eggs and a glass of milk, neither of which could then be bought in the shops. She declared that the impression gained by the 'paying guest' that Berlin could carry on indefinitely under the British blockade was deceptive. The queues for bread, butter and meat were long, and women were standing for hours to obtain their weekly ration of butter the size of a walnut for each member of the family. The children were happy, but not thriving, on the ersatz honey. When visiting a friend unexpectedly for supper, Mrs Bullitt was given some 'large white balls which tasted like dough', some small stewed prunes, and fried potatoes as a luxury. The weekly meat ration was half a pound per person, and cream was obtainable only on a doctor's prescription. Soon after, Mrs Bullitt dined at the Esplanade and found the food 'really too awful'. As she had neither meat nor bread cards she was reduced to eating a concoction of eggs with asparagus (the latter being 'fat, white and tasteless'). But, as she found in July, the houses of the rich could still produce the finest fare. Staying in Hamburg with the Warburgs, the wealthy banking family, she enjoyed a 'most royal dinner' of roast beef (her first in Germany) followed by many other courses, including nectarines from the Warburgs' country hothouses, and strawberries with unstinted sugar. This was when sugar was generally short. That month continuing rains were threatening the next potato harvest. The peasants were paddling round their potato fields in boats trying to save some of their crops. One farmer lamented that one more week of rain would make things 'very bad'. But in August, when Mrs Bullitt's husband saw Herr Karl Helfferich, the Minister of the Interior, he was told optimistically that Germany could continue indefinitely as far as food was concerned, that the harvest would be up to 30% better than for 1915, and that Germany would be far better off in the coming year than in the last. Meanwhile, press propaganda was persuading the public to take comfort from their privations by proclaiming the benefits of frugal diet. In June, for example, a long article in the *Vossische Zeitung* demonstrated that over-eating was a cause of baldness.

The creation of a War Food Office in May, with an experienced administrator, von Batocki, as its director, had not greatly improved matters. Known as the 'Food Dictator', von Batocki had too many difficulties to surmount. 'If he could not create plenty from shortage', writes one historian, 'he could at least bring the cold comfort of an equal misery to everyone.'[14] Von Batocki was charged, in fact, with favouring Prussia at the expense of the South German States, and many Bavarian towns announced that visitors from Prussia must not expect to receive the same rations as local people. Meanwhile the shortage persisted. Milk and butter output was affected by the scarcity towards the end of the year, and lack of fats became a serious problem. Though fish was still abundant, it was growing increasingly dear, and the meat shortage was causing a run on eggs. The September egg ration of two eggs per week was reduced in December to one every two weeks. Late in 1916 great efforts were made to augment the number of pigs, and notices were posted in the villages to encourage the fattening of these animals. With the potato yield decreased by some 50% by the disastrous harvest, recourse was now being had to turnips, the homely root vegetable that for many Germans would become something like a staple food in the notorious 'turnip winter' of 1916–1917. Among all but the very rich, food was now the dominant topic, and the cause of a mounting dissension between the townspeople and the wealthy land-owning farmers. To Germans, who were customarily such hearty trenchermen, the war had indeed brought a drastic belt-tightening. By the end of 1916 the old pre-war plenty and variety of diet was but a fond memory banished under a bewildering mass of price-fixing and card-rationing regulations – the War Food Office had produced over two hundred and fifty new controls – which themselves did not guarantee that reasonably-priced supplies would be available.[15]

Shortage of food was accompanied by that added trial which no German who lived through the war years was likely to forget: the food substitute.[16] The phenomenon occurred in Britain, but not nearly to the same extent. As scarcity made itself felt, there was hardly an article of diet that was not replaced or supplemented by some more or less palatable surrogate. German ingenuity went to every length to produce artificial foods that looked or tasted something like the real thing. Food exhibitions were held in Berlin and elsewhere, demonstrating the great range of such ersatz eatables and beverages. Bread, at first largely adulterated with rye flour, gradually embodied ingredients like oats, Indian corn, barley, beans, peas and buckwheat meal. Cake was made from clover meal and chestnut flour. Meat was substituted by the rice lamb chop, the nut cutlet, the vegetable beefsteak – a pale green concoction of cornmeal, spinach, potatoes and ground nuts bound with egg – or sausages made from offal. Butter was 'stretched' by a powder made from starch and sodium carbonate, or replaced by a mixture of curdled milk, sugar and colouring material. There was an egg substitute, of maize and potato-meal. Artificial jellies contained gelatine and colouring matter. Pepper was adulterated with ashes. There were substitutes for salad oil made from plant mucilage and sap, labelled 'Salatan' and 'Salatin'. Many attempts were made to develop substitutes for fat – an abiding deficiency – from rats, mice, hamsters, crows, cockroaches, snails and earthworms, even hair clippings and old leather boots, but none was very successful. Sand and plaster of Paris were utilised for the 'mineralisation' of foods. Unscrupulous bakers adulterated cakes with sawdust. Of drinks and beverages, there were countless artificial lemonades, while coffee went through several stages of substitution. First it was mostly replaced by roasted barley and oats, flavoured by coal-tar products. With sugar it was fairly nourishing and palatable. Then came the *Kaffee-ersatz-ersatz*, of roasted acorns and beechnuts, with just enough roasted barley to provide flavour. But with acorns and beechnuts reserved to feed porkers, a third substitute appeared, made chiefly of carrots and yellow turnips. Tea was a matter of linden tree blooms mixed with beech buds and a few tips of pine for flavour; or the leaves of blackberry, raspberry, sour cherry, bilberry, cranberry, nettle and so on.[17]

Nevertheless, despite the mounting signs of undernourishment, the Germans were not yet in desperate want. In an attempt to counter the false hopes being raised in Britain by tales of famished, rioting Germans, an Englishman returning to Britain from Germany published an article in the *Daily Mail* at the end of July, giving his view of the true position. 'The Germans are not starving,' he wrote. 'They are not getting nearly so much to eat as they were used to and would like, but as they mostly over-ate in peacetime, they are now on a more *normal* living standard than they were before. Conditions are unmistakably inconvenient and unpleasant – imagine Germans being short of potatoes – but anybody in England who thinks the Germans are being defeated by hunger is dwelling in a paradise of idle dreams.'[18]

But now, as other shortages appeared, the ersatz was extending beyond food to textiles and other everyday materials, to affect much of Germany's civilian life. Already in the previous winter clothing and clothing fabrics were growing scarce. With cotton unobtainable and wool now a luxury, clothes had to be darned, patched and turned to prolong their existence to the utmost. All the best leather was commandeered for the army, and the remainder, for civilian use, closely controlled. In February all stocks of clothing, clothing materials, linen and so on were requisitioned and an Imperial Clothing Office established soon after, to handle and distribute clothing, so that it was impossible to buy a suit, dress or pair of shoes without an official permit. Women were restricted to two dresses, two blouses, three items of any undergarment, six handkerchiefs and two pairs of boots. In order to secure a permit for a new article of dress, they had to declare on oath that they did not possess more than the allowed quantity of the item in question and surrender their worn garment if called upon to do so. Meanwhile strenuous efforts were being made to produce synthetic fabrics. A cotton substitute was produced consisting of nettle and willow fibre, with a small admixture of wool or cotton. A paper-cloth was evolved to replace manilla, jute and even garments like women's and children's coats. Attempts to find a leather-sole substitute were less successful, and finally a wooden sole was adopted. Ersatz rubber for heels was obtainable, but of little value. (It also proved useless for tennis balls, it was noted.) In the military sphere, fruit-stones were brought into service to yield the glycerine from which was produced the oil for explosives.

Despite all the austerities and the spreading war-weariness, the Germans retained an undiminished faith in their war leaders. (These, at least, could be relied on, even if the Deity had failed them by denying them quick victory.) At the start of 1916 the Kaiser was still immensely popular. Beginning to age and with a streak of white hair now showing above his temples, in his simple grey uniform and helmet he was said to look every inch a soldier. He was cheered wherever he went, and an observer had earlier noted the reception that met him on his return from the Eastern front, when men threw their hats into the air, women fluttered handkerchiefs, and the cheering seemed to make the buildings shake. But the war, it seemed, was beginning to weigh on him. While engaged on his favourite pastime of tree-felling at Potsdam, he was seen to 'stop and look fixedly before him, lost in his thoughts'.[19] Like King George V and President Poincaré, he was setting an example in frugal living. With the Empress, he had been one of the first to adopt the German war bread and make other economies, including the abandonment of elaborate court functions.[20] Politically, his power was still absolute and, as one writer commented, 'the public always received his words like those of a prophet'. Hardly less venerated was that formidable military figure, Field-Marshal von Hindenburg, Commander-in-Chief in the East, now aged sixty-eight and in 1916 celebrating the fiftieth anniversary of his entry into the Prussian Army. Tall and dominating, his furrowed features marked by small penetrating eyes and crowned by hair stiffly en brosse, he gave the impression of brute animal strength. The nationalist press indulged in exaggerated eulogies of him. One paper declared: 'No German till the end of time will forget the iron hand, the steel brain, the glittering, effulgent spirit of our great Hindenburg.'[21] Another asserted that he rose head and shoulders over his contemporaries like a new Knight Roland, and stood beside Bismarck as the man who had engraved his name on the destiny of the nation. The sight of him, on one occasion attending divine service with his staff, 'praying aloud, asking God for help and power to enable him to carry out his work to a victorious conclusion', was said to be 'overwhelming'.[22]

Coupled with this extravagant leader-worship, another antidote to war-weariness was the continued propaganda glorifying war and stimulating hatred of the enemy. The nobility of the struggle was being constantly underlined by professors, men of letters, poets, even priests. 'Hate' lectures were an institution, typical of which was that of the Berlin University professor who, speaking to a crowded hall at Munich, said: 'We must hate the very essence of everything English. We must hate the very soul of England.'[23] Equally uncompromising messages resounded from church pulpits. At Whitsun the fire-eating Pastor Falk, of Berlin, attacked Anglo-Saxon civilisation and stressed Germany's urgent mission to destroy Britain. In Hamburg, Pastor Ebert preached that God had not placed the sword in Germany's hand for nothing, and nowhere could it be seen that He had commanded them to lay it down. 'God has given us all the weapons,' he declared, 'to defeat the enemy' (by which was chiefly meant Britain).[24] To stir up anti-British hate, a poster was issued showing an ogre-like 'John Bull', under which appeared the caption, 'This man is responsible for your hunger.' All this was in accordance with directions given to pastors of the State church to concentrate their attacks on Britain rather than France or Russia. But by mid-1916 the hate was spilling over to include the Americans, on account of the help they were giving the Allies. In July the Berlin Ambassador James Gerard reported that everyone in his Embassy was reaching 'breaking point' under the strain of living in a hostile country; and, soon after, that one of his attachés had broken down, unable to carry on in the inimical atmosphere. In September the wife of an American newspaperman was attacked in the street, and two secretaries from the Embassy assaulted because they were speaking English.[25]

The 'hate' and 'war-glorification' themes were being re-inforced by blatant truth-distorting propaganda. Isolated from news of the outside world, the Germans were at the mercy of a machine that reiterated that the Allies, and not they, had started the war and that Germany was being attacked by the whole of Europe. The women of the upper and middle classes were, it is said, particularly influenced by the official stories.

They believed the papers implicitly, and it was futile to argue with them about the war. They were convinced, for example, that German reverses suffered at Verdun and on the Somme were no more than tactical retirements. In June the Baroness von Bissing, wife of the German Governor of Belgium, was heard to say: 'It is a pleasant little joke of France and England about our invading Belgium first, but I *know* that England and France were there before us.'[26] But towards the end of the year working-class women, at least, were beginning to lose interest in the claims and urgings of official propaganda. Travelling to and from work in the trains and trams, they were discussing, not German victories or the heinousness of Britain, but the stark topics, 'peace' and 'food'. A hint of this mounting restiveness came in August with rioting in Hamburg, where crowds, largely of working women, demonstrated with cries of 'Down with the Kaiser' (perhaps the first sign of popular disillusion with Germany's great leader) and calls for an end to the war.[27]

In general, Germany's mood in this year (if such an imponderable thing as national morale could be measured), was one in which all illusions were finally shed and a spirit of dogged acceptance took over. With news of victory and reverse, hopes could rise and fall fairly mercurially. The battle of Jutland in June – treated by the Germans as an outstanding triumph – called forth wild rejoicings. People celebrated with champagne, the streets were gay with flags, church bells were rung and schools were closed to mark such a signal defeat of the hated British. But soon after, on tidings of the successful Russian offensive and the evacuation by the Austrians of Czernowitz, euphoria gave way to gloom. Worry over the food situation increased the dejection, especially when it was seen that the expectations of a good 1916 harvest would not be fulfilled. So, in the later months of the year, morale began to drift downwards, and in some rural areas workers became so apathetic that it was difficult to get them to harvest their own crops.[28] The depressing aspect of the Home Front had its effect, too, on troops returning on leave. The shabby, straitened condition in which their families were living did nothing to improve their own morale.

In these wartime days, the stubborn German spirit was well symbolised by the capital, Berlin. With none of the romantic, winding by-ways of London or Paris, Berlin was a modern, hard-looking city of straight broad streets and had a generally utilitarian appearance. Moreover, since the beginning of the war, Berlin had assumed a new importance and prestige in the nation's life. Hitherto it had been looked down on by industrialists of the Ruhr or Upper Silesia, or the great estate-owners of East Prussia as the seat of an officious bureaucracy, interfering in the lives of the people who actually did the country's work. Now, however, it had become the undisputed administrative hub of the national war-effort, setting the tempo for the rest of Germany. But amid the city's growing drabness, there were still centres of almost peacetime luxury and glitter. One such was the Esplanade Hotel, whose vast flower-decked reception hall, spacious thick-carpeted lounge and marble-pillared, chandelier-hung dining-room with its red silk curtains were a meeting-place for the capital's leading figures and notables passing through. The privileged women who lived there performed not very arduous war work. They spent the morning in nursing, running soup kitchens, visiting workshops. Afternoons were leisurely, and the high point of the day was after dinner, when ministers, military authorities, diplomats, court officials and serving officers from the front foregathered to exchange gossip with the ladies and discuss politics and the latest war news with inside knowledge.

But places like the Esplanade did not altogether escape the war's rigours. Its guests were subject to food rationing like everybody else. And as 1916 brought more shortages, they shared other restrictions. In May soap was rationed, the allowance being one pound a month for laundry, with 100 grammes of toilet soap. To save soap, women took to washing their clothes once a fortnight, and it was felt to be asking a great favour to borrow soap at a friend's house to wash one's hands. In Berlin the continuing scarcity of copper and other metals was evident when the copper lightning rods of churches were stripped in February, an attempt was made to remove the brass reading desk from the American Church and the fittings from the Japanese Embassy. The cotton and wool shortage had produced a greater simplicity of dress. Women were wearing robes of clinging pre-war style, mostly black, relieved by dark browns and greys. But some, less patriotic, were adopting extravagantly full skirts, a fashion which officialdom discouraged by ordering dressmakers who employed more than one worker to render their accounts to the police, so that their use of scarce materials could be controlled. But despite the stringencies, the big Berlin department store of Wertheim's was doing more business than in peacetime. And, in their moments of leisure, hard-working Berliners were seeking distraction as eagerly as the citizens of London or Paris. On a Sunday in May a record crowd attended the Berlin races, betting more money than ever before in the country's racing history.[29] Theatres were crowded, and even a semblance of the old night-life was continuing, most of the customers being officers on leave, who roared out hearty patriotic songs. Dancing, however, was banned, and at a party in June at the American Consul-General's, German guests opted to play cards while the Americans danced, and it was thought prudent to keep the blinds drawn. It was still possible, amid the prevailing frugality, to eat luxuriously. Supping at a restaurant, Edward Bullitt and his wife were given the German café-goer's favourite peacetime delicacy, peaches in a glass of champagne.[30]

If it was impossible for Germans, like their fellow-civilians in Britain and France, to appreciate the full reality of war, they had their sobering reminders of it in the sight of troops departing for the front. An observer in Berlin records how her tram was halted by a marching regiment bound for a railway station. Each soldier wore a bunch of flowers at his belt, a sign that they were destined for the trenches. The column was accompanied by young girls and old men and women, even small children who had joined the ranks to hold their father's hands. Watching the procession, four women in the tram – all in black – began to sob.[31] But still there remained the almost unbridgeable gulf between fighting soldiers and civilians. A Berlin resident tells of a youth on leave in February who had gone through terrible experiences at the front and who, to his parents' dismay, was unhappy and preoccupied, and no longer interested in the things that had once amused him.[32] There were countless similar examples. It was as if he, and tens of thousands like him, French and British as well as German, bore a knowledge that could never be communicated to those at home, while at the same time they found themselves isolated from a civilian world that saw the war in an irreconcilably different light from that in which the soldiers saw it. By mid-1916, after two years of war, the phenomenon had become established in all the belligerent countries.

In October a Frenchwoman repatriated from Germany reported her impression that Germany lacked nothing, but that everything was meticulously regulated.[33] Total regulation there certainly was, but, despite that, many commodities were now simply not available. By the autumn of 1916 the country was being squeezed and strained for every scrap of usable material. Wastage had virtually disappeared because there was nothing left to waste. Garbage-saving had been in force since 1914. Households had been scoured for copper and brass, and recently an appeal had been launched for people to bring out their gold. Church bells were being smelted, old iron was fetching fancy prices. Used paper was at a premium. Horse-droppings were being collected as fertiliser, while the streets themselves were left unswept and dirty. To save fuel, summer-time had been introduced, public transport drastically reduced and early closing decreed for shops, cafés and restaurants. And to meet the grave coal shortage, villagers had been allowed to lop the dead wood in the State forests. The summer had seen a huge berry-gathering drive, followed by a massive harvesting of nuts and mushrooms. The countryside itself presented a dismal picture. Buildings lacked whitewash; their shutters were dilapidated and walls streaked with damp. Gardens were neglected and such stock as remained looked uncared-for. Clothing was becoming an increasingly serious problem. With textiles desperately scarce and the best materials going to the troops, civilians were put to all kinds of shifts to garb themselves. Every old garment was pressed into use or sold to the ragman for re-working, and recourse was had to 'shoddy' (the waste arising from the manufacture of wool). It was found that, with a little added fibre, one old suit could be converted into two. Profiteers reaped rich rewards by selling 'shoddy' as new and asking steep prices for a suit that might disintegrate in the first rain-shower. If the customer complained, he would be told to blame the war.[34]

This picture of Germany as Christmas 1916 approached is reinforced by an observer's impressions.[35] There was, he notes, an almost total absence of young men from the towns and countryside. Through the streets ran ancient horse-drawn cabs and taxis – four-fifths of the latter electrified and, owing to the rubber shortage, almost none with solid composite rubber tyres. Laughter was rare, there was no applause in theatres, night-life had virtually disappeared and dancing was unheard of. Beer-cellars were doing better business than supper restaurants, but the beer was weak and watery. No spirits could be sold after 9 p.m. Food and drink were largely ersatz. The great staple of German diet was tuna fish, disguised as roast beef, steak, veal chops and so on. There were substitutes for coffee, sugar, beer, milk, butter, eggs and condiments. But on so-called meatless days meat could be obtained from black-market restaurants. Evening clothes were hardly ever seen, and their wearer would be viewed with suspicion. Despite the enormous casualties, little mourning was worn, this being in deference to a wish expressed by the Kaiser early in the war. But fashion-conscious women were still obtaining Paris-styled clothes, called 'Viennese' by the couturières, through neutral Berne. There were collecting stations everywhere, for anything from old bottles to paper, bits of rubber, string and rags. And a feature reminiscent of Britain at the end of this year was the nation-wide cultivation of allotments. In an effort to combat the food shortage, Germans were utilising every spare plot of ground, mostly to grow potatoes.

The food difficulties were graphically reflected in the crowded poorer quarters of Berlin's East End. The butchers' shops were almost bare of meat, and long queues – some of them for horse-flesh – were common. The number of empty shops was growing, many small provision-sellers being put out of business by the centralised distribution of food. Bakers did little business except at morning and evening. The dwindling supply of cattle and pigs had allowed the conversion of some slaughter-houses into People's Kitchens, to which thousands of Berliners came for the stew that could be bought at 5d. a quart for taking away. In another district the huge Alexander Market was regularly serving 30,000 people. The pervading dreariness of the East End was in contrast to the city's West End and central area where, as one writer put it, 'the café lights were bright and music made the restricted menu cards easier to bear'.[36] Along with the lights, music helped to bolster war-wearied spirits. The strains of military bands were commonly heard, sometimes accompanying columns of lightly wounded soldiers to and from hospital.

In Germany, as in Britain and France, old moral standards were fast collapsing under the stress of war. Illegitimate births had risen spectacularly, accounting for more than 10% of the population increase. Accepting the situation, all the German State governments, except the more strait-laced Prussia, abolished the 'illegitimate' birth certificate and accorded the soldier's unmarried 'wife' or 'widow' the right to call herself Frau (Mistress) instead of the customary Fräulein (Miss). Yet, while denying these women the consolation of social recognition, Prussia at least granted them financial support. The question whether the children of unmarried women whose 'paramours' were not soldiers should receive the benefit of legitimisation caused considerable controversy. Clergy and other puritan or conservative elements strongly opposed this, on the grounds that free love would thus be encouraged. But prejudice was overcome and, under the law, all children of unwed mothers were deemed legitimate, all mothers being eligible to receive the appropriate financial help. The problem highlighted the vast wastage which the war was imposing on the manpower of Germany. By the end of 1916 the total losses of the Central Powers in men killed or incapacitated were some five million. With women of marriageable age in Germany and Austria numbering about twenty million, there were left only four marriageable men to every five women.[37]

It was Germany's parlous manpower situation that led, in December, to a new and unprecedentedly drastic step to mobilise the nation's labour force: the passing of the Auxiliary Service Law. Though German manpower was already stretched tight, it was now clear that if the nation was to go on fighting the screw must be turned yet further. More men must be found for the army, to make good the grievous battle-losses; and these, apart from the new eighteen-year-old intakes, could come only from the war-factories and mines – which themselves needed to maintain or even augment their work force in order to meet the ever-mounting demands for war material. The campaigns of 1915 and the first half of 1916 had increased the pressure on every source of labour, including foreign workers, women and even children. The recent battle of the Somme, with its crying need for accelerated munitions output, had taken matters to the point of crisis. The German war-effort was in danger of foundering through lack of hands to produce the raw materials and guns and shells to match the now massive Allied output. Field-Marshal Hindenburg, appointed Chief of the Great General Staff in August in succession to General Falkenhayn, assessed the position with his colleague General Ludendorff, Quartermaster General, and demanded what amounted to total civil conscription. In November a Supreme War Office (Kriegsamt) was created, headed by General Groener, to administer such a measure. Groener declared in a

speech that Germans must 'subordinate their wills unquestion-
ingly to the needs of the Fatherland'.[38]

The Auxiliary Service Law, promulgated on the 5th December, was largely the work of the Secretary of State and Vice-
Chancellor, Dr Helfferich, but in order to make it more
palatable for the long-suffering Germans to swallow, it bore
the name of their revered Field-Marshal, being known as the
'Hindenburg programme'. It certainly needed some such
promoting. As described by one writer, the measure was 'the
most comprehensive scheme for mobilising a nation at war in
military annals'.[39] It provided for the compulsory employment
of every male German (women and children were not mentioned) between seventeen and sixty years, not already in the
fighting forces. Such employment could include the government service, war industries, agriculture, forestry and the like.
It was no less than a mass levy which, said a Cologne paper
rather ominously, was ushering in 'the last phase of the war'.[40]

Thus, after some two-and-a-half years of war, did Germany –
to an extent not approached by Britain or France – have to
subordinate everything to the one purpose of war-making.[41]
No man (with a few specified exceptions as to categories of
employment) or plant or machine or piece of equipment that
could contribute to the war-effort was exempt from conscription. From the manpower angle, it was a matter of placing the
available pool of men in the jobs in which they could effectively
serve rather than finding more (for there were virtually none).
It meant wholesale switching of employment and ruthless
streamlining and rationalisation, such as the closing-down of
long-established firms and the amalgamation of factories in the
same kind of business. Though women were not officially
included in the scheme they could in fact be recruited through
Directresses of National Service appointed at each Army
Headquarters throughout the country. The immediate result
of this great surge of effort was encouraging. In May 1917
General Groener was to report a substantial rise in German
steel and iron production and a threefold increase in munitions
output. The raised volume of production was to continue for

the rest of the war – but at a ruinous cost to the national economy. In her desperate bid to meet the voracious demands of war, Germany was to use up her precious raw material resources. Meanwhile for her much-restricted, much-regulated people, this was one more burden to bear.

The Hindenburg programme was only one indication of how seriously the Government viewed Germany's overall situation. Compared with 1915, 1916 had been a militarily disappointing year. Verdun had remained untaken, the British were hammering at the Somme, and in the East the Russians under General Brusilov had broken the Austrian front and pushed into the heart of Galicia. The only victory the Germans could claim was a naval one, in the battle of Jutland at the end of May. Politically, Rumania's entry into the war against Austria-Hungary at the end of August had been a disconcerting shock. It was to stiffen the national leadership that Hindenburg and Ludendorff had been recalled from the East in August to assume the supreme military role under the Kaiser himself. The most urgent problem was to determine a future strategy that would relieve the mounting economic pressure that was beginning to strangle Germany. One answer seemed to lie in the launching of a campaign of unrestricted submarine warfare against Britain, thus subjecting her to the same threat of starvation as was facing Germany herself. The military and naval authorities were in favour of this, as was a growing section of the public. The Chancellor, Bethmann-Hollweg, at first reluctant, finally agreed after persuasion from the Reichstag. But first it was decided, at his suggestion, to try another recourse: a peace approach to the Allies. The fall of Rumania's capital, Bucharest, on the 6th December, gave Germany a pretext that enabled her to act from a seeming position of strength, and the Peace Offer was issued six days later.

So, in a call for peace, ended this depressing year for Germany. If a dominant theme could be described which expressed the dearest wish of German civilians in the dark days of this December, it was that which had already been heard among the working women in the streets – 'peace and food'. Christmas was a time of little rejoicing. 'Berlin has recently become more melancholy,' wrote James Gerard, the American Ambassador. The American colony gave a party, with a Christmas tree, for poor Berlin children. 'One little kid got up and prayed for peace,' noted Gerard, 'and everyone wept.'[42]

Part Four

1917: THE WIDENING CRACKS

Chapter 10

THE GENERAL SCENE

Exhaustion grows

FOR 1917 Germany decided on a defensive policy on the Western Front while proceeding if possible to eliminate Russia in the East. And to relieve her own growing strangulation by the British blockade, she planned as her main offensive weapon against Britain a campaign of unrestricted U-boat warfare – a campaign that brought Britain close to starvation. Meanwhile the Western Front was once more the scene of great battles, initiated by the Allies. First, in April, the French launched a heavy offensive on the Aisne, whose failure caused the French Army to mutiny. And then, from August to November, the British maintained a prolonged assault known as the Third Battle of Ypres, which caused vast losses and brought virtually no results. Meanwhile Russia, exhausted by the war and in the throes of revolution, had ceased to count as a military force.

1917 was, in the words of President Poincaré, *l'année trouble* – the year of confusion. It was the year when, after twenty-nine months of colossal and unremitting effort, war-weariness and exhaustion began to take serious toll of the belligerents. All their previous exertions had come to nothing, and against the recent background of vast struggle and carnage at Verdun and on the Somme, in the West they now faced another year of war on battle-lines that were almost unchanged. And on both sides the military leaders were still without new plans for breaking the trench-bound deadlock that had persisted since the end of 1914. On the Home Fronts, as in the fighting zones, the war had now become part of life. Civilians who at the close of 1915 had dared hope for an end to it during 1916 now saw it dragging into yet another year with no sign of decision. In all three countries the earlier enthusiasm and optimism had subsided into a grim resignation and a tired determination to see it through. But now civilian endurance was to be tested still further by growing shortage and privation, which in Germany and Britain would threaten the hard-pressed Home Front with starvation. And even if the feeding difficulties were somehow surmounted, the further straining of other already diminishing resources – notably manpower – would present all three belligerents with increasingly critical problems. Most ominous, on both sides would now appear signs of defeatism or revolt.

Hitherto the main thought of both sides had been outright victory – nothing short of conquest by force of arms. But with the rosy dreams of victory fading and exhaustion growing, now at the start of the year peace talks were in the air. The first peace-approach, from the Central Powers, had been made in December 1916. This declared that, though they were prepared to fight on to the end, they wished to stop the bloodshed and believed that their proposals (which in fact were entirely unacceptable to the Allies) would provide a basis for a lasting peace. A week later the United States President, who himself had been considering the possibility of peace, had circularised the belligerents with his own Note, inviting them to state their peace terms. Replying to the Central Powers late in December, the Allies had curtly rejected their proposals, and in January, in answer to the President, they set forth their war aims, which included the restoration of Belgium, reparation for territorial invasions and seizures, liberation of German-dominated countries and expulsion of Turkey from Europe. It was obvious that these would not even provide grounds for discussion, and late that month the President addressed the Senate in a speech which appealed for 'peace without victory', a proposal which met with no welcome in Britain. Further peace-moves, by the Emperor Charles of Austria in May and by the Pope in August, were to be equally unproductive. In this island, at least, the general mood was still for 'war to the end', whatever the weariness and the sacrifice.

But in this third full year of war two events were to occur that would radically change the prevailing picture: the Russian Revolutions in March and October and the entry of the United States into the war in April. The first would give comfort to the Germans by its elimination of their eastern enemy and the consequent freeing of powerful German forces for use in the West, and the second would immensely hearten the Allies with the promise of massive aid, in men, materials and ships, towards continuing the struggle. Militarily the two events tended to cancel each other out, though the more immediate advantage was with the Germans owing to the inability of the Americans to arrive in strength until 1918. But if the potential military effect of the Russian Revolution caused the Allies some concern, in France it was to have a disturbing impact on the Home Front, by encouraging and fomenting the pacifist-defeatist agitation that was already stirring beneath the civilian surface in the spring of 1917.

Chapter 11

BRITAIN

The spectre of starvation

B Y 1917 no British citizen could fail to be aware how tightly he was hedged about by rules and regulations. Thanks to DORA, frequently enlarged, supplemented and amended, a whole range of actions, so innocent in peacetime, were now beyond the legal pale. Apart from prohibitions against 'careless talk' and so on, there were scores of 'don'ts' which themselves seemed silly but which added up to a very necessary code of safeguards for the protection and promotion of the war-effort. A civilian must not, for instance, send abroad any letter written in invisible ink; trespass on railways or loiter near railway arches, bridges or tunnels; buy binoculars without official authorisation; fly any kite that could be used for signalling; buy whisky or other spirits on Saturday or Sunday, or any other day except between noon and 12.30 p.m., pay for any intoxicating liquor for another person, except as host of that person, at lunch, dinner or supper; give bread to any dog, poultry, horse or any other animal.[1] More obviously sensible than most was the rule restricting the entry of civilians into special military areas around the coasts. In a wider field the absolute authority of DORA had been demonstrated two years before, when under it the Government had been empowered to mobilise any or all Britain's general industrial resources – which meant in effect that the Government could direct manufacturers to produce what it ordered.

Under Lloyd George's new Coalition Government, State control was now taken still further. The mounting scale and complexity of war-administration had shown the need for new Government departments, with responsibilities in specific areas. In 1915 Lloyd George himself had shown the way in this field by heading the newly-formed Ministry of Munitions, thus taking over – with immense benefit to war-production – what had been part of the task of the over-burdened Lord Kitchener. But 'control' in itself was not the only necessity. Under Asquith's premiership it had often hampered rather than assisted the industries with which it was concerned. Increasingly a call was heard for 'business heads' to be brought into Whitehall. Lloyd George strongly favoured this idea, and one of his first moves was to introduce business men into the Government, appointing them to new Ministries or departments – such as Shipping Control (Sir Joseph Maclay), Board of Trade (Sir Albert Stanley), Local Government Board (Lord Rhondda), Food Control (Lord Devonport), and National Service (Neville Chamberlain). This inevitably meant more bureaucrats; and to accommodate the new army of clerks a dozen large London hotels and club-houses were requisitioned: the National Liberal Club and Constitutional Club, the Victoria Hotel, St Ermin's Hotel, Hotel Cecil and others, and several new office blocks.

Among the new Ministries, that of National Service started work in March under Neville Chamberlain as Director-General, to administer the National Service Scheme. The aim of the scheme was to introduce a system of National Industrial Service, by which a new industrial army of volunteers was to be created to fill the vacancies caused by conscription of the workers for military service. Though launched with great publicity, the scheme did not prove a success. At least 500,000 volunteers had been hoped for, but by mid-April only 163,000 had registered. And by August a mere 20,000 were placed in full-time jobs. Not only was the scheme abortive but, as the second such registration held during the war, it was criticised as a waste in view of the vast amount of clerical work involved. Meanwhile the army was making its own inexorable demands. In March a comb-out among younger miners began. In April General Sir William Robertson, Chief of Staff, made a speech stressing the needs of the army – 500,000 more men by July – and appealed to 'every man and woman in the country to do a full day's work of an essential nature'.[2] And as a sinister sidelight, that month all doctors of military age were called up to man new hospitals abroad, a move made necessary by attacks on hospital ships.

General Robertson's appeal coincided with a time of marked labour unrest. Through the winter there had been constant disputes in the engineering and munitions factories, largely on the issue of dilution by unskilled men and by women. These culminated in April and May in widespread unofficial strikes at Rochdale, Barrow and elsewhere involving nearly 200,000 men and causing the loss of 1,500,000 working days. In Lloyd George's view, though agitators were partly responsible, they would have been powerless unless there had been genuine discontent upon which they could play. 'The workers were sound at heart,' he wrote. '. . . But there was a real danger that the hardships, anomalies and annoyances of the times might be worked up by trouble-makers to wear down their sense of patriotic duty.' Indeed, those who readily condemned the 'cussedness' of the workers at these times tended to overlook their generally fine war record. They had surrendered many hard-won privileges including the right to strike, and in the cause of war-production were enduring difficult conditions and much discomfort and disruption of their normal lives (though their lot was of course infinitely preferable to that of the fighting men). In an effort to alleviate the unrest, in June Lloyd George set up eight area commissions to investigate and report on the causes of discontent. Their reports adduced a number of factors: high food prices in relation to wages (behind this grievance lay the sinister shadow of the 'profiteer'), and the unequal distribution of food; the restriction on the mobility of labour; the calling-up of young workers who had been understood to be immune under the Military Service Acts; lack of adequate housing in some districts; liquor restrictions; industrial fatigue due to Sunday and overtime work; want of confidence in the fulfilment of Government pledges; lack of consideration for women workers by some employers; delays in granting pensions to soldiers; inadequacy of the compensation payable under the Workmen's Compensation Act. The commissioners made various recommendations to improve matters. 'Their findings', wrote Lloyd George, 'proved invaluable to the Government in its task of dealing with the grievances of the workers, and allaying discontent.'[3]

Official concern at the labour situation was expressed in March by Sir William Weir, Director of Air Supply, and colleagues to the writer Arnold Bennett. They spoke of it as 'acutely bad', and claimed that the unofficial strikes were being fomented by alien influences working through the shop stewards. Weir and his colleagues, however, agreed that the margin of labour was adequate. They felt that even after the Government had taken the men they needed for the army, enough workers would be left in the essential occupations to carry out the necessary work – 'provided they would produce their maximum output, which (and this was in depressing contrast to Lloyd George's view) they don't and won't'.[4] At the same time they all spoke enthusiastically of the output of France's workers. Nevertheless, industrial unrest was sharply increasing in France – as shown by the record of 689 strikes in 1917 involving 293,000 workers, compared with the 98 strikes in 1916 affecting 9,000 workers. This year's 688 'trade disputes' in Britain, involving 860,000 workers, showed a general rise over earlier war years (though they were still fewer than in the immediately pre-war period).[5] But in view of the current strains and pressures, the overall picture for 1917 might well have been worse. Indeed, in summing up the situation for the year, an eminent historian rather surprisingly writes: 'All in all, British labour was probably less disturbed than in any previous year of its history.'[6]

The writer who noted that 'by 1917 Britain was a country of women, old men, boys and children, with a sprinkling of men in khaki', was not greatly exaggerating.[7] In any event this was the year when the women's war-effort approached, if not actually reached, its maximum. With more and more men being conscripted for the forces, including the large numbers being combed out from the war-factories, the demand for women in every sphere of work continued to grow. But though thousands of them were already working in munitions, at the start of the year their presence in the 'shops' was still being opposed by prejudiced employers. To counter this, the Government threatened to refuse contracts to firms which rejected women. Nottingham was said to be a stronghold of resistance; and elsewhere, when women were taken on for certain forms of dock work, the dockers talked of striking. But in April wages for munition workers were still low, being only £1 for a forty-eight-hour week. To meet the increased cost of living, they were now raised to 24s.[8] Marked improvements were being made for the welfare of these workers. For the mothers there were crèches, pleasant with tiled walls and blue cots, where the babies were cared for by volunteer nurses and women doctors and could spend the day on wide open-air verandas. Factory canteens were provided to cater for workers unable by reason of their working hours to prepare home meals. But it was found that even when off-duty the workers tended to buy ready-made meals rather than cook their own. Ham-and-beef and fish-and-chip shops now did a roaring trade.

The danger in which these munition-workers laboured was brought home to the country in January, when a disastrous explosion occurred at Silvertown, East London, causing over four hundred and fifty casualties, including sixty-nine deaths. In a detonation that was heard over a large part of the capital, four large factories and several smaller ones were destroyed, and streets of houses demolished.

But besides the 'munitionettes', the other factory workers, the clerks, nurses, land girls, policewomen, transport workers and the rest, there was now another great army of women war-volunteers to be seen in Britain's towns and countryside: the women of the uniformed services. Formed largely to take over the men's non-combatant duties in the armed forces, these services were the WRNS (Women's Royal Naval Service or 'Wrens'), the WAAC (Women's Auxiliary Army Corps) and the WRAF (Women's Royal Air Force). The largest body was the

WAAC, running into some thousands, with its uniform of khaki coat-frock, soft felt hat, gaiters and brown shoes. The WRNS girls were in naval blue and the WRAF in a lighter 'air-force' blue. Along with the uniformed VAD and Land Army women, they brought refreshing colour to the drab British scene and demonstrated that there was now no sphere of war service in which women were not 'doing their bit'. That they were performing indispensable work could be seen from the jobs in which the WRNS, for instance, were serving – as wireless telegraphists, coders and decoders, naval writers, electricians, and gas-drill instructors. By their wholesale participation in the war, women could now be said to have thrown off the chains of inferiority and inequality which had bound them for so long. An acknowledgement of this was made in the House of Commons at the end of March, when by an overwhelming vote approval was given for woman's suffrage (to be included in a scheme of electoral reform which was to be introduced at the end of the war). Mr Asquith made a fine speech proposing the motion, in which he recanted the firm opposition he had made to votes for women before the war. Next day, in support of their right to suffrage, a great gathering of women of all professions and callings, many of them in uniform, paraded in Whitehall. A historic victory, fought for so hard in earlier years, had been won. But for the war, which had given women the chance to prove their worth, it might have been delayed much longer.

Amid its booming war-activity, ever-tightening regimentation, increasing shabbiness and the resigned determination of its people, Britain in 1917 seemed decades away from the peacetime nation of 1914. Almost month by month its face was being transformed. It was undergoing great population shifts as country people flocked to the munition centres and townsfolk went to agricultural work. There was a constant migration to London. With full employment, match-sellers and bootlace-vendors had disappeared. There were no outcasts sleeping on the Embankment. The capital was full of mushroom buildings in the parks and on the roofs of Government offices. Many homes of servicemen were shut, their furniture stored in disused chapels and warehouses while the wives went to live with parents. Town mansions and country houses were now hospitals and convalescent homes. Railway travelling, subject to new restrictions, was increasingly comfortless: trains were fewer, fares had risen by 50% and passengers were limited to 100 pounds of luggage. In March, newspaper posters were banned; which was just as well in view of one poster recalled by a contemporary, which announced with equal emphasis: 'Battle Raging at Ypres. Gatwick Racing – Late Wire.'[9] But racing itself was soon to suffer. In May it was suspended by the Jockey Club at the instance of the War Cabinet. And this year the University boat-race, Henley and Cowes Regattas, county cricket and the football league final all disappeared from the sporting calendar. The autumn saw London taxi fares raised from 8d. to 1s. 2d. for the first mile. On a more warlike note, it was announced that air-raid shelter accommodation for about a million people was now available in London. And, in November, in anticipation of coming shortage, coal rationing was announced.

In London, Soho was prospering not only with its night clubs but as a lunching-centre where girl clerks from nearby offices met their soldier-friends for a reasonably cheap meal at the small foreign restaurants. West End ready-made dress shops flourished, supplying girl wage-earners with dance frocks to meet the current craze. Men's tailors, on the other hand, fell into difficulties. Those accustomed to give long credit found themselves with numerous bad debts owing to so many of their officer customers being killed. In the search for pleasure dictated by life's uncertainty – and aided by the earnings of girls who had not gone out to work before – conventions were openly flouted, and elders were shocked by the dress and behaviour of forward young women. In January a writer in the *Nineteenth Century* denounced the 'flappers [this was the new word] with high heels, skirts up to their knees and blouses open to the diaphragm, painted, powdered, self-conscious, ogling'. Careless of sexual taboos, young girls gripped by 'khaki fever' haunted the army camps. To many chance liaisons – even brief innocent encounters – there was a pathetic side, exposing a sad fatalism among the young. A writer quotes this letter of a young 'Society' girl: 'Life was very gay. It was only when someone you knew well or with whom you were in love was killed that you minded dreadfully. Men used to come to dine and dance one night, and go out next morning and be killed. And someone used to say, "Did you see poor Bobbie was killed?" It went on all the time, you see.'[10]

As a refuge from current cares, the theatre continued to thrive, catching the popular mood with light plays and revues – whose scantily-clad girls and generally free-and-easy tone provoked many protests. The fortune-telling craze persisted despite efforts to suppress it. People took increasingly to gambling, the favourite card games being bridge and poker. The general restlessness and the disappearance of so much of normal social life led to a mania for meetings. It was as if people could not bear to sit at home, perhaps alone, but had to seek company. Hence they attended gatherings for charity schemes, war savings, recruiting. A notable feature of the times was the transformation wrought in the traditional social hierarchies. The young Robert Graves, now an instructor to a cadet battalion at Oxford, found himself solemnly saluted whenever they met a don at St John's College, wearing the grey uniform of the General Reserve. And holding a commission as a fellow-instructor with Graves was a college scout.[11] A sad but inevitable result of the lengthening war was the general acceptance of sights that previously would have shocked and horrified. A writer recalls the spectacle, at Brighton, of hundreds of wounded men on crutches, with one leg or no legs, whom passers-by hardly remarked.

In the prevailing climate of violence, uncertainty and social flux, it was not surprising that juvenile delinquency was rising. The same thing was happening in Germany. There were sundry reasons why youths should be tempted to lawlessness. With fathers away soldiering and mothers possibly on war work, family life and parental authority were lacking. Schooling

was affected by shortage of teachers. Employment was easy
and wages high. For leisure hours there was the exciting
distraction of the cinema. In France and elsewhere, men were
daily killing each other in thousands. The whole environment
invited indiscipline and delinquency. Educationists and youth
leaders were concerned at the growing problem. The answer
seemed to lie in the various boys' organisations – the Boys'
Brigade, Church Lads' Brigade, Boys' Naval Brigade, Boys'
Life Brigade, Boy Scouts and Sea Scouts – in whose activities
the lads' interests and energies could be constructively engaged. An appeal by the Home Secretary for the co-operation
of these bodies led to their being linked more closely with the
national war service, in the case of the Boys' Brigade, which
already in 1914 had provided messengers between the War
Office, Government departments and so on. The timely intervention of the other organisations now succeeded in checking
the rise of delinquency.[12]

Equal disquiet was being caused by the rising tide of 'immorality', by which was meant sexual laxity. This too was
specifically a war phenomenon, stemming – among Britons,
Frenchmen and Germans alike – from the large number of
broken homes, the crowding of men in camps and barracks,
the new freedom of women, the loosening of social restraints,
constant mobility, and the strains and tensions of wartime life.
If there had never been such 'immorality' before, it was
because in no previous war had existence seemed so cheap and
old taboos so meaningless: and never before had there been
such inducements to live for the moment and take what
pleasure one could while one could. For thousands of girls,
and their men who might not live to see the end of the war, a
brief fleeting sexual liaison was better than none at all. Hence
the mounting illegitimacy rate, which by 1918 would have
increased by 30% as compared with before the war. In June,
at a conference at the Caxton Hall, London, on the moral
conditions in the streets of the capital, the Chief Commissioner
of Police stated that in the last three years some 19,000 women
had been arrested on soliciting and similar charges.[13] The

police and the various welfare societies were all disturbed at
the state of things in London's parks and open spaces. The
divorce-rate (along with the marriage-rate) was rising steeply.
This year's Trinity Sittings showed the highest number of cases on
record: 394, of which 330 were undefended.[14] To serious-minded
critics, the whole fabric of society seemed to be threatened.

But in 1917 there was, at least, one healthy outlet for
Britons' energies. That spring and summer, spurred by the
gravity of the food situation, the allotment campaign got into
its full stride. In May the number of allotments and vegetable
plots under cultivation was said to be 500,000. Work on the
allotment was now the great patriotic activity: the British had
become a nation of gardeners. City men hurried home to
change, and emerged from suburban houses in old clothes and
stout boots looking like agricultural labourers, to tend their
bit of soil. Gardening tools became scarce. Private gardens
were turned to use, and with flowerbeds given over to potatoes,
parsnips and beans, it was said that by summer there was
hardly a garden in the country not contributing to the food
supply. Members of tennis clubs dug up their courts and went
to work with fork and hoe. Schools joined the campaign.
Eminent examples were set by the Royal Family and by
Lloyd George, who grew a fine crop of King Edward potatoes
in his garden at Walton Heath. On fine evenings and Saturday
afternoons in the London suburbs, food-growers would be out
in their thousands: Dulwich, for instance, had more than
3,000 plots. To speed the work, the Archbishop of Canterbury
issued a pastoral letter sanctioning Sunday labour; and church
services were held on the allotments, the men and women
leaving their digging to assemble round a white-surpliced
clergyman. 'Tea on the allotment' became a regular Sunday
event. When thieves began making depredations, allotment
patrols were organised and growers took turns to guard their
own and neighbours' plots. Severe penalties were imposed for
thefts – £100 fine or six months' gaol. 'Britain had only two
passions,' wrote a contemporary, 'to thrash the Germans and
cultivate its soil.'[15]

But Britain could still relax. Whit Monday on Hampstead
Heath presented a sight of thousands of young women enjoying
a brief hard-earned leisure. Most, as a diarist noted, were
probably munitions workers. They had never, in his experience,
appeared so well-dressed before. They had 'laid aside their furs
and velveteens and high-laced boots for the summer finery of
coloured sports-coats, white and pink dresses and low shoes'.[16]
Only a few wore the huge blue and pink feathers, up to now a
favourite adornment for hats. The general wear was now a
cloth toque. The spectacle led the writer to ponder on the
changes brought about by the war. The holidaying crowds
showed no sign of the squalid poverty so common before.
More had been done, he reflected, for the social betterment of
the working classes by three years of war than for many
generations. Alongside the vast destruction and misery caused
by the war, there was a greater well-being among society's
poorer members than had ever been known. The needs of war
had in fact brought prosperity to every class, even the professional men like barristers and accountants, who had been
absorbed into important war-work. In these reflections the
diarist was pointing to one of the war's great ironies. But he
overlooked one social group, namely the *rentier* class living on
fixed incomes who were hard-hit by the steadily mounting cost
of living.

A prime factor in raising living costs had always been food.
If increasingly dear, at least it had remained reasonably
plentiful. But in 1917 Britain's food began to be in acutest
danger. German submarines were taking a toll of shipping
that threatened to become crucial. In the last four months of
1916, 632,000 tons had been sunk. In November Mr Runciman,
President of the Board of Trade, had reported to the War
Committee that 'a complete breakdown in shipping would
come before June 1917'.[17] Then on 1st February, the Germans
produced a new menace. Armed with a new long-distance
cruising submarine or U-boat, they declared unrestricted
warfare against all merchant ships sailing to and from Allied
ports. A desperate move dictated by Germany's growing

strangulation as a result of the Allied blockade, it underlined for Britain the urgency of rigorous food economy measures. Already under Lord Devonport, appointed Food Controller in December 1916, new restrictions had appeared. Devonport set up in London's stately Grosvenor House where, as one account goes, 'the suggestive flesh of the famous Rubens paintings were covered up to protect the morals of the girls recruited as typists'. Stopping short of compulsion, he launched an extensive Economy Campaign and introduced a voluntary rationing scheme. He cancelled the order limiting the number of hotel and restaurant courses for lunch or dinner (because people had allegedly abused it by eating too much bread and meat) and instead asked consumers to limit themselves to 4 lb of bread a week, $2\frac{1}{2}$ lb of meat and $\frac{1}{4}$ lb of sugar. He also banned tea-shops from serving teas at more than 6d. and imposed two potato-less days a week and one meatless day in hotels and restaurants.

With these and other measures, 1917 started gloomily. The potato shortage (following the bad harvest of 1916) was sufficiently marked for a university professor to recommend in February the eating of the skins and all: in peeling, he claimed, one-fifth of the potato's food value was lost. To prevent destruction of poultry and vegetables the Food Controller's department even advised the shooting of foxes – a practice already adopted by Masters of Foxhounds.[18] Sugar scarcity now necessitated restrictions to brewers, confectioners and grocers. In January beer output was cut to half that of pre-war, and sweet and chocolate production reduced. On 'sugar days' London grocers' shops attracted long queues of women. Home jam-making became almost impossible, a situation that later caused the waste of quantities of fruit normally used for jam. Soon sugarless housewives were to take to substitutes like syrup made from sugar beet, glucose and concoctions known as 'Consip' and 'Sypgar'.[19] In February sugar disappeared from the tables of Lyons' cafés: instead, a bowl of it was brought round by the waitress. Most serious was the wheat shortage. In January orders were made for the further dilution of wheat-flour with rice, maize, barley or oatmeal. This provided the public with more breadstuffs, but at the cost of eggs, bacon, pork and other meat (the poultry and animal food being diverted to bread). The gravity of the sugar and wheat situation was such that in April Britain's sugar stocks were diminished to less than ten days' supply, and the Ministry of Food announced that, without economy in bread consumption (it was calculated that nearly 10,000 tons were wasted weekly in Britain), there was danger of bread supplies not lasting until the harvest.[20]

Still opposed to compulsory rationing (one reason being that it would swell the bureaucratic army), in the matter of economy Lord Devonport preferred to rely on the public's sense of honour and discipline. His envoy Kennedy Jones, Director-General of the Food Economy Department at the Ministry of Food, led a countrywide campaign calling for reduced bread consumption. In April bold-lettered posters appeared in London and elsewhere, enjoining: 'Eat Less Bread and Victory is Secure.' Travelling lady lecturers demonstrated the virtues of bread surrogates: ground-rice scones, maize-flour puddings, oatcakes for breakfast. Mid-April brought an official announcement that, in view of the need for national economy, and particularly in breadstuffs, the King, Queen and Royal Household had adopted the (voluntary) scale of national rations since early February. This proved a valuable incentive, and citizens inspired to follow the royal example proudly sported a badge of purple ribbon. It was now that the meatless and potato-less days were decreed for public eating-places. But the order did not prevent the well-to-do from making an excellent meal. For its meatless day one hotel provided a six-course lunch of varied hors-d'œuvres, salmon, eggs in casserole, vegetables, entrée and sweet. As a gesture to economy, potatoes ceased to be sold at the Army and Navy and Civil Service Stores, or served in the Houses of Parliament. For private houses the voluntary principle continued. Lloyd George himself observed the injunctions. Dining with him at Downing Street in April, his friend Lord Riddell, the newspaper magnate, observed: 'So far as the food, service, and appointments are concerned, it looked as if a small suburban household were picnicking in Downing Street – the same simple food, the same little domestic servant, the same mixture of tea and dinner.'[21] The writer Arnold Bennett also conformed. 'Yesterday, for the first time,' he noted in early May, 'we had no bread on the table at dinner. People who want it must ask for it from the sideboard. Wells gave me this tip. The value of these dodges is chiefly disciplinary. If the whole of the well-to-do classes practised them, the wheat problem would be trifling.'[22]

The bread-economy propaganda evidently worked, for by the end of May consumption was reported to be 10% below that of February. But the general food prospects had looked so grave that in March arrangements were made to set up communal kitchens. Soon after, the first National Kitchen was opened in Westminster Bridge Road by the Queen, who herself served a number of customers. One of the day's dishes was cornflour and rhubarb jelly. Fortunately, the subsequent decrease in the U-boat sinkings made the continuation of these kitchens unnecessary. Meanwhile the food crisis was being vigorously tackled by the Board of Agriculture. In January a special Food Production department was set up, with Sir Edward Lee in charge and telegraphic address 'Growmore', to increase Britain's food-growing to its maximum capacity, with the aim of making her self-supporting and independent of overseas supplies. This meant putting three million extra acres under cultivation. County Executive Committees were appointed, with extensive powers. To overcome the manpower shortage Home Defence men and even serving soldiers were being used, together with prisoners-of-war and, of course, women Land Army volunteers. Another source of help was holiday-makers. Scarce machinery was augmented by commandeering and by a rush order for five hundred tractors from the United States.[23] Supplementing this great effort were the allotment workers. If their 'back-garden' plots were infinitesimal compared with the broad farmland acres, their cultivation was invaluable because intensive.

One of the keenest allotmenteers was said to be the King himself. An accepted rule of the Royal Household was that he and the Queen and royal guests should play their part on the 'food front'. After lunch they would divide into two groups, one to help serve meals to munition workers, the other to do some allotment digging. 'The King and Queen', it was remarked, 'dug as heartily as anyone.' This was in line with the conscientious lead the King was giving in all forms of war economy. From the start of the war he had as far as possible banished luxury and ostentation from his household. The royal footmen had gone, mostly to the army. Alcohol had long been renounced, and food was plain and simple. Every palace resident was 'rationed' with the statutory 4 lb of bread and 2½ lb of meat weekly. But early in May the King took a further step by issuing a Proclamation: 'We ... do ... exhort and charge all heads of households to reduce the consumption of bread in their respective families by at least one-fourth of the quantity consumed in ordinary times. To abstain from the use of flour in pastry ...'[24] This injunction was read on Sundays in the country's churches and chapels. It was a measure of the crisis now facing Britain – a crisis underlined by the sinking in April of 526,000 tons of British shipping, the highest loss in any month of the war. How Britain's larder was being depleted was shown by the catering on Hampstead Heath on Whit Monday, some three weeks later. The old plenty had vanished, and the fare for this popular cockney holiday was now thin indeed. 'No pre-war piles of pork pies and pigs' trotters, or round parti-coloured sugar sticks and thick bars of chocolate,' recorded the diarist MacDonagh. 'Little wheaten bread. A chunk of treacly brown cake was commonly served.' Shell fish were fairly plentiful, but coconuts scarce. There were no apples and few bananas. Oranges cost 5d. each.[25]

After the record sinkings of April, the monthly toll decreased – thanks to the convoy system introduced in May, by which groups of merchant ships were escorted clear of the U-boat zone by a protective destroyer screen. This measure did nothing less than save Britain from defeat by starvation. But with losses still running at a perilously high rate (the monthly sinkings remained at well over 300,000 tons until September), the emergency persisted. In June the sugar situation caused fresh trouble. Working people, having to queue long hours for it, were angry that better-off people were allegedly obtaining as much as before the war. The replacement that month of Lord Devonport by Lord Rhondda as Food Controller heralded stricter controls generally. Shortages made themselves felt in odd and unexpected ways. It became an offence to throw rice at a wedding. Starch in laundry work was restricted. Feeding stray dogs – and the London pigeons – was forbidden. There was controversy over the continued provision of pet foods, with dog-lovers and others in heated opposition. A man was fined £50 for collecting crusts for pig food after making the vain defence that otherwise these would have been wasted as navvies would not eat crusts. Local food controllers were appointed, and butchers ordered to display price lists. In September a 'cheap' (subsidised) loaf appeared, and in October bakers were permitted to add potato to their flour in the proportion of one to seven. 'Bun hogs' invaded the West End cakeshops to buy up buns and cakes which were reduced in price after 6 p.m. That winter the time-honoured muffin was to vanish: no longer would the familiar muffin man, his baize-covered tray on his head, be heard ringing his bell around the small streets of Britain.

Queues grew more frequent, with butchers', bakers', grocers' and greengrocers' shops besieged by lines of women and children patiently waiting in inclement autumn weather. Meat became scarce and prices rose. There were complaints of the offensive attitude of shopkeepers, who were accused too of favouring special customers. But whatever the difficulties in the shops and humbler homes, the smartest London hotels were still havens of plenty. In November a journalist dined luxuriously at the Ritz and published an article describing his lavish six-course meal. He had no trouble obtaining four rolls of bread (an illicit quantity).[26] But at least that month the traditional Lord Mayor's Banquet – held despite some objections – showed a slight concession to the times. The guests sat down to clear soup, fillets of sole, casserole of partridge, roast beef and sweets, served with punch, champagne and port. 'Such was the demand for roast beef', noted MacDonagh, 'that the two carvers were kept very busy cutting the huge barons into slices.' Though the top table staged its usual show of gold plate and orchids, much of the banquet's customary glitter, the bright uniforms, medals and jewels, was absent. The soldier-diners wore khaki, 'the colour of the mud in the trenches', wrote MacDonagh.[27] The banquet might have seemed justified by the November toll of shipping losses – at 175,000 tons the lowest since January. But in December the lost tonnage leapt to 257,000, dispelling any false hopes that the U-boat menace was mastered. At mid-month there was a marked shortage of tea, sugar, butter, and bacon. If the middle-class dining-table now showed no actual sign of want, it had become uninspiring. A December day's menu in a suburban home was as follows: Breakfast – Oatmeal porridge without milk, tea with milk and sugar, potatoes fried in fat; Dinner – Salt brisket of beef, carrots and potatoes, milk pudding, cheese; Tea – Bread and jam; Supper – Maize semolina.[28] In poorer homes the fare was perforce less adequate. The situation was now such that compulsory rationing could not be deferred much longer.

The war was also making further inroads on the citizen's drink. Dearth of raw materials had produced a marked beer shortage. Public houses were rationed, and if they sold too quickly they found themselves 'dry' by the weekend. To recoup themselves, publicans had raised prices. In some quarters this had caused trouble. Thirsty Liverpool dockers, enraged at being charged 8d. a pint for their beer, wrecked some public houses and boycotted others. To quiet the discontent, in the summer the Government was forced to allow the brewing of a third more beer than had been intended.[29] Meanwhile the temperance cause was being strongly urged. At a meeting of the Strength of Britain Movement at the Albert Hall in May, the chairman asserted that £512 million had been spent on drink since the start of the war. A resolution for the Government to prohibit the manufacture and sale of alcohol during and immediately after the war was enthusiastically carried. And the Bishop of London declared that it was hypocritical for the King's recent proclamation on food economy to be read in the churches if the public did not live up to it. The poor housewife was exhorted to save every crumb, he added, while countless tons of potential food were turned into beer and spirits. To this that ever-popular figure, Harry Lauder, added his support.[30] But it is certain that, in 1917, a worse handicap to the British effort than the 'demon drink' would have been the catastrophic blow to morale, had liquor been banned.

In the matter of spiritual sustenance, the Church was still, in general, emphasising the evils of the enemy and advocating the continuation of the fight for the Allied cause. In 1916 the assembled bishops had declined to entertain appeals made to them to intercede for peace. In refusing such calls the Archbishop of Canterbury had said: 'So long as the enemy assure us that they are committed irrevocably to principles which I regard as absolutely fatal to what Christ taught us . . . I should look on it as flimsy sentimentalism were I to say that I want immediate peace.' The Bishop of London had added that to talk of a patched-up peace at that stage 'was nothing else than treachery'.[31] Earlier, Dean Inge of St Paul's, had, on the other hand, been accused of giving comfort to the enemy by saying that if he were a betting man he would wager two to one on a peace before Christmas. He had given further offence when he declared that 'time given to prayers for victory would be better occupied for the purpose of making munitions'.[32] But now in 1917, after a heavy daylight air-raid on London in July which had caused many casualties, the Bishop of London stoutly rebutted the angry public cry for reprisals. He did not believe, he said, that the mourners would wish that sixteen German babies should be dead to avenge the dead British babies. Soon after, an assertion of Christian brotherhood came from the House of Laymen in Convocation. They passed a resolution that 'in view of the example of Germany and of the tendency of the war to inflame national sentiment, it was necessary to reaffirm the primary allegiance which Christians owed to the Catholic Church . . . and that they were bound to love all the disciples of Christ of whatever nationality as brethren.'[33] But while convinced Christians forswore hatred, the man in the street continued to nurse it – notably after occasions like the July raid. The young Edmund Blunden, on leave from France that month, noted: 'I remember principally observing . . . the crystallisation of dull civilian hatred on the basis of "the last drop of blood"; [and] the fact that the German air raids had almost persuaded my London friends that London was the sole battle front.'[34] At the same time the King was giving notice of his own sentiments about the enemy by changing the title of the Royal Family to 'The House and Family of Windsor' and relinquishing all German titles and dignities.

Despite growing war-weariness, the popular attitude to the war coincided generally with that of the churchmen: the struggle must go on; there must be no weakening, no talk of peace. The Government's forthright rejection in January of the German approach and the American President's proposals had been in tune with this mood. At the same time a minority voice had continued to demand an end to the war or at least a clear statement of Allied war aims. But such views made virtually no impact. While France was this year beset by defeatism and calls for peace were heard in the German Reichstag, the British people remained doggedly behind the war. The speeches of pacifist leaders like J. A. Hobson and E. D. Morel fell largely on stony ground, and the alarming-sounding resolutions of the Independent Labour Party and revolutionary sentiments expressed at the Socialist Conference at Leeds in June presented no real threat. A truer view of the workers' feelings about the war could be gauged from the refusal of the Seamen's Union to man the ship that was to take Ramsay MacDonald and his co-delegates to the International Socialist Conference at Stockholm in August. (This refusal induced the Government to rescind the permission to attend that it had previously given.) The year's most sensational peace-move from within Britain came from Lord Lansdowne, distinguished statesman and a member of Asquith's late coalition. In November Lansdowne published a letter in the *Daily Telegraph,* throwing doubt on the possibility of decisive victory and recommending the consideration of peace proposals. This met with a storm of protest from the Conservative press, was called by Lloyd George 'ill-advised and inopportune', and in general proved abortive.[35] Meanwhile great stimulus had been given to the prosecution of the struggle by the entry of the United States into the war in April, and the arrival in Britain, in mid-August, of the first American contingent. Impressive in their physique, the 'doughboys' marched through London greeted by cheering crowds – just as they had been in Paris, on their arrival there the previous month. 'It comforted our hearts and raised our spirits to see them and think of what they meant in succour and comfort,' noted MacDonagh.[36]

Militant sentiments could be stirred in other ways too. In September enormous interest was created by the trial of an army officer, Lieutenant Malcolm, on the charge of murdering a certain 'Count' De Borch. Malcolm had shot De Borch on discovering him in a compromising situation with his wife. The defence was that he had killed the 'Count' in self-defence. But the underlying plea involved a question of honour. Lieutenant Malcolm was shown as a wronged husband confronting the villain who had tried to seduce his wife while he himself was away fighting for his country in France. When the jury pronounced him not guilty 'a roar of joy burst forth from the court'.[37] It was a verdict that, for the public, served to enhance the image of the man in uniform, the patriot to whom Britain owed so much. The case provided a welcome distraction from the dreariness of the civilian war. But just now there were other less agreeable distractions. Late September saw four heavy air-raids on London. These plainly affected the steadiness of already war-strained Londoners. Though they carried on normally they seemed to one observer like people who had experienced an earthquake or the like. 'Even the men one met in business looked pale and nerve-racked.'[38] Worst of all in the raids was the ordeal of the very poor. Crowding the tubes in search of shelter, they presented a pathetic sight. Arnold Bennett was shocked to see the women and children herding into the underground lifts and thronging the steps. A friend told him of a young woman shelterer who was in labour, and whom he had managed to get taken to hospital.[39]

Christmas 1917 was, understandably, the gloomiest of the war. To all the other causes of depression and despondency was added deep discouragement at the futility and fearful slaughter of that third Battle of Ypres, the Flanders campaign which from August to early November had produced 240,000 British casualties. More thousands of homes were now bereaved. A vast new quota of wounded filled the hospitals. Nowhere was there any ground for cheer or optimism. Though there was a spirit of 'grin-and-bear-it' abroad, it was noted, 'most folk looked worn-out and sorrowful'[40]. But life had to go on. In the North, it was reported, more money was being spent than ever before. The London theatres were full, as were the West End hotels, though these had made no special Christmas preparations. For the families at home the Ministry of Food had planned a special Christmas dinner: French rice soup, filleted haddock, roast fowl and vegetables, plum pudding and caramel custard – to cost 10s. for four people. The inmates of a Maidstone workhouse, on the other hand, patriotically rejected Christmas pudding in favour of cornflour. Nor did the diarist MacDonagh adopt the Ministry menu. His family circle celebrated with Denny's Irish gammon, cabbage and potatoes, plum pudding and a glass of claret. In this muted mood the British nation looked to a coming year in which victory seemed as remote as ever.

Chapter 12

FRANCE

The darkest hour

WHATEVER similarities there were in the wartime civilian scenes of Britain and France – and there were many, as there were also between both of these and that of Germany – the harsh fact always remained that France's own soil was a battleground. Beyond the boundaries of uninvaded France lay a wilderness of devastation that was also France. Not only economically but psychologically, this placed her on a different plane from Britain. In a sense that was not true of Britain, she was fighting for her existence, and the sacrifices she was making in manpower alone were demonstrably greater. Though accepting regimentation and limitation of personal freedom more readily than Britain (as in her tolerance of universal military conscription since 1870), she was yet more of a nation of individuals and a more volatile and emotional people than Britain. She was also less amenable to discipline. She could perhaps hate more strongly – and she found good reason to hate her traditional Teutonic enemy – just as she could more easily feel enthusiasm or fall into apathy. These traits together with her deeper and closer involvement in the war were liable to produce a more vulnerable morale than that of the British and expose her more readily to defeatist influences when things went badly. All this was relevant to France's situation in the dark New Year of 1917.

Since the first shock and disruption of August 1914, France's war output had overcome various difficulties and steadily expanded, until now it was at a satisfactory level. It had in fact just about reached its peak, for henceforth it would begin to be hampered by new strains that would be increasingly felt until the armistice. Apart from the crying lack of manpower (France's population was the smallest of the three belligerents, and her army the largest in proportion to her population) there would be raw material shortage, problems caused by the diversion of transport and shipping to the United States war-effort, and damaging labour unrest. The latter, though partly incited by pacifist agitators, was a measure of the underlying weariness that was afflicting France. In meeting the fresh challenge of 1917 she would be handicapped by faltering morale as much as by physical deficiencies. The previous November President Poincaré had noted a 'vague malaise' permeating the country. This may have been due to the experience of Verdun, which had not only half-crippled the French Army but left a deep trauma on the whole nation. But perhaps there was another factor, suggested by the *poilu* who in December, in a letter to the press, had lamented the disunity between front and rear and appealed for a single France – of soldiers united with civilians. The writer was pointing to an alienation that had been growing through the war years and had obvious dangers for a concerted national effort. Now, in January, Henry Bordeaux expressed his concern over the matter in conversation with the President. The military leaders, he said, had not sufficiently appreciated that the war should engage 'the whole strength of the country and not just the military strength'. As an example Bordeaux cited the matter of leave, remarking that in permitting leave only after eleven months of hostilities, the generals had broken many family bonds and suppressed many births. Poincaré replied that he himself had insisted on leave being granted, after a great struggle with General Joffre.[1]

But Joffre was now no longer the army's all-powerful chief. He had been relieved of his command in December, slipping unobtrusively away from the GHQ over which he had presided so autocratically from the start of the war – a figure whose once towering reputation had steadily declined since the Marne, and who had finally been unable to survive the attacks of press and parliament for his allegedly incompetent handling of the Verdun campaign. Promoted Marshal of France and appointed as Military Adviser to the Government, Joffre now faded into semi-obscurity; while in his place a new military hero, General Robert Nivelle, famous for his own successful part in the Verdun battles, became Commander-in-Chief. Nivelle was soon to introduce a new concept (far more disastrous than any strategy of Joffre's had ever been) into offensive operations. But meanwhile French civilians, shivering in the coldest winter for decades, were undergoing fresh discomforts and privations.

With Paris gripped by frost, frozen pipes left many Parisians without water, and plumbers were in pressing demand. But worst of all was the coal shortage, due to the cessation of supplies from Britain.[2] This for the first time brought real hardship. The situation was so serious that the city authorities had to allocate their own small stocks to consumers who came to fetch it from the depots. Sometimes supplies ran out altogether. All over Paris queues waited in chilling cold for scant rations. Often people had to go away empty-handed after standing for hours. In parts of the city coal-carts were besieged and their loads shared out by fuel-starved citizens (who paid strictly for what they took). A 20-ton supply, dumped in the road for delivery to a Ministry, had to be protected by armed guards. When coal was first sold in the Opéra courtyard, a thousand-strong crowd assembled to receive a mere 20-lb allocation. A typical scene was a queue of two hundred women waiting at the Galerie d'Orléans, near the Palais-Royal, for a bag the size of a pillow-case. An observer noted that though all looked pale, they were apparently not unhappy – on the contrary, they were 'full of lively chatter'.[3] There were long queues on the quays and elsewhere, the women standing with children who cried with the cold. It was common to see well-dressed men and women in mourning pushing carts or wheelbarrows in search of coal or wood. Lack of central heating, through fuel shortage, produced the novel sight of frost-covered shop windows. In the hot-house of the famous Jardin d'Acclimatisation all the tropical plants, maintained at great cost, perished for lack of heating. But Parisians could at least laugh at their predicament. One newspaper cartoon showed a liveried footman deferentially ushering along a carpeted passage a coalman carrying two sacks of coal, and saying: '*Par l'escalier d'Honneur*' (By the grand staircase). And in a whimsical demonstration of the inestimable value now placed on this rare mineral, the smartest jeweller in the Rue de la Paix placed in his window a lump of coal, surrounded by diamonds.

It was impossible to get lamp-oil and candles were scarce. To the fuel-less conditions was added the trials of dirt. A dearth of cleansing staff meant that dustbins lay unemptied in the icy streets until afternoon, causing windblown garbage to clutter the pavements. And people were queuing not only for coal. Sugar was now rationed, and huge lines stood outside the grocery stores awaiting their quota. As other shortages appeared, similar lines would wait for milk, chocolate and potatoes. In Paris and elsewhere, this frigid winter would be remembered above all as the time of the queue. A cameo of these days was provided by Corday: In a central boulevard two queues standing opposite each other across the road. 'Both had the same dingy and humble appearance.' One was waiting to buy potatoes, the other to take up shares in the new War Loan. Nearby two burly gendarmes stopped a diminutive soldier, 'exhausted by three years of war', and asked to see his papers. [4]

But still the paradoxes persisted. From the Madeleine to the Place de la République, Paris on these winter evenings was, in the words of Corday, a scene of 'tremendous gluttony'. The restaurants, ablaze with light behind their heavy blinds, were crowded with diners. 'Laughing eyes, glowing cheeks, busy jaws, waiters darting to and fro. Not a single empty seat.' [5] A few score miles away, Corday reflected, men were standing in the trenches. He concluded that posterity would find the pictorial documentation of the war very defective. Not only would the squalid life of the trenches go unrecorded, but also the scenes of Paris enjoying itself – as too would the city's gloomier side, the darkened interiors of houses, the candle-lit fruit-stalls, the loaded dustbins, the queues. Yet the ordinary people stood up well to the discomforts. The worst spirit was shown by the small shopkeepers, who – exhibiting the same traits as their opposite numbers in Britain – took pleasure in bullying and browbeating their customers, and especially middle-class women who were unaccustomed to wartime shopping conditions.

The queues outside the provision shops betokened further difficulties for fuel-starved Frenchmen. After some thirty months of war, food shortage was at last making itself felt, as a result both of enemy occupation of French territory and of intensifying U-boat activity. With only sixty-five sugar factories out of over two hundred still productive, the first serious scarcity was of sugar.[6] Apart from restrictions for consumption in the home, early in February sugar in restaurants was limited to 10 grammes per customer, while tea shops and sweet shops were closed two days a week in the Paris area and Seine departments. More generally, restaurants were now forbidden to serve diners with more than two dishes, including only one of meat. Subsidiary dishes were banned, and the menu for each meal was limited to two soups and nine dishes (for example, one egg dish, two of fish, three of meat and three vegetables). Bread was strictly regulated as to shape and weight. Fancy bread was prohibited, as was *patisserie* for two days a week; cakes for cafés were limited, and flour for biscuit manufacturers reduced. A 'stale bread' order in February restricted the amount of new bread sold. This indispensable item of French diet was indeed suffering strange vicissitudes, becoming in time hardly recognisable from the fresh, crusty and pure white product of pre-war years. A Paris resident has described it as going through wonderful colour changes, from a sour, damp and indigestible grey to an unappetising brown. It was made with successive mixtures of different flours infinitely less palatable than English war-bread. The flabby crust was just eatable if covered with butter or jam. Even the French, it was said, gave up eating it, as was their custom, between every two mouthfuls of a meal. This caused a great waste of flour, because large quantities were left unfinished at table.[7] More disquieting was the claim that some of this war-bread was injurious to health. It was alleged that bread with only 85% of wheat turned black owing to growth of vegetable fungus, which caused boils and gastric disorders while destroying the nutritive properties.[8]

Increasing scarcities were accompanied by steeply rising prices. In early March, the cost of fish soared by 50% in Paris on a single day. Sometimes commodities such as milk and even condensed milk suddenly ran out. But in May Parisians suffered a fresh blow; their first meatless day. On its eve there was a rush to butchers' shops to lay in stocks for two days. Amid scenes of disorder the butchers resorted to selling the meat by auction. Thieves took advantage of the chaos, and by 10 a.m. most shops were out of stock.

But for all these privations, by comparison with Berlin the French capital seemed just now 'a land of abundance'.[9] This was the finding of James Gerard, who as United States Ambassador to Germany left Berlin for Paris in February, when the United States broke off diplomatic relations with Germany, as a preliminary to declaring war on her in April. As to eating, he noted, even the two courses served in restaurants could be supplemented by a second helping. After Berlin, Gerard was struck by the liveliness of Paris. Taxis, plentiful in Paris (though petrol was regulated in April), were almost non-existent in Berlin. The soldiers thronging the Paris boulevards looked far happier than the 'heavy-footed Germans who so painfully tramped down the Unter den Linden'.[10] Gerard was surprised to see the many wounded in the streets, a sight unknown in Berlin, it being the Government's policy to conceal the war-injured from the German public. The cold, however, was inescapable. The whole city was suffering intensely from the fuel shortage. In Gerard's frigid hotel, guests made do with wood fires in their rooms. The theatres, now limited to three performances a week with evening dress banned, were entirely unheated. Gerard attended one play wrapped in a fur overcoat, but found the cold so bitter that he had to leave after twenty minutes. Paris at night was a place of gloom. The streets were darkened as an air-raid precaution, and interiors were subject to strict lighting restrictions. Private houses were reduced to a single electric bulb for each room, a rule whose violation brought a penalty of three weeks' loss of light. The dining-room of the fashionable Ritz Hotel, with lights only on its tables, was a sombre shadow of its pre-war chandelier-lit brilliance.

America's entry into the war on the 6th April (caused by continued sinking of her ships by U-boats) was a tremendous stimulus to sagging French morale. In the Chamber it was greeted with characteristic Gallic eloquence by the elderly Alexandre Ribot, who had succeeded Briand as Prime Minister in March. 'The banner of the Stars and Stripes,' he declared, 'is about to float beside the Tricolour. Our hands are about to join and our hearts to beat in unison. It will be for us, after so many sufferings heroically endured, so many bereavements and losses, a renewal as it were of the courage which has sustained us during this long ordeal. The mighty, decisive assistance of the United States will not be merely material; it will bring us especially moral succour and true comfort.'[11] The words of the tall, patriarchal Premier were received with rapturous applause. In the Chamber at the time was William Sharp, US Ambassador to France since 1914. 'As my presence in the Chamber furnished the only visible means by which Members could render their homage to the United States,' Sharp relates, 'the entire membership, rising as by one impulse upon the mention of the name of America by their distinguished Premier, turned towards the diplomatic gallery where I was sitting. Again and again they bowed and cheered.'[12] Parliamentary enthusiasm was echoed throughout France. Soon after, the great event was fêted in a Paris hung with American flags. A 101-gun salute was fired from the Eiffel Tower while one of France's best-known baritones sang the Marseillaise in front of the LaFayette statue. In mid-June the American Commander-in-Chief, General Pershing, arrived in the capital, to be hailed by welcoming crowds who cheered him for hours outside the Hotel Crillon. National gratitude to the new ally was shown on the 4th July, when American Independence was celebrated by a parade of American troops through Paris and an impressive military review at the Invalides.

But in early April Frenchmen had another cause for encouragement. A great French attack was imminent, that might, it was said, break the persisting deadlock and even bring the end of the war in sight. This was the project of the new Commander-in-Chief, North-East, General Robert Nivelle, who on replacing General Joffre had wasted no time in reshaping existing Allied offensive plans for 1917 in favour of an ambitious plan of his own. Nivelle was a dynamic commander who (as he had shown at Verdun in 1916 under General Pétain) believed in hitting the enemy hard and decisively. Now, instead of a combined Anglo-French attack on a broad front, much of the old pattern, there was to be a massive, concentrated assault on a forty-mile front between Soissons and Reims by the French, shortly preceded by a diversionary British attack in the north. So confident and persuasive was Nivelle that he had managed to win the agreement of the Allied leaders to his plan, though some generals were dubious about it as being over-bold. But on the battle-weary French troops, whose already low morale was now further depressed by the bitter winter conditions they were enduring at the front, it had had an electrifying effect. Infected by the confidence of their new commander and inspired by his virtual guarantee of success, suddenly they regained hope. Now, they felt, there was a chance of ending the stalemate and achieving the breakthrough that had eluded them since 1914. Morale rose dramatically in anticipation of the great attack, which was scheduled for early April.

In resurrecting the army's wilting morale, Nivelle had to contend not only with war weariness and arctic weather. There had been a more sinister factor: anti-war propaganda from the pacifist-defeatist groups that had recently been operating in the rear in growing strength. The previous November a wave of pacifist propaganda in the war factories and industrial plants had coincided with similar activity among the troops. The traffic, largely through tracts and leaflets, had continued in the New Year, sponsored by bodies like the Committee for the Renewal of International Relations, the Committee of Syndicalist Defence, the Syndicate of Teachers, the Federation of Metal-workers. Circulating surreptitiously among the troops, the tracts had proclaimed that the French troops were fighting for an unjust cause, that Germany was not the real enemy, victory was impossible, and only peace would solve France's problems. Other material reached the armies through men who had attended inflammatory meetings while on leave and brought back accounts of them to their units. At the end of February Nivelle sent the Minister of the Interior, Malvy, a report of these activities coupled with a strong demand to suppress the menace by seizing the subversive tracts, banning the revolutionary meetings and silencing the extremist leaders. Soon after, he interviewed Malvy in Paris, but obtained no satisfaction. Malvy virtually told him to handle the matter himself. Malvy's laxity – or worse – would later become apparent; but his attitude reflected the Government's current difficulties in the handling of labour relations. If they took action against the leading pacifist agitators, they ran the risk of provoking unrest among the war-workers. Fortunately for Nivelle, he was able to instil his troops with such certainty that a breakthrough would be achieved – he even promised success within forty-eight hours – that the defeatists' efforts were nullified. But they remained a potential threat both to the army and the Home Front.

Meanwhile, in Paris, the coming offensive was an open secret. With no regard for security, it was optimistically discussed in bars, cafés and restaurants. Such 'careless talk' was not calculated to help the result for which every Frenchman so fervently hoped. It merely fed the listening ears of enemy agents (confirming the intelligence that the Germans had already gleaned from actually observing the preparations for the attack). So, with the public keyed-up at the start of April for a great victory, the *déception* (disappointment) was all the more shattering when the assault, launched on the 16th in atrocious weather, foundered with heavy losses. After eleven days' savage fighting, at the cost of 96,000 French casualties including 15,000 dead, the German front was still virtually unbroken. This reverse had disastrous repercussions. At the front Nivelle's troops, bitterly angered and disillusioned at the failure of the offensive on which they had been induced to build such extravagant hopes, mutinied. Between the end of April and the beginning of June, elements of fifty-four divisions rebelled, deserted, refused duty, called for peace, threatened to march on Paris and confront Parliament. In the rear, as weary and despondent civilians saw their rosy expectations dashed, the mutinies were echoed by a surge of unrest, expressing itself in demonstrations, street parades, strikes and labour troubles. Like the troops (and indeed like their fellow-workers in Britain) the French workers had their well-defined grievances. France's labour legislation and factory laws had been suspended on the outbreak of war, and the situation had been aggravated since then by poor wages, difficult working conditions and the steeply rising cost of living. The workers' restiveness had been intensified by the Russian Revolution that had shaken the world in March. By the end of June stoppages in war factories around Paris and the provinces numbered 170, involving 70,000 workers, while the full year would show a total of 689 strikes, affecting 293,000 workers (compared with a mere 98 strikes in 1916). Even the political unity proclaimed in August 1914 was splitting apart as Socialists reverted to their old pacifist leanings and increasingly criticised the conduct of the war. In these spring and early summer weeks France was in greater disarray than at any time in the struggle.

By a feat of secrecy that was one of the remarkable things of the war, almost no news of the mutinies penetrated the rear. (Even the British Commander-in-Chief, Sir Douglas Haig, and the Prime Minister, Lloyd George, knew little of them until afterwards.) But French civilians were already aware of the uneasy spirit of the troops, the disenchanted sons and husbands who came on leave voicing their various plaints and grievances; and this had added to the general war-weariness of the Home Front. It was an underlying mood, vague and ill-defined in itself, but potentially fertile ground for the pacifist-defeatist cliques which hovered in the background of France's war effort, always looking for opportunities to plant their disruptive propaganda. Even more open to exploitation was the rebellious mood of Nivelle's troops – though in their state of angry despair they needed little outside provocation. At all events it was now that the anti-war agitators moved in, both on the Home Front and among the troops, to take advantage of the situation. Much of their campaign against the soldiers, by tract, leaflet and clandestine news-sheet, was directed into the Army Zone itself, but they were active in Paris too. In and around the large railway termini, especially the Gare de l'Est and Gare du Nord – stations for the front – lurked their agents, mingling with the troops in transit to distribute anti-war pamphlets and urge them to desert. Near the stations were illicit clothing agencies, at which deserters could obtain civilian clothes. This year the toll of desertions, either spontaneous or induced, was to reach the record total of 27,000.

In their attempts to subvert the Home Front the saboteurs dropped into civilian letter-boxes, in Paris and the provinces, manifestoes like this: 'Frenchmen! Groups of friends of peace, true and good French patriots, are conducting at this moment throughout the country a vigorous though clandestine campaign in favour of peace. Do not look on them as enemy agents, German propagandists, paid to sow discord among the French. No: those who, in the café, at the theatre, in the street, will speak to you of peace, are not the agents of Germany. They are very good patriots, much more respectable, honest and franker than the gang of degenerates and careerists who are leading France to the abyss. The friends of France are conducting their purely national campaign in a clandestine way because they are convinced that the hour for declaring themselves has not arrived.'

But the mass of ordinary Frenchmen were unlikely to be

seduced by the defeatists' calls. If they now ardently wanted peace, it was not at the cost of deliberately sabotaging the war-effort. At the same time the fervent patriotic spirit of August 1914, inspired by the hopes of a short war and a speedy victory, had long since faded. It had been replaced by a resignation increasingly tinged with cynicism, the result of the disparity between the war as portrayed by the official propaganda machine and as they themselves were experiencing it. The huge toll of bereavement, the growing drabness and austerity of life, the stories of what things were really like at the front brought back by men on leave, all added up to make the officially inspired picture less credible and reliable. Reports of starvation in Germany, descriptions of the enemy as a brutish ogre and of the *poilu* as a brave hero, accounts of the invincibility of the Allies, of triumphant French and disastrous German offensives, did not tally with the seeming endlessness of the war and the persistent non-arrival of victory. The blandly optimistic propaganda line permeated not only the press, but novels and plays. The gap between fiction and reality that soldiers from the front had so quickly perceived – and which added so powerfully to their sense of alienation – rapidly became an 'abyss' that even civilians could not ignore.[13] Soon the whole popular press was suspected of printing eyewash (*bourrage de crâne*), and to find out the truth about the war people turned to the smaller, independent papers which rejected the official line and did not fear to criticise people and policies. Such papers were *L'Œuvre*, *Le Pays*, and above all Clemenceau's hard-hitting *Canard Enchaîné*. Another was *La Vague*, started by the deputy Pierre Brizon in 1916, which achieved great success for its printing of letters from fighting soldiers – an activity which the General Staff might well have suppressed, but in fact allowed to continue as it provided a useful indication of the soldier's mood.

Linked with the growing popular cynicism was a concern about the aims for which France was really fighting. Only clear and acceptable war aims could justify the huge sacrifices which she was making. And in any case was there no means of achieving these aims except by a war whose end could not be foreseen? As a way out of the dilemma, was a compromise peace possible? These issues were taken up by papers like *La Vérité*, which demanded a statement of war aims as a basis for a negotiated peace. Such questions were perfectly valid, but they could easily be turned to the advantage of France's enemies. This was the situation as perplexed and troubled Frenchmen moved towards the war's fourth year in the early summer of 1917.

The actively defeatist groups that were attempting for their sundry reasons to undermine France's fighting capacity were a motley assortment. They included pacifists, internationalists, and labour and extremist left-wing factions; the doctrinaires who saw no point in fighting to preserve what they called the imperialist capitalism of bourgeois France; the Marxists who wanted peace because it would usher in the dreamed-of dictatorship of the proletariat and banish class-differences; the professional anarchists who welcomed a German victory because it would ruin France and bring in its train civil war; the pro-Germans and outright enemy agents. Many were aliens or of alien origin, for whom Paris, as Europe's most cosmopolitan capital before the war, had been a natural magnet. They were to be found behind the doors of certain Paris *salons*, in trade-union and small newspaper offices and even a few Government bureaux. Their intensified activity at this critical stage underlined once more the error made by the French Government in late July 1914, when it had decided not to detain most of the known anti-war agitators and extremists listed in the dossier *Carnet B*. The view was then taken that wholesale arrests might cause trouble among the workers being called to the colours, and thus hinder mobilisation. This was against the advice of that stubborn old Radical, Clemenceau, who when consulted by Malvy had replied: 'Put the whole lot in prison! You'd be a criminal not to!' Fuel had been added to the saboteurs' cause by the world-shaking Russian Revolution in March, with its encouragement to disruption and anarchy. That some at least of the saboteurs were in direct enemy pay was shown by the incident of *Le Bonnet Rouge*, the newspaper which had caused the Government trouble in 1916 and was now again among the most active illicit propaganda sheets.

On the 14th May M. Duval, editor of *Le Bonnet Rouge*, was arrested in a Paris-bound train on the Swiss frontier and found to be carrying a cheque for 150,000 francs drawn on a Swiss bank and signed in the name of a certain Herr Marx (later identified as the German paymaster of German agents abroad). The cheque was confiscated but Duval was allowed to proceed, un-arrested, to Paris. Soon after, the cheque was returned to him by M. Leymarie, head of the *cabinet* of the Minister of the Interior, Malvy, Duval's explanation that the money was a repayment to him of a pre-war business debt having apparently been accepted. This was the first hint of a series of scandals involving, among various others, Duval and his *Le Bonnet Rouge* colleagues, Leymarie and the Minister of the Interior himself. Duval was arrested in July on the orders of the Prime Minister, Ribot, and at the end of August Malvy, after a slashing attack by Clemenceau in the Senate, was forced to resign, thereby bringing down the Ribot Government. The full extent of the internal dangers threatening France was to be revealed in the notorious 'treason' trials that took place the following year.

Meanwhile, as the mutinies of the troops intensified, the now discredited Nivelle was replaced by General Philippe Pétain, the cool and cautious leader who, as Nivelle's superior at Verdun, had turned the tide of battle there and since won fame as the Saviour of Verdun. At the same time, on the Paris boulevards the first signs of labour unrest were appearing. This began in mid-May with a parade of *midinettes* demanding higher wages to meet the rising cost of living. (Complaints against '*la vie chère*', suggests the diarist Louise Delétang, were not always as genuine as they were made out to be. 'Today', she noted at the end of May, 'there was a queue at shops selling asparagus and strawberries, and the roasts and legs of lamb are more in demand than the cheap cuts.'[14]) In their voluminous navy blue costumes and outsize hats the banner-carrying girls made a light-hearted spectacle. For the next week their parades continued, swelling in size to immobilise altogether 15,000 sempstresses. As soon as these returned to work, more girls from other workshops came out, marching and picketing the Ministry of the Interior. The demonstrations were mostly good-humoured, but beneath their surface lay a grimmer note. Mrs Coolidge, the wife of an Embassy official in Paris, encountered in a modiste's shop a girl strike-leader who came in to urge the assistants to join the strike. 'She spoke most dreadfully,' recorded Mrs Coolidge. 'It is really the Boches who are at the bottom of it.'[15] Agitators joined the marches, shouting revolutionary slogans. Soldiers, too, were accompanying the demonstrators. Police patrolled the streets in force, forming cordons to guard buildings and bar the passage of crowds. Sometimes scuffles broke out and arrests were made. 'It has been a question of labour so far,' noted Mrs Coolidge, 'but the bad element is beginning to mix up in the mess, so that it may be transformed into a minor revolutionary movement.'[16] On the 1st June the Council of Ministers was shown a pacifist tract issued by the *Fédération des Métaux* which, in Poincaré's view, was sufficiently inflammatory to infringe the law; and an investigation was thereupon ordered. Next day, in the Elysée Palace, the President listened anxiously for two hours to the shouts of marching demonstrators. At the French Army GHQ, Compiègne, General Pétain was being kept informed of the situation in Paris by his liaison officer, Colonel Herbillon. Pétain, his hands full with trying to quell the mutinies, was convinced that these were being provoked by the Paris agitators. At his behest Herbillon called on Leymarie at the Ministry of the Interior to name the suspected troublemakers and demand action against them. Leymarie replied somewhat helplessly that if the leaders were arrested there would be revolution.

Early in June fresh disquiet was caused by a Paris street affray involving French colonial troops. To the anger of the crowd the men had opened fire and caused several casualties. This coincided with a secret session of the Chamber in which, during a tense and stormy debate on the crisis, defeatist views were voiced and the possibility of peace mentioned. From the young Socialist member for Aubervilliers – Pierre Laval – came a startling speech alluding to the street brawl. 'Whether you like or not,' he declared, 'a wind of peace is blowing through the country. If there are any more disorders like this, I very much fear that the cry for peace will get stronger.' This produced a tumult of protest. Later, Laval raised the delicate matter of the international Socialist Conference at Stockholm – an issue then exercising the French as well as the British Government – and made a powerful plea for French participation. 'After so many deaths, after three years of war,' he said, 'we must understand that the country is tired, and look for the best means of bringing about the recovery of this great nation. And these means, gentlemen? The means of giving hope to the troops and confidence to the workers – whether you like it or not – is Stockholm!' After more uproar the new War Minister, Paul Painlevé, spoke, concluding thus gravely: 'At this moment, gentlemen, we are living through hours as grave as those which we knew on the 4th August 1914. We will surmount them – if the morale of the army and the morale of the country are not broken!' This brought resounding cheers, and the sitting ended with a five-to-one majority vote against a motion to send delegates to Stockholm.[17] The Assembly was expressing its determination to continue the struggle. But the debate reflected the anxious, uncertain mood pervading Parliament and the public in these June days. In his diary President Poincaré commented sombrely: 'Order is everywhere threatened. The fever is spreading. Must we await a new victory of the Marne to be healed?'[18]

From current preoccupations Poincaré was wont to snatch a brief escape in the tree-bordered gardens of the Elysée, accompanied by his wife, their black-haired bitch, Babette, and Miette, their little Belgian griffon. Farther afield, Parisians relaxed amid the beauties of Versailles. At the start of June an observer noted there: 'a sky like silk, boats on the canal, soaring plumes of water, café tables where the New Rich drink

French refugees at the Gare du Nord, 1918

Recruits leave Paris, 1917

Police on riot duty, Berlin, 1918

champagne for tea: a brilliant display of festivity and pleasure, and the war so far away.'[19] This was the moment when, at the height of the mutinies, only two dependable French divisions (near Soissons) stood between Paris and the enemy, a mere seventy miles distant. As always, whatever the crisis, the capital presented its paradoxes. At a revue with 'bare backs, bare breasts, bare legs, in infinite perspective', Corday was struck by a song which declared that, when peace returned, Frenchmen would sigh for the days of danger. 'What heroes they feel when comfortably sitting in the stalls!' he remarked.[20] Amid an evening crowd of soldiers and painted prostitutes strolling on the boulevard, Corday was shocked to see a drunken one-armed *poilu* 'begging for a copper or a cigarette and mouthing the word "Peace . . . Peace" '.[21] In April he had met a soldier just back from the Aisne battle front. The man was shocked at the gaiety of Paris. He expressed his sense of isolation from the Home Front when he said, in reply to Corday's suggestion that men like him would have to speak out after the war, that he and his fellows knew nothing at all, being too busy fighting, 'while those who would speak out would be the men who read about the war in the newspapers'.[22]

Enduring their winter ills, Frenchmen had had no difficulty in hating the enemy who was seen to be responsible for them. The American Embassy official in Paris, James Coolidge, reported that members of the American Embassy in Berlin who had arrived in Paris in February were impressed by two things: the large number of taxis in the city and the bitterness of the hatred against the Germans.[23] But hate was whipped up to a new pitch after the enemy, in making a strategic withdrawal in February from their northern positions to their 'Hindenburg Line', left a huge area of total destruction. The French country-side was devastated, towns and villages left in ruins, fruit-trees felled, livestock killed, furniture smashed. After a visit to the area, M. Viviani and a colleague issued a proclamation, with Senate approval, in which they 'held up to universal execration the authors of the crimes committed by Germany in these regions'. Viviani's colleague, M. Chéron, declared that 'hatred of Germans is henceforth the holiest of duties'.[24] After this it was easy for further hatred to be visited on the enemy for an 'atrocity' which they did not in fact commit. This stemmed from the notorious 'Kadaver' story, in which it was rumoured in April that the Germans were boiling down the corpses of their soldiers for fat. In France and Britain alike the story was widely – and perhaps eagerly – believed, creating a horrified disgust that magnified still further the conventional image of the enemy as a monster of barbarity. It arose from a report in a German newspaper from a correspondent on the Western Front which ran: 'We are passing the great Corpse [Kadaver] Exploitation Department Establishment of this Army Group. The fat that is won here is turned into lubricating oils, and everything else is ground down in the bone mills into a powder which is used for mixing with pig's food and as manure – nothing can be permitted to go to waste.' But in the Allies' wide exploitation of the story the needs of anti-German propaganda outran the respect for truth. For it should not have been difficult for anyone with knowledge of German to appreciate that the German word 'Kadaver' meant not a human but an animal corpse. The corpses in question were those of horses.

On the industrial front, fresh strains were now evident. The pressing demands of the arms factories meant the further diversion of coal, raw materials and labour from less essential industries. Problems were raised by the transport difficulties of private factories, and great efforts were made to find substitutes for scarce coal. Wood, sawdust, and peat were all tried, but with unsatisfactory results. Progress was, however, made in methods of using coal, the management of steam generators and the development of hydro-electric machinery. Wherever considerable water-power was available, in the Pyrenees, the Alps and the central mountain ranges, the building of hydroelectric installations was started (many being completed only after the war). The manpower shortage was now such that troops were being withdrawn from the front. Owing to the success of the U-boat campaign with its consequent threat to home food-production, the greatest need was for agricultural workers. From April to the following January, 300,000 farm hands were to be returned to the land, while 32,000 men went to the mines, 3,000 to navigation, 8,000 to the railways and 5,000 to the educational services. Care had to be used in granting exemptions, in order that inexperienced young workers should not leave the trenches while older trained men remained, and that public opinion should be satisfied that no unfairness was involved in the withdrawals.[25] The Government therefore ruled that only men over forty-one (or in some cases over thirty-five) should return to the Home Front. And to ensure the proper allotment of labour supply to the farms and factories, economic committees were established in each department, in co-operation with the military. Thus in this critical year the men flowed back from the front to keep France's industries running – the flour-mills, sugar-factories, gas-works, potteries, and all the manufactures and services on which the nation's life depended.[26]

The manpower dearth imposed a yet greater call on France's women. They were now a commonplace sight in almost every job they could physically perform. There were the Paris postwomen, neat in their black overalls and black straw hats, carrying their little square boxes. There were the tram conductresses, ticket collectors, gardeners tending the lawns and flower-beds in the Tuileries and elsewhere, even the street-cleaners clad in black overalls, big hats and clogs, wielding their heavy hosepipes. One field they had not invaded was that of the uniformed services. Frenchmen liked their women to be feminine, and even the needs of war did not overcome traditional distaste for seeing them aping the male in para-military uniform. They never became really accustomed to the appearance of Britain's Wrens or Waacs, or America's dark-grey uniformed YMCA girls, in the Paris streets. The only uniform tolerated was that of the Red Cross, though such was the French sense of delicacy that at one time there was agitation to withdraw young girls from hospital service on the grounds that they were unfitted for the disagreeable sights to which they would be exposed in the wards. Strange tales circulated about women factory-workers. It was said that they ate little but kept themselves going on spirits and wine, being chiefly happy if they could trot about on fashionable high heels.[27] In a different vein, the war was revealing a moving testimony to the fidelity of war-widows to the memory of their dead husbands. A Frenchwomen told an English friend that she did not know of a single war-widow who had remarried, however unhappy had been her married life. Such remarriage would have brought social ostracism on the woman. French people generally were shocked at the number of English war-widows who had quickly found new husbands.[28]

By July the worst of the army disorders was over. With a mixture of severity and judicious attention to the troops' genuine grievances (and the French Army had many, including wretched welfare conditions, poor pay, inadequate leave, harsh discipline, overtaxed fighting capacity), General Pétain had nursed their ailing morale back to a state of convalescence. But he sternly warned the Government that he could guarantee no permanent recovery unless the Home Front agitators were suppressed. The air was cleared somewhat at another turbulent session of the Chamber at the end of June in which deputies angrily castigated the High Command for its ill-judged offensive and generally ventilated the nation's ills. And as evidence of the defeatists' activities accumulated, the Government at last began to take action against them. After Duval's arrest, his colleague Almereyda was detained, and *Le Bonnet Rouge* was suspended indefinitely. A round-up of troublemakers was started, bringing in 1,700 suspects by the end of the year. At the close of November Malvy, who after his resignation three months before had been sensationally accused by the ultra-patriotic editor of *L'Action Française*, Leon Daudet, of informing the enemy of French military plans, was formally charged with treason.

But though much of the earlier industrial disturbance had now abated, the spirit at some war-factories was still restive, strongly influenced by the tumultuous events in Russia that culminated in the October Revolution (in which Lenin seized power with the aim of making the country a totally Communist state and ending the war with the Central Powers). That autumn there were sporadic strikes at Lyons, Bourges, and in the Loire area. On a visit to provincial war-plants the Minister for Armaments, Albert Thomas, was greeted at one factory by shouts of 'Down with the war!'[29] In mid-November sabotage occurred in munitions factories and electric power stations in Paris. Fortunately for France, she now had a Premier capable of handling such trouble – seventy-six-year-old Georges Clemenceau, who had just succeeded Paul Painlevé (Prime Minister for three months after the fall of Ribot). Clemenceau informed the leader of the *Confédération Général du Travail* (CGT) that he had commandeered the three Paris racecourses and that if the sabotage continued he would bring troops into the city to stop it. Not all the threats came from the pacifist left. Indicating some right-wing plot, late in October dumps of arms were found at the offices of *L'Action Française* and else-where. This discovery prompted a Government inquiry. 'The depots of arms', noted Lord Bertie of Thame, 'represented a general discontent by many people . . . at the cliques which pretend [*sic*] to rule the country.'[30]

The coming of the war's third anniversary prompted anxious questionings. 'Is the fourth year of war illuminated by a ray of hope?' Louise Delétang asked herself. 'More and more one foresees the dragging-out of the fearful nightmare since the Americans are not yet ready.'[31] Meanwhile France was faced by further stringencies.

The cost of living was soaring towards an increase of 80% on its pre-war figure, severely affecting the rentier and salaried middle classes and the farming community (though industrial workers were protected by a minimum wage law). In Septem-ber newspapers were doubled in price to 10 centimes. To control coal distribution and prevent hoarding, coal tickets were now introduced, allotting each family a fixed quota. And large stocks of firewood from the forest of Dreux, south-west of Paris, were stored in the Paris yards against the coming winter. At the end of November bread rationing was announced for towns of more than 20,000, the ration being fixed at 300 grammes per head, with an addition for special workers. Saccharine was now in common use as a substitute sweetener. But in Paris there seemed to be plenty of everything – at a price; and there were enough people with the money to buy. This was the time, *par excellence*, of the profiteer, the *mercanti*, who had grown rich on war contracts and was living well. Observing the general scene, Michel Corday believed that people had become even more resigned to the war than they were a year before. Another witness was struck by the 'orgy of luxury' in women's dresses and accessories that contrasted so sharply with the common wartime sobriety of costume. Never had the counters of the large drapery shops been so besieged as now by well-off women eager to buy the flimsiest, most delicate lace-edged garments. There was a craze too for the military look. Women affected airmen's hats, and brooches fashioned out of the Croix de Guerre, and had their sleeves embellished with imitations of wound stripes. Favourite colours for costumes and summer frocks were khaki, horizon blue, hospital blue. Sweets were packed in boxes simulating shells, grenades and trench helmets. Such costly fads and fancies were to lead to the luxury tax, introduced in April 1918.[32]

If this was but a minority indulgence amid the generally tightening austerity, it seemed that some Frenchmen at least were not longing for peace. Lunching in September with the eminent man of letters, sixty-three-year-old Anatole France, at his home near Tours, a wholesale clothier of that city asserted that the vast majority of his fellow-townsmen, both workmen and dealers, were happy to see the war go on, owing to the high wages and profits they were receiving. They were conditioned by the 'reactionary' press, whose line was 'war to the end'. In short, the speaker declared, it was only the men at the front who were pacifist.[33] But that autumn there was another, more sombre spirit abroad. France showed her deeper feelings on that Catholic anniversary, All Souls' Day, the solemn Day of the Dead. The occasion was marked by long processions marching, in grey November weather, to lay wreaths on the tombs of dead soldiers. Black-clad mourners filled the churches and cemeteries. Acknowledging the beauty behind the idea of the Day of the Dead, a writer questioned whether it was 'wise to allow the whole nation deliberately to plunge itself into a gulf of dark despair'.[34] But at the end of the year a political change was afoot that gave room for growing hope. In November Painlevé, France's latest Prime Minister and successor to Ribot, resigned to give place to Georges Clemenceau. None of Clémenceau's wartime predecessors – Viviani, Briand, Ribot, Painlevé – had had the grip or leadership necessary to command the nation's united support. But Clemenceau was a leader of a different calibre. In the political wilderness since 1914, and confined to denouncing national slackness and inefficiency through the columns of his papers, *L'Homme Libre* and *L'Homme Enchaîné*, he had, before becoming Premier, launched the much-overdue attack on the saboteurs and shirkers who had been hampering the war-effort almost unhindered. A merciless enemy of all anti-patriotic elements, fearing no party or faction, setting his face inflexibly against any thought of a negotiated peace, he now proceeded energetically with his campaign, liquidating the defeatist cliques, silencing the pessimists and doubters and renewing France's bruised and battered fighting spirit. His one aim was victory. 'Home policy? I wage war! Foreign policy? I wage war!' he bluntly stated. 'All the time I wage war!'

Like Painlevé, Clemenceau included no Socialists – the party that now made no secret of its wish to end the war and seek a negotiated peace – in his Government. He further showed his fighting determination by himself taking on the Ministry of War. The full effects of his leadership would appear when France faced her supreme test in 1918. Meanwhile Corday assessed the national attitude to the war as 1917 ended. While a minority wanted to treat the Russian armistice (currently concluded at Brest-Litovsk) as a peg on which to hang a general peace, the overwhelming majority, it seemed, were prepared to carry on while awaiting the arrival of American aid.[35] To President Poincaré the situation gave only the most limited grounds for optimism. Never, he commented in his journal, was the union of all Frenchmen so necessary. Since the beginning of the year there had been disputes between politicians, between generals, and even mutiny in the army. If the state of crisis continued, what would happen to France? Poincaré admitted that Clemenceau's accession to power – and the President had little liking for the new Prime Minister – had produced some recovery in national morale, but this was still incomplete. 'We are still in profound darkness,' he wrote. 'The year started in mist. It is ending in fog. No matter. Let us go on hoping all the same.'[36] But at Christmas-time in Paris there seemed as much gloom as hope. 'In many parishes,' recorded Louise Delétang, 'there was no midnight mass. The streets were badly lighted, the churches cold, and there was constant fear of the Zeppelins.'[37]

Chapter 13

GERMANY

The great run-down

GERMANY started the year 1917 with her hopes dashed by the Allies' uncompromising rejection of her peace approach. There was nothing for it but to continue the struggle. For the hard-pressed population there was the daunting prospect of persisting and increasing privation. Everything that made life tolerable was becoming desperately short – adequate clothing, heating, food. This was the time when, for lack of other nourishment, hungry stomachs had to put up with the humble turnip – the notorious 'turnip winter'. In Berlin's January cold the food queues lengthened. An observer noted that in a line of three hundred people, all showed the ravages of hunger. The facial skin of the younger women and children was drawn tight over their bones, their features were bloodless, their eyes sunken and their hair dull.[1] 'We are all growing thinner every day,' wrote Princess Blücher in January, 'and the rounded contours of the German nation have become a legend of the past. We are all gaunt and bony now . . . and our thoughts are chiefly taken up with wondering what our next meal will be, and dreaming of the good things that had once existed.'[2] A month later she commented: 'Now one sees faces like masks, blue with cold and drawn with hunger, with the harassed expression common to all those who are continually speculating as to the possibility of another meal.'[3] Not only was food scarce, but prices had risen disproportionately to wages. It was calculated that this winter, while wages had increased by fifteen points, food and other prices had mounted by sixty-seven points. It was now unusual to see a fat person: such individuals were even regarded with suspicion. In Berlin

an observer noted a stout lady being followed by a crowd of
jeering boys. For erstwhile fat people an unfortunate consequence of loss of weight was that their clothes hung on their
attenuated frames 'like sacks'.[4]

James Gerard noted in the New Year that everything pointed
to a coming food crisis, of a seriousness that even the authorities
could not gauge.[5] Another writer felt that the 'drama of the
battlefield' had changed to the 'drama of the larder'.[6] Potato
cards now had to be presented in hotels and restaurants, and
on two occasions in January angry Berliners stormed the city's
food markets. In the anxious quest for food, people were
becoming callous to the sufferings of others. In one food queue
a woman was seen to collapse, overcome with fatigue and grief
at the loss of her son, while the women standing around did
nothing to help her. One of the chief articles of meat now seen
in the butchers' shops was black crows. The country was faring
little better than the towns. Smuggling across the frontiers was
common, considerable quantities of food were being concealed,
and in some areas the police were regularly searching the
farms. 'At Krieblowitz,' reported Princess Blücher, 'we tried
now and again to kill one of our pigs, but it won't do as a rule.
There is none of the feasting and revelry which generally
accompany this solemn ceremony. The whole province of
Silesia watches the act with hungry faces, counting how many
mouthfuls we each appropriate for our own share, and Hindenburg stands sternly in the background, demanding a portion
of it for his munitioners, whilst we are deprived of our meat
tickets for weeks to come as a punishment for the few succulent
morsels we may manage to get . . . If we are lucky we are doled
out one egg every three weeks. Our bread is being "stretched"
in every way possible, and is now mixed with some of those
numerous subterranean vegetables coming under the rubric of
the turnip, of whose existence we never dreamed before.'[7]

It could, however, be said that no matter how grave Germany's food position became in the coming months, this alone
would not force her into defeat. The Germans, as one writer
said, were 'frugal, thrifty, patriotic'. A typical day's meals at

this time – if they could actually be obtained – were described as follows: breakfast, a cup or so of coffee substitute, or tea substitute without milk and with a minimum of sugar, together with one-third of the daily bread ration (about two-and-a-half ounces); lunch, a plate of soup with a slice of bread, two ounces of meat, two ounces of vegetables, a small pudding or cake and a cup of coffee substitute; afternoon tea, substitute coffee or tea, a half-ounce wheat-flour cake; dinner, no soup or pudding, but a modicum of meat and vegetables with a little cheese and the rest of the bread ration, possibly washed down with a glass of watery beer.[8] This might keep body and soul together for all but heavy workers, but the availability of many items was highly uncertain and everything had to be queued for. On the average, Germans were now reduced to one quarter of the meat they consumed before the war. While rich and poor alike were subject to the same rationing, for those with money there was a rampant black market which defied the price controls. To ease the feeding problem, mobile War Kitchens were soon introduced, which provided very palatable stews against ration coupons. These became unpopular because people thought the portions doled out were too meagre. And there was grumbling at the so-called favouritism by the women helpers. More successful were the People's Kitchens, which provided a greater variety and in which customers could sit and eat their meals in comparative comfort. In Berlin over 7,000 social workers were engaged in instructing women in the art of cooking without milk, eggs or fat, and ensuring that the children had their fair share of milk. But some at least of the food troubles were due to administrative incompetence. In April the bread allowance was reduced, causing a violent wave of protest and even strikes. The worried authorities thereupon promised the public additional meat in compensation, and despite the objections of farmers ordered all milch cows in certain districts to be slaughtered. As a result, for a week or so there was such a glut of meat that some had to be thrown away to prevent it spoiling in the warm weather. As a further consequence, milk ran short – to produce further grumbles from a populace already severely lacking in this commodity.

But as calamitous as the food shortage in the bleak New Year of 1917 (the start of a record cold spell that affected much of Europe) was the coal famine. Frenchmen too were suffering bitterly from lack of fuel, but they at least had more food than the Germans, an advantage that to some extent made up for empty hearths. The German coal crisis stemmed partly from the fact that in 1916 the Central States had exported some four million tons to neutral countries and occupied territories, in order to keep their industries operating.[9] Every ton of this was vitally needed at home, and though pressure on slender stocks had eased during the summer, no surplus had been built up. So, when winter came, the bunkers were almost empty. Belatedly, the Government introduced drastic economies. Industries not directly contributing to the war-effort were ordered to discontinue all night work and overtime. Shops, cafés, hotels and restaurants had to reduce their fuel consumption to one-third of normal. Shop-window lighting was virtually banned. Shops had to close at 7 p.m., and cafés and restaurants first at midnight, then at 11 o'clock. Hotel lights were put out at midnight, all unnecessary heating was prohibited, and their provision of hot water cut to two hours daily. In each corridor and at each stair-landing or lift-door one small bulb was allowed. For apartment houses (in which most Berliners lived) it was 'lights out' at 9 p.m. At nights the streets were gloomy with every other light extinguished. A strange sight for Berliners was the elephants from Hagenbeck's famous circus drawing the coal carts from the railway stations. Nevertheless, Berlin was less hard-hit than Munich, where all public buildings and theatres and cinemas were shut for lack of coal.

Coal, or its absence, became the topic of the moment. It 'seems suddenly to have disappeared from the face of the German Empire', commented Princess Blücher in February.[10] It was common to see groups of shivering, hungry Berliners picking their way through the snow-covered streets in the hopes of meeting a coal-lorry from which they could buy a score of briquettes, to ensure them a warm room for a day or so. Many disgruntled, coal-less people stayed in bed. At the Esplanade Hotel there was an untoward incident when some of the heating maintenance men refused to leave their beds, complaining that their food tickets had been taken for the guests, and refusing to get up until these were returned. Like frost-bound Paris, Berlin suffered an epidemic of burst water-pipes, with no plumbers to repair them. In the streets the snow lay un-disturbed, except when occasionally cleared by teams of schoolboys or women volunteers. Cars were hardly to be seen. Instead, a few ancient droshkies patrolled the roads, drawn by half-starved beasts that did not rise if once they fell. But for the people of Berlin there remained one means of combating cold and depression – the theatre, cinemas and music-halls. Through this dismal winter they were crowded. 'The Art world', said one observer, 'did yeomen service to keep the people from going insane'.[11] The theatres presented a remark-able repertoire. There were three houses continually playing Shakespeare, and others performed the plays of Oscar Wilde and Bernard Shaw. It was noticeable that no war plays were featured, though there was a taste for sombre and tragic drama. One popular piece was *Maria Magdalena*, portraying life in a small town, in which the mother died of apoplexy on the stage, a lover was killed in a duel, the rival lover committed suicide and the daughter jumped down a well. The curtain fell with only the old father and the cat alive.

But lack of food, coal, clothing and common amenities were only a symptom of the deeper malaise that was overtaking Germany in this third winter of the struggle. After some thirty months of total war, the mighty German machine was begin-ning slowly but surely to run down. Such was the pressure on the nation's manpower and material resources that its highly complex life could no longer be maintained at an effective level. It was a process that operated in widening circles. At its centre lay the growing failure in the railway communications system. The regular track-gangs had been depleted by mobilisation and replaced by less skilled Russian prisoners-of-war and even women. The track-servicing had deteriorated, resulting in a reduction in the speed of trains. Expresses had been discontinued on all except trunk routes (there were fewer expresses between Berlin and Vienna, and they were slower), ordinary passenger trains had been restricted to twenty miles an hour, half their normal speed, and freight trains to twelve miles an hour. This had severely diminished carrying capacity. The call-up had also affected rolling-stock maintenance. And through lack of grease for lubrication and oil for repainting, freight-cars had become dilapidated and weather-worn, their bearings rusted. Left unrepaired, they were discarded and replaced by new ones (wood being plentiful). Passenger-coaches suffered similarly. Their upkeep and cleaning was neglected, they lacked soap and towels and were often without water. Motive-power was involved too. Deprived of proper maintenance, engines leaked at every joint, with a loss of some 40% of efficiency. In cold weather, stations were muffled in escaping steam. Accidents and breakdowns increased alarmingly. Freight movement was seriously impeded, its volume reduced to one quarter of the normal. This led to wastage, notably in winter, when perishable foodstuffs might be held up and exposed to cold in transit. There were instances of train-loads of potatoes, frozen and rendered unfit for human consumption.[12]

Closely linked with the rail-communications decline was the coal shortage itself. The slender stocks – enough for some three weeks – available at the start of the winter had caused a heavy demand in industrial centres and large towns. Congestion on the ill-maintained lines from the coal mines had followed. The disruption had been increased by snow and frost, with the result that the coal had not got through. This had slowed down essential war-production as well as affecting the civilian population. One consequence in the towns was the reduction of electric tram services (their power being dependent on coal), which in any case were suffering from lack of manpower to keep the rolling-stock repaired. (New rolling-stock was scarce

as most of the manufacturers had turned over to war-production.) The communications-breakdown had extended to the
roads, whose untended macadam surfaces were potholed and
in rain became waterlogged. Thus a farmer conveying foodstuffs to the railhead could carry only a reduced load. He was,
moreover, short of draught animals (it was estimated that by
the end of 1916 half the horses on Central European farms had
been commandeered for the army). On the under-manned
farms themselves, tools and equipment were deteriorating
through neglect. And in town and country, buildings generally
were falling into disrepair through want of labour and maintenance materials like paint and varnish. In the industrial
field, partially-closed premises such as textile mills resulted in
abandoned plant and valuable machinery left to rust.[13]

So the tale of wasting assets and scarce, overstrained resources
spread and multiplied. On the basis of how the kingdom of
Saxony was affected, the writer, George Schreiner, calculated
the economic loss being suffered by Germany and Austria
together. This, he estimated, amounted to nearly 9,000 million
dollars (or about £1,900m.). Some fourteen million able-
bodied men, mobilised for war service, had been withdrawn
from their normal place in the economic sphere. Not only were
they consuming at a vast rate, but they were virtually non-
productive except for war purposes. To this non-production
could be added a massive deterioration of transport, industrial
and agricultural resources due to abandonment of repair and
upkeep. With no opportunity of effecting the customary
thorough maintenance, the Central States were now 'living
from hand to mouth'. 'Decay and rust', concluded Schreiner,
'had got the upper hand.'[14] The withdrawal of manpower from
normal productive and servicing activities was of course a
feature common to all the belligerents. What differentiated
Germany from Britain and France was the fact of the blockade
– the strangling Allied ring which forced her into an ever more
rigid self-sufficiency, without hope of renewal of supplies from
outside.

If the increasing shabbiness and hardship of life intensified the general depression, the enemy's tightening grip on Germany toughened the resolve of the stouter-hearted not to give in while the fighting men remained unbeaten. As one observer said, people cursed and sneered at the blockade in the same breath. A hint of success in the headlines would restore their flagging spirits, and then, standing wearily in the food queue, they would complain at the length of the war and rail at British treachery. But it was noticeable that there were no more cheers for troops marching through Berlin, bound for the front. And the troops trudged silently, no longer singing. Everywhere, the old enthusiasm and sense of heroic endeavour had gone for ever. It was a question now how long heavy burdened Germans would continue to accept the sacrifices asked of them before the underlying wish for peace became dangerously vocal.

But in February public despondency suddenly vanished under the impact of heartening news. On the 1st of that month Germany, launching the new and deadly weapon that had been reserved pending the outcome of her peace approach to the Allies, opened her unrestricted submarine campaign against the British. Most Germans hailed the move as the sure prelude to final victory. 'Hollow chests filled out again, heads were held erect,' wrote a contemporary.[15] British internees at Ruhleben, near Berlin, were informed by exultant guards that perfidious Britain was at last to receive the punishment she so richly deserved. The U-boats, they were told, would bring her to the verge of starvation, probably within six months. March brought further good tidings, with the Russian Revolution – signifying the withdrawal from the war of a powerful enemy, which would enable Germany to mass greater forces against the Allies in the west. Hardly had this news been absorbed when morale was rudely shaken by an equally momentous event, the entry, on the 6th April, of the United States into the war on the Allied side. But even if, on balance, Germans could take comfort from these happenings (the United States could not be militarily effective for many months), they still had little to feed on but hopes. And these could not satisfy stomachs that sadly lacked physical nourishment.

Meanwhile, as the Auxiliary Service Law began to take effect, Germans found themselves under ever more rigorous regimentation. Though the measure applied only to men, an intensified propaganda campaign was now mounted to recruit women and children into the programme. Germany's women, like those of Britain and France, had already shown their patriotic spirit by volunteering in their thousands for industrial and agricultural work, and a whole range of clerical and other tasks in which they could release men for the army or the most essential war employment. The most stalwart of them were driving heavy vans or labouring like navvies, with pick and shovel. Children too had been pressed into the war effort, notably to collect salvage. Sallying forth under a priest or teacher, parties of them would gather anything from which useful material could be extracted, from kitchen refuse to bottles and old rubber. And in the cause of food economy they would scour the country-side for nuts and berries. It was women's growing feeling that they, like the men, should be liable for national service that had encouraged the authorities to call upon them now in a more organised way. To muster them into appropriate work, a women Director – in each case a well-known feminist leader – had been appointed to each of the country's six army com-mands. Soon large numbers of these new volunteers were toiling in the munition factories, steel works and mines, performing almost every task hitherto reserved for men. In Germany the women's revolution had gone at least as far as in Britain or France.

But the 'Hindenburg programme', calculated as it was to squeeze the last ounce out of Germany's productive capacity, relied in the final resort on the human element – the continued and even greater efforts of the workers. And on the men in the arsenals, factories and mines the strain of war was now beginning to tell. After two-and-a-half years virtually free of industrial disturbance, the country was suddenly hit by a wave of strikes. The industrial truce between employers and workers agreed in 1914 was going the way of most truces, political as well as industrial, so solemnly sealed within the belligerent countries in the first days of the war. The German workers' endurance was faltering as a result of causes only too predictable: onerous working conditions, mounting privations and general war-weariness. Superficially at least, the situation was similar to that in France, which was suffering an almost simultaneous outbreak of labour trouble. But in France, whereas the physical hardships counted for less (the food position was not so desperate), there were factors at work that were not affecting Germany: intense despondency at the failure of the much-vaunted Nivelle offensive in April and the subversion of anti-war agitators. But whatever the causes, it seemed as if, in these two highly regulated countries, the accumulated stress of some thirty months' unrelieved war-effort must now find an outlet.

The first four months of the year saw strikes in the Ruhr, Berlin and elsewhere.[16] A basic pretext was the insufficiency of food. The Ruhr disturbances were so serious that the troops were called in. Here the workers were demanding that either they receive more food or that they be paid higher wages to obtain food on the black market. In the Ruhr coal mines a further cause was the temporary unemployment produced by the transport crisis. The reduction of the bread ration in mid-April provoked a wave of strikes in Berlin and Leipzig. On the 16th some 220,000 workers struck in the capital, staging huge non-violent demonstrations. After negotiations, they were promised an increase in the meat ration, on which most strikers returned to work. The Leipzig stoppages had a more political character, for besides demanding more food and coal the strikers called for a Government declaration stating, among other things, its readiness to conclude a peace without annexation. The strike quickly ended after a Government undertaking to raise wages and reduce the working week to fifty-two hours. Meanwhile more Berlin workers had struck, making claims similar to those of the Leipzig men. Only after their workplaces – two branches of the German Weapons and Munitions Factories – had been occupied by troops and the strikers ordered to return under pain of fines and imprisonment, did the stoppage end. There was more trouble in June, notably in the Rhur where, in the calls for peace and political reform, a new radical note was evident. July brought strikes in Düsseldorf and Upper Silesia, the latter resulting in losses of half-a-million tons of coal. A feature of the stoppage – unexpected in a regime so rigidly military as that of Germany – was that though courts-martial and heavy sentences for the ringleaders were used to break the strikes, the authorities stopped short of the death penalty.

An added irritant for workers, and civilians generally, was the housing difficulty.[17] The housing shortage, due to lack of new building and the wartime shifting of the population, had been steadily growing for over a year. More recently it had been aggravated by the repatriation of families from Britain and the colonies. Rooms were scarce even in small university towns, where the thousand or more students who lodged during college terms in peacetime had dwindled to a few hundred. To ease the problem, a census had been taken of all available accommodation and compulsory billeting introduced. This proved highly unpopular as it caused considerable disruption in apartments and houses which did not lend themselves to sub-division into separate living-units. Much inconvenience and annoyance ensued from different families having to use the same kitchen, scullery, cellar and even lavatory. In these cramped and crowded conditions, gossip, scandal and spying became rife, upsetting neighbourly relations. Billettees of lower social standing or different religious faith, or hailing from another part of the country, were resented by the people on whom they were lodged. In the smaller provincial centres the traditional friendly *Kaffeeklatsch* – the afternoon coffee party with friends – became the occasion for rumour-mongering and hostile tittle-tattle about newcomers. The officials of the Special Housing Board, responsible for billeting and requisitioning of rooms, had a thankless task. They had to make decisions that might arouse furious criticism, and were open to bribery and charges of favouritism.

These might be minor trials, but they counted in the realm

of morale. The very rich, too, had their troubles. They are reported to have been leading, at this stage of the war, 'a rather colourless life'.[18] Charity work no longer had great attractions. Bazaars were out of fashion because everyone had tired of them, and though it was possible to make money from concerts, teas and receptions, there was not much of use to be bought with the money. It was said, moreover, that with widespread Government control and everybody working hard, nobody needed much assistance. Such openings as there were for voluntary work, like superintending co-operative dining-rooms or centres where women and children could rest and warm themselves, required greater experience than most Society women felt they possessed. Even for the rich, travelling was now virtually impossible, not only owing to the state of the railways and scarcity of fuel, but on account of the pro-liferation of passes, visas, authorisations, and health and good conduct certificates needed. It was a mark of the German regime that wealth and position gave no exemption from these formalities: rich and poor were treated alike. Only officers and soldiers were immune.

With the coming of autumn and the darker nights, the short-ages and privations bore yet harder on the Home Front. Lighting presented a problem, for there was little gas or electricity, and even methylated spirit was scarce. In the Government's continuing search for metal, the churches were particular sufferers. Everywhere bells and organ pipes were being removed for melting into ammunition. In a small Silesian town where the three-hundred-year-old bell was requisitioned, the sorrowing townsfolk staged a funeral service for it before handing it over, covering the bell with flowers and wreaths and escorting it to the military headquarters in a procession headed by a priest. Owing to lack of oil, the cherished Sanctuary lamps in Catholic churches had to be extinguished. The plague of ration cards was, in one Berlin resident's words, bringing everyone 'to the verge of lunacy'. The scarcity of fodder threatened to drive horse-cabs off the Berlin streets. In one instance a cab-driver reported that he had been out for twenty-four hours without being able to find a scrap of food for his scraggy horse. Food was now such a sensitive matter that a policeman could stop a shabbily-dressed woman in the streets and insist on examining the parcel she was carrying, to see if it contained provisions. Even in the country it was almost impossible to obtain butter. The peasants had to hand a quota over to the military authorities, and if this was not produced the monthly sugar allowance was withheld. As the countrymen were eager to get the sugar for their jam-making, they would not sell their butter to would-be purchasers, even at an exorbitant price. In Berlin the shortages were such that in October no eggs, butter, coffee or tea was available at one of the capital's best hotels, though meat and various kinds of fish, including salted herrings, were to be had.[19]

In an attempt to fortify Germans against such conditions, the hate campaign had continued unabated. An instance of this was the speech of the Prussian general in command at Limburg, in occupied Belgium, in which he had declared early in the year that there was nothing like getting up in the morning after having passed the night in thoughts and dreams of hate.[20] Likewise, postcards showing Zeppelins in the act of murdering the sleeping babies of an enemy city were proudly circulated. The Americans as well as the British were targets for German venom – even before America's entry into the war. American correspondents in Berlin were forbidden to send out reports of such 'hate' speeches and articles. On an occasion in January one American reporter had had at least half the matter he was dispatching erased by the censor.[21] As for the State church, it could only endeavour to keep the spirit of hatred alive and offer Germans continued exhortations to fight on. War-weary citizens looking for some hint in favour of peace from a Protestant pulpit were doomed to disappointment. Even if individual pastors secretly approved the peace move initiated by the Pope in August, anti-Catholic hostility – let alone loyalty to the State or fear of higher authority – would prevent their publicly supporting it. ' "We hope for a good German peace from God, and not a bad international one from the Pope," was their war-cry at present,' commented Princess Blücher in October. Yet, according to the Princess, there was one small group of peace-minded pastors who at this time were courageously collecting signatures for a Peace Protest.[22]

Nothing more markedly demonstrated the nation's growing disillusion with the war than the waning popularity of the Kaiser. By the start of 1917 his reputation had slumped heavily. In the opinion of the Princess, people in England could hardly realise the covert scorn with which Germans were now speaking of him. 'Send him to the East where there are some prisoners to march past, and he will be pleased; and again to the West where there is a little success to show him, and he will be as pleased as ever,' was one remark she heard. 'In reality he is but a lay figure, crowned and clad in shining armour, and moved here and there at the will of the military power which he has created,' she commented.[23] And by July the Princess was reporting that the Kaiser was becoming more and more the shadow of a king, and that his abdication was being discussed as a possibility much to be desired. He was giving in to all the demands of the Socialists, she added, but at the same time making so many palpable blunders that a man in high office declared that it looked almost as if his counsellors were in the pay of England, so insane was their advice.[24]

But despite the mounting discouragement, the sporadic strikes and demonstrations, the mass of the people remained mutely at the service of their masters. Long conditioned by orders, controls, censorship and propaganda, they were not yet ready to repudiate the iron military regime under which they lived. If the Kaiser's prestige had declined, Hindenburg was still a revered and trusted figure who might yet lead their unbeaten armies to victory. 'Hindenburg has never yet deceived us; he will not deceive us now,' proclaimed the Leipzig *Nachrichten* in May. 'We shall fight and conquer with him. Only let us trust in our Hindenburg. Surely that is easy enough. Then our day must and will come, the day of Germany's splendour, the day of groaning and lamentation, and the gnashing of teeth and tearing of hair in London and Paris, in Rome and in Washington, in all the capitals of the accursed of God. Only our trust in our Hindenburg must be perfect.' In any case, all except the more perceptive minority had little alternative but to believe the blatant propaganda that (apart from the stories of soldiers returning home on leave) was their only source of information and opinion. But the success of the propaganda resulted less from its efficiency than from the people's isolation within the beleaguered fortress which Germany had become. Some of the material fed to them was anything but skilfully conceived. It was often full of contradictions and contortions. As an instance, when the food situation became acute early in 1917, the press correspondents were assembled by the Government and told that, however badly the Germans themselves might suffer, it must be emphasised that the privations of the British were ten times worse. This, however, was soon belied by the plentiful food parcels seen reaching the British internment camp at Ruhleben – to explain which, the authorities promptly gave out that the food was a bluff by the British, to conceal the fact that the country was on the brink of starvation.[25]

But there were some Germans, notably businessmen, who not only rejected the official propaganda line – on the matter of anti-British hate, for example – but were prepared to express themselves candidly. One such was Herr Dernburg, the well-known Berlin banker and industrialist, who in August 1916 had addressed a meeting at Libau, in Latvia, at which many German officers were present, urging a speedy economic agreement with England. 'I can understand that officers are enraged against England,' he said in closing, 'but we shall not go far with that. I know the English well; they are not so bad. Before all, there are economic reasons why we must reach a good understanding with England as soon as possible . . .' More significant, by 1917 even the highly regulated press was beginning to sound a note of restiveness and dissatisfaction at the conduct of the war. There was growing criticism of the leadership, a frank canvassing of peace possibilities, an open admission of food riots. 'The decision to remove from the occupied territories in France and Belgium all draught animals and all machinery and plant with the object of utilising them in Germany is a monstrous one,' declared the *Berliner Tageblatt* in May. 'We want no more of these draconian performances. The violation of personal rights perpetrated by the deportation of Belgian workmen to Germany was enough. The German masses are determined to tolerate no repetition of such scandals, and . . . the Government will find that the last word is, after all, with the common man on the land and in the street.' That same month the *Chemnitzer Volks-Stimme* wrote: 'Despite official contradictions, we are in a position to state that serious street disturbances occurred last week at Stuttgart, where food stores and public kitchens were pillaged by mobs of working people, who were driven to these excesses by hunger.' In May, too, the *Breslauer Volkswacht*, in pressing the Chancellor to reply to the peace urgings of the Social Democrats, said: 'If he fails to do so we shall most energetically demand his dismissal . . . The time has passed for bandying words. There must be an end to the horrible bath of blood, and obstacles to its removal must be destroyed wherever they may be found.' From the influential *Frankfurter Zeitung* came a plea for a reasonable peace, when it wrote in June: 'Two-thirds of the entire world have taken up arms against Germany. How long are we [to], how long could we, continue fighting all these forces; and if we did, what would be the gain? The conditions, in fact, are such that we ought to admit that any peace that would restore to us our territorial position, and would guarantee us our independence and our freedom of development, would be an honourable peace for Germany.'[26] The quotations could be multiplied. Such bold questionings would have been inconceivable in previous years. They were indications of a mood that would eventually gather strength to topple the German leadership.

While discontent simmered in the columns of the press, the Government was being shaken by a political crisis that destroyed the last vestiges of the truce of 1914. It turned on the vital issue of German leadership in the light of Germany's increasingly difficult war situation. Left-wing sentiment in favour of some kind of peace had been encouraged by the Russian Revolution in March, and the Peace Party considered that the time had come for renewing the overtures to the Allies that had met with failure the previous winter. Hindenburg, Ludendorff, and their High Command colleagues, intent on continuing the war, identified the Chancellor, Bethmann-Hollweg, with peace sympathies and now sought to get rid of him. Suspecting him of intriguing with the Socialists and Catholics to end the war on terms which nullified their military conquests, they managed to persuade the Kaiser to dismiss him. He was succeeded in July by a Wilhelmstrasse official, Georg Michaelis, a man more likely to serve the High Command's interests. But in order to avoid an open breach with the peace advocates in the Reichstag, Michaelis supported a Peace Resolution, presented there on the 19th July and carried – despite fierce opposition from the war-minded Junker Party – by 212 votes to 126. The resolution was in any case vague and ambiguous. It seemed to stand on German rights and make few clear concessions. Sponsoring it in the Reichstag, Michaelis said: 'If we make peace we must, in the first line, make sure that the frontiers of the German Empire are made secure for all time . . .'[27] The resolution made little impact abroad. Commenting on it, a historian has said: 'Germany had seemed to say to her enemies: I have tried to destroy you; I have failed; therefore let us be friends again!'[28] But the new Chancellor was not to remain in office long. His downfall, in November, stemmed from an event small in itself but, as a first straw in the wind, ominous for Germany; mutiny in the German Navy. Demoralised by inaction and resentful at other grievances, in July some sailors at Kiel staged hunger strikes and deserted ship. Unwisely, Michaelis charged certain Social Democrats with encouraging the trouble, and thus forfeited the confidence of the Reichstag. His successor was the elderly Count von Hertling, Minister President of Bavaria. The appointment satisfied all parties, and the High Command, too, saw in Hertling a President who would accept its direction. For the moment, Germany's political stability was restored; and, with peace agitation silenced, the nation's leaders prepared to fight on.

But, for the ordinary people, there were still forlorn hopes of peace, born of the Russian armistice signed in December. 'Christmas was, of course, but a sorry season,' recorded Princess Blücher, 'although the unexpected and seemingly successful peace movement in Russia undoubtedly created a brighter atmosphere for people here than they have known since the war began. Brest-Litovsk, mingled with the divine proclamation of "Peace upon earth and goodwill amongst men", moved our hearts to a new throb of hope.'[29] Meanwhile, winter brought a culmination of distress. 'One of the most terrible of our many sufferings was having to sit in the dark,' wrote a German after the war to a friend in England. 'It became dark at four in the winter. It was not light until eight o'clock. Even the children could not sleep all that time. One had to amuse them as best one could, fretful and pining as they were from under-feeding. And when they had gone to bed we were left shivering with the chill which comes from semi-starvation and which no additional clothing seems to alleviate.'[30]

Part Five

1918: THE FINAL EFFORT

Chapter 14

THE GENERAL SCENE

Approach to breaking-point

•

ON the defensive in the West during 1917, the Germans now marshalled all their forces in the series of massive Western assaults that were to be their last. On the 21st March they attacked the British with forty divisions on a fifty-mile front, advancing over forty miles in less than a week. They resumed the offensive in April, and on the 27th May mounted a heavy assault on the French, to reach the Marne less than forty miles from Paris three days later. Early in June they attacked again near Compiègne, winning further ground – and in July made one more effort that carried them across the Marne. This marked the peak of their advance. On 18th July the Allies counter-attacked, reinforced by nine American divisions. Under relentless assault the Germans now began to fall back, in a retirement that accelerated into a general retreat after the appearance on the battlefield of the new British armoured tanks on the 8th August. By mid-September they had been pushed back almost to their own frontiers; and from then on their fighting morale and powers of resistance steadily weakened as they faced inevitable defeat in the field.

With 1918 came the supreme and final effort of the belligerents. Such had been the inroads on their resources of manpower, materials, food, transport and other services – and indeed morale and fighting spirit – that a continuation of the struggle beyond another year had become impossible. With Russia out of the war and the various 'sideshows' (the campaigns on subsidiary fronts) being relatively unimportant, it was clear that now the war must be ultimately decided by an 'all-or-nothing' confrontation between Germany and the Allies on the Western Front. In a last desperate bid to gain victory, or avoid defeat, Germany would muster all her remaining strength. Britain and France, almost equally strained, would be saved the prospect of disaster only by the timely aid of their new ally, the United States. But even now, after three full years of trench warfare in which none of the great battles had achieved an appreciable breakthrough, the generals had evolved no new means of overcoming the stalemate: the technique would still mainly be the throwing of massed infantry, aided by heavy artillery, against barbed wire and machine-guns. To satisfy the voracious demands for fighting men, the three belligerents would call upon literally their last reserves.

On the Home Fronts, virtually every employable pair of hands not wanted to hold a rifle would be recruited to man the war-factories and replace the men called-up. To all three belligerents the fact that this was a total war, fought in the rear as well as on the battlefronts, would be inescapably apparent. This would be felt particularly in Germany, now brought to her knees by the Allied blockade. Not only was she near starvation and reduced to a miserable existence of ersatz makeshifts for clothing and so on, but with her transport and industrial system fatally impaired through lack of maintenance, repair and renewal, her whole life was grinding to a halt. And her people, so long rigorously regimented by their military masters, were now at the end of their tether and ripe for revolt. If Britain and France were less desperately affected, Britain's precarious food situation now necessitated strict rationing and she, like France – also undergoing food rationing – was nearing exhaustion. Fortunately for France, she had largely overcome the crisis of morale that had affected her in 1917, but the fortitude of Parisians was to be tested once more by the enemy's long-range bombardment of the capital, a three-months' ordeal that left no doubt that in this war the Home Front could be directly in the firing line. It would be Germany's plea, after her defeat in November, that the collapse of her own Home

Front had led to her defeat on the battlefield. It was indeed the fate of the German Home Front to break down under its unparalleled privations, while the British and French Home Front, subject to lesser hardships, managed to survive. But it is certain that quite independent of the German rear, the German Army was finally beaten in battle.

But at the start of the year, even while the three belligerents were marshalling their resources for a supreme effort, across the Atlantic thoughts were being directed towards the establishment of peace. In a historic address to Congress in January, President Wilson enumerated fourteen conditions of peace – the famous 'fourteen points' – which were to be the basis of the peace negotiations that took place after Germany's defeat in the following November. In September the President added five further points outlining the five permanent needs of peace. But before Germany sued for an armistice, American troops would have reached France in massive force and taken a decisive part in the final battles.

Chapter 15

BRITAIN

'We must fight to a finish'

In Britain the bleak New Year of 1918 opened with a day of national prayer. On January's first Sunday the churches were crowded, and at a service at St Paul's, attended by the Lord Mayor and Sheriffs and many wounded soldiers, the Bishop of London preached a sermon stressing the rightness of the nation entering the war in 1914. Preaching at Westminster Abbey, the Archbishop of Canterbury declared 'We persist and must persist in our task.'[1] But in some high quarters there were doubts about Britain's capacity to go on. Lord Riddell expressed his misgivings to Winston Churchill, Minister of Munitions. If the war continued for another year, Riddell declared, Britain might collapse in her effort to defeat Germany. She would be burdened with further colossal debt and have lost another million dead or wounded, in addition to losing much of her merchant shipping and trade. But Churchill saw things otherwise. 'We must fight to a finish,' he replied laconically. 'You never know when the Germans will crash.'[2]

If Churchill's view reflected the country's dogged mood, for civilians at this sombre time there were two main and immediate thoughts: coal and food. Both were becoming increasingly scarce, and queues for them were now a regular part of the scene. Coal had been rationed since October, at the weekly rate of 2 cwt for three to five rooms, 4 cwt for six to seven rooms, and 8 cwt for more than twelve rooms. With coalmen departed for the forces it was common in the poorer districts to meet perambulators or soapboxes serving as coal carts. The shortage was such that it was a punishable offence to waste cinders, and newspapers published recipes for making briquettes with

King George V and Queen Mary at Claremont Talbot's works, 1918

Women at work in a lens factory

Miss Mary Taylor recites *Feed the Guns*, Trafalgar Square, 1918

clay, coal-dust and tar as a cooking fuel. One woman without coal, it was recorded, drove around London with a laundry basket begging a few lumps from friends to make a fire for her sick mother. People with coke-burning boilers were fortunate: they could have baths, and the generous ones invited friends round to do likewise. In these coal-scarce days citizens evolved all kinds of water-heating devices and cooking-boxes, learning to cook in ways that economised both fuel and food.[3]

The food situation was now at its most serious. The various steps taken from August 1917 onwards to secure economies and fair distribution – the setting up of Food Commissioners and Food Control Committees, orders fixing maximum meat, butter, flour, potato and milk prices, a new scale of voluntary rations – had proved useful, but still the shortages persisted and the queues lengthened. In the poorer neighbourhoods of London and elsewhere the working women stood for hours outside the shabby small shops with their baskets, string bags and reticules of American cloth, patiently and even cheerfully waiting for a scrap of meat or a few vegetables. Middle-class housewives, now without servants, were queuing too. The queue problem had led to a further order in December requiring the registration of customers, the aim being to prevent any retailer accepting more customers than he could quickly and conveniently serve. And now, in January, the Food Ministry mounted a fresh economy campaign. Slogans appeared, enjoining: 'Eat Slowly. You Will Need Less Food', and 'Keep Warm. You Will Need Less Food.'[4] It became illegal to throw bread scraps to gulls on the Thames Embankment. That month a meat crisis developed. Unable to get supplies from local butchers, people crowded to Smithfield in the hope of a Sunday joint. Even here many stalls were empty. As substitutes, eggs were available at 3s. 6d. a dozen, and reasonably priced herrings and sprats. But rabbits, previously costing 4s. 9d., disappeared when their price was fixed at 2s. 9d. Nor did the queues diminish. Over January and February the London police counted 500,000 people standing in queues every Saturday.[5] As other shortages suddenly appeared, for margarine, tea, sugar, women would trek from shop to shop seeking supplies. With growing suspicions that the rich were getting more than their share, queuers began to show resentment. Sometimes, when full delivery-baskets were seen quietly leaving a tradesman's back door, protests arose and the baskets were looted. More serious, the poorer mothers and their children, unable to obtain enough basic necessities, were beginning to show signs of malnutrition.[6]

At the end of January Londoners found themselves subjected to two meatless days a week. But this just touched the fringe of the food emergency. There was now only one recourse: compulsory rationing of all main foodstuffs. One item – sugar – was already just rationed, after prolonged scarcity. (Robert Graves, married in January, had to save a month's sugar, along with butter, for his three-tiered wedding cake. Even then the cake had a plaster case of imitation icing.[7]) The general order came a month later, applying to London and the Home Counties; and a further order, early in April, brought in the rest of the country. Rationing covered butcher's meat and bacon, butter, margarine and lard. Two cards were issued to every registered consumer, one for meat and bacon, the other for the fats. They contained detachable coupons allowing for a weekly 15 ounces of meat, 5 ounces of bacon, and 4 ounces of fats, which could be used either for household purchases or meals in restaurants and cafés. Fixed meat prices when Londoners were rationed in February were: beef 1s. 10d. per lb, steak 2s. 2d., mutton or lamb 1s. 10d., chops 1s. 8d. per lb. The April rationing order came in none too soon, for by then meat was so scarce that some butchers were open for only one hour a day.[8] Hoarding attracted a £100 fine. In the London area the benefits of rationing – improving, as it did, food distribution in relation to known local demands – were immediately apparent. Queues almost disappeared. 'Not for months,' noted MacDonagh, 'has the housewife done her shopping in circumstances so agreeable to her requirements and purse.'[9] There was no room now for misplaced generosity. Probably everyone was acting like Arnold Bennett who, as he noted in February, had taken to asking guests who were invited to dinner to bring some food with them. The prevailing frugality was apparent even at that Mecca of lavish eating, the Mansion House. The first anniversary of the American entry into the war was celebrated by a luncheon there, attended by four hundred distinguished guests. No meat was served, and the fare – soup, fish, eggs, vegetables and fruit – was said to be the plainest ever offered. The final rationing step came in July, when the existing cards were withdrawn and national ration books distributed, containing coupons for all previously rationed foods. With milk restricted under a separate scheme, the only items remaining unrationed were tea, cheese and bread. All this was not achieved without the issue of a flood of regulations which 'drove those engaged in the food trade to despair'.[10] But by the end of July – thanks to rationing and to the fairly steady decrease in the sinkings of food ships bound for Britain – all fear of starvation by the German blockade was ended.

Under the urgency of the war-effort, many ordinary refinements of life had vanished for the duration. For men, elegance in dress was absolutely 'out', and well-worn shabbiness the accepted thing. If any young man had appeared in the West End in evening dress, as MacDonagh commented, he would have 'risked a jostling'.[11] And a general untidiness was creeping over the scene. Owing to lack of cleaners, roads were often unswept for days. One small improvement was the disappearance of dead matchsticks from streets and railway carriages. A dearth of matches was limiting users to some half-dozen a day, and whereas in 1914 they had cost 2d. a dozen boxes, now they were 2d. a box. In March lighting was banned in entertainment places and restaurants after 10.30 p.m. Along with the stringencies, there was a strong anti-waste drive. Waste paper collections in April reached 3,000 tons. Meanwhile food production was proceeding vigorously. At the start of April the King directed that the flowerbeds around the Queen Victoria Memorial outside Buckingham Palace were to be planted with vegetables instead of the customary scarlet geraniums. And this Eastertide saw extensive vegetable growing in the Royal Parks, Kew Gardens having two hundred acres under cultivation. On the suburban commons allotmenteers were out in force, furthering the movement that in the last months had taken in 3,000 additional acres. For Easter holiday-makers there were no extra trains, and some travellers had to wait all day before getting away. Hampstead Heath was bereft of its usual crowds – a sign of the sturdy response of many young munition workers to the call of Winston Churchill to carry on with war production.

But Easter 1918 was shadowed by fresh anxieties. In Flanders on the 21st March the Germans launched their great spring offensive. It was the start of their last tremendous bid to win the war, a gamble on which they were staking everything. Directed mainly against the British – the men of General Gough's Fifth Army – the assault was pressed with terrific weight, and when it slowed down ten days later the enemy had at one point broken the British front to advance forty miles. In Britain the course of the battle was followed with growing concern. Those hours in which the public read the terse but alarming reports of the German progress were among the tensest of the war. Saint-Quentin, the point of breakthrough, was a name on everybody's lips. The official explanations that the British retreat was according to plan brought little comfort. On the critical Sunday before Easter there was a rush to buy the papers containing an ominous despatch from Sir Douglas Haig. Hyde Park was thronged with people fearfully discussing the news. Crowds gathered outside Charing Cross to watch, and cheer, the lines of Red Cross ambulances with their freight of wounded from the front. At south coast towns the rumble of the guns was plainly heard, and on the high ground of Wimbledon one could perceive 'a curious atmospheric sensation – a kind of pulsation in regular beats . . . It was the guns,' recorded MacDonagh, 'the terrible cannonade of the Great Battle in France which was shaking the earth literally.'[12] And as the wounded poured back, contingents of men were being hurried to France, even from the training camps, to reinforce the depleted British lines.

In a desperate effort to raise more soldiers, Britain now made her most drastic call on her manpower. In mid-April Parliament hurriedly passed a Military Service Act conscripting men up to fifty-one years. Not only the fathers, but the grandfathers, were being summoned to take up arms. May brought an order calling up all men born in 1898 and 1899, regardless of the effect on industrial output. Next month the 1895 to 1897 classes were called, the sole exceptions being 'pivotal' shipbuilding and shale oil workers. So gravely was Field-Marshal Lord French, Commander-in-Chief, United Kingdom, viewing the position in April that he was making all necessary preparations to repel an invasion, and considering forming a compulsory militia for all men up to sixty years.[13] Meanwhile the urgent comb-out from industry had continued, and in June the Minister of Munitions reported that in six months 104,000 munitions workers had been released for military service. But now, as the British armies in Flanders faced supreme crisis and the need for throwing every available man into the battle became paramount, there was no alternative but to take yet more workers from industry. In the past the Government had always met opposition from the Unions in its attempts to conscript industrial workers. But whatever the Union's reasons for being reluctant to co-operate, now these were over-ridden in Labour's heartening response to the Government's call.

The Prime Minister, Lloyd George, had personal experience of this in the changed attitude of the Miners' Federation. Hitherto the Federation had stubbornly blocked the Government's request to take 50,000 young men from the mines. But in April, at the height of the emergency, he invited its leaders to Downing Street in a further effort to persuade them. He had had a map prepared showing the depth of the German advance and the number of enemy divisions facing the British. Before starting the discussion he invited them to study the map with him. They examined it 'with increasing gravity of mien', and when they sat down to talk it was clear that they would offer no more objections to the transfer of the miners. Robert Smillie, their hard-headed and uncompromising chairman, led his colleagues in agreeing to the Government's request. Later, when the comb-out had started, Lloyd George received worried calls from the Coal Controller, who reported protests from the miners – not because they were being conscripted but because they were being left in the mines while their comrades were being called. The Premier was further cheered by what he found on a tour of Scotland. Whereas on a visit there in 1917 he had met considerable unrest and some pacifist spirit among the workers, on a further trip in the spring of 1918 he encountered a totally transformed mood. In the streets and factories and at public meetings he saw 'a grim resolve imprinted on the faces of the people'. Pacifist talk was hardly heard and the operatives were working hard and uncomplainingly. At a Sunday service Lloyd George listened with grim approval to a sermon on the text: 'Gad [an Old Testament tribe], a troop shall overcome him; but he shall overcome at the last.'[14]

As spring passed into summer and the Germans pressed still farther westward, the crisis deepened. In mid-April, spirits at home were chilled by Haig's ominous orders to his troops: 'With our backs to the wall and believing in the justice of our cause, each one of us must fight to the end.' By the end of May the enemy reached the Marne. In mid-July they crossed it, threatening Paris once more as in the dangerous days of 1914. For Britain and France this was the climax of the war. With the United States Army not yet fully deployed on the continent, their fate depended on the outcome of the great battles raging in northern France. Meanwhile the British people went about their business in a mood of dour unexcited acceptance. The nation was stripped for war almost to the limits. But if every available man was now drawn into the war-machine, there was still a reservoir of women. A campaign was now mounted for more women volunteers. In April London saw a recruiting rally for the Women's Land Army, whose strength was already 260,000.[15] In May there was a big rally for female hospital workers. In June a 3,000-strong procession marched through London, representing all branches of women's war work. The parade of uniforms – from those of the para-military and nursing services to those of the bus conductorettes, the brown-smocked, gaitered Land Army girls with their cockaded hats, the brown-jacketed girl foresters in their bright green caps, the white-gowned munitionettes – made a colourful sight. Amid all this workmanlike garb, feminine dress had sustained one wartime casualty. An observer noted that there was not one petticoat to be seen. The demonstration showed a firm patriotic spirit. Commenting on the feminine attitude to the war at this time, one writer declared that the nation's working women were more determined to carry on the struggle than the working men. A meeting in June of the Women's Co-operative Guild at Bradford, at which a resolution advocating peace by negotiation was defeated, typified the general temper.[16] But though women were winning high praise for their war service and showing an unsuspected capacity for taking on and mastering men's jobs, they were still suffering from inequalities, even in highly professional spheres. For instance, women doctors in the RAMC received lower pay than their male colleagues and, whatever their seniority and qualifications, ranked below the latest-joined RAMC subalterns and took orders from them.[17]

But women were soon to gain their full reward for the sterling war services they were rendering. Already, at a Speaker's Conference sitting at the end of 1916, it had been decided that 'some measure of woman suffrage should be conferred'.[18] This was confirmed early in 1918 by the Representation of the People Bill, when a seven-to-one majority voted to accord the vote to women. And in November their political emancipation was completed by a Bill making them eligible, at the age of twenty-one, for election to Parliament. Even now the anomaly remained that women could not actually vote until they were thirty. But the long and strenuous fight had finally been won.

In the current atmosphere of threat and danger there was

a sudden burst of animosity against minorities that were not supporting – or were imagined to be actively hindering – Britain's total war-effort. There was a renewed witch-hunting of aliens, conscientious objectors and pacifists. In July, partly as a result of a reference by Lloyd George in the Commons to a number of anonymous, violently anti-German letters, there was a public outcry for the internment of all enemy aliens, whether naturalised or not. The press took up the call, and in view of the popular mood the existing regulations against aliens were drastically tightened. Steps were taken to revise exemptions from internment, to review naturalisation certificates issued during the war, to exclude enemy or neutral aliens from Government offices, and wind-up enemy banks. But the obsession with the 'enemy' in Britain's midst intensified, to reach the proportions of a mass-phobia. A hysterical 'Intern Them All' campaign was mounted, and in August, after a great supporting demonstration in Hyde Park, a monster petition containing over a million signatures was borne to Downing Street, escorted by bands and a great procession that included thousands of discharged servicemen. The hounding of conscientious objectors was no less savage. 'In general society', writes a contemporary, 'you could scarcely mention their existence, much less claim acquaintance with individual c.o.s, so great was the disgust and abhorrence.' There was a widespread social ostracism of objectors, even when they undertook civilian service. Their lives were made a burden to them, sometimes by their own families. The Home Secretary admitted in the Commons that thirteen conscientious objectors in prison and three in work centres had been certified as insane. Even suspected pacifist sympathies were liable to bring harsh penalties. There was the case of seventy-one-year-old Arnold Lupton, imprisoned for six months for having in his flat one hundred copies of a peace pamphlet proscribed by the authorities.[19]

London in these last months of the struggle had taken on a wartime look that seemed permanent. A *Times* article described it in May as a place of temporary government buildings as huge as balloons, with little low sheds filling in all the odd spaces. The streets were thronged with khaki, relieved here and there by the blue suits and red ties of the wounded. Among the once strange sights now grown familiar were the women window-cleaners in their peg-top trousers, the work-manlike VAD nurses and the agile conductorettes. Everything was difficult, from obtaining food to getting home at night in the murky darkness, unilluminated save for the probing searchlights. Another picture cites the great mansions in Mayfair, Belgravia and Bloomsbury, now passed into the temporary occupation of soldiers from the far ends of the earth. Mayfair had become the clubland of Dominions and United States troops, while the historic Norfolk House in St James's Square was given over to service-women from overseas. That summer there was a great run on the theatres. The public had money to spend and never was it in greater need of distraction. It was thus hard to get a seat at even the worst plays. War themes were popular, and in the spring a spy play featuring a pigeon, Pierrot, working for the French Intelligence, had drawn good houses. On Sunday, 4th August, the fourth anniversary of the war's outbreak, there was a service at St Margaret's, Westminster, attended by the King, the peers, and Members of Parliament. 'Many of the latter looked frail,' noted a writer, 'and seemed older, while the younger men were missing, and there were a good many members in khaki.'[20] As autumn set in it seemed, said another chronicler, as if the war would last until there were no more men left to fight. The streets were dark, as were people's clothes, for though mourning was now little worn, bright colours were rare and the shops stocked mostly black and grey materials. Fears of starvation were past, but food was still scarce, and so dear that only the rich could afford much more than the necessities.[21] Other prices too, for clothes and household goods, had risen, and there were further reductions in coal, gas and electricity supplies. For householders, bureaucracy had produced one more exercise, the filling of a form stating the number of rooms possessed, and other particulars. Regarding the nation's manpower and employment situation, one noteworthy sign of the times was that in September the rate of pauperism, at 122 per 10,000, was the lowest for the war.[22] Another sign, equally telling in its way, was adduced by Arnold Bennett. 'The sensual appeal', he noted in October, 'is now really very marked everywhere, in both speech and action, on the stage. Adultery everywhere pictured as desirable, and copulation generally ditto. Actresses play courtesan parts with gusto.'[23]

This continuing revolution – it was hardly less – in taste and morals showed how deeply war had eroded the old accepted standards. It was also a measure of the people's increasingly avid search for diversion from the war's drab and depressing realities. There was now no hiding the intense war-weariness affecting the country. It was seen in the growing industrial unrest that caused widespread strikes from July onwards.[24] Though ostensibly arising mostly from wage disputes, these betrayed a collective underlying mood of strained nerves and exhausted patience among workers who had toiled hard and long to serve the war-effort. (If labour now seemed to be exploiting the nation at its time of greatest crisis, in fact most of the strikes took place after the tide of battle had turned in France and the Allies were starting to push the enemy back. That historic moment was the 8th August, called by the enemy commander, General Ludendorff, 'the black day of the German Army'.) The first trouble came at the end of July with un-official strikes of 35,000 engineers in the Midlands, in protest against an 'Embargo Order' prohibiting the engagement of additional skilled labour without the sanction of the Ministry of Munitions. A general strike was avoided only when the Government threatened to conscript the strikers. Work was resumed on the 2nd August. Then, in mid-August, came a stoppage of 11,000 London tram and bus workers and their sympathisers, which secured a 5s. per week increase for women workers. On the 21st 150,000 Yorkshire miners struck over the wages of surfacemen. In September there were stoppages among cotton-spinners and railwaymen. But the most spec-tacular strike was that of the Metropolitan Police at the end of

August. On the night of the 30th some 14,000 London 'bobbies' stopped work. Their two main demands were an increase of pay (including their war bonus) and the recognition of their union, the National Union of Police and Prison Officers. Certainly during the war, London had never seen such an extraordinary occurrence. For nearly three days the huge metropolitan area from Barnet to Epsom and Dagenham to Staines was unprotected by its familiar blue-uniformed guardians of the law. While a deputation of leaders conferred with the Prime Minister, Downing Street was invaded by a good-tempered crowd of policemen. They sang songs to while away the time, fraternised with a lorry-load of troops whose rifles they held as the men dismounted. The police were granted their demands on condition that they returned at once to duty. Their absence from the London streets produced no sudden outbreak of crime. 'The strike has its place in social annals in that, at least, it afforded proof of London's ingrained respect for law and order,' recorded MacDonagh.[25]

It was only at this late stage of the war, when weariness was overtaking Allies and Germans alike, that the British Government was making full use of the propaganda weapon. Under the aegis of that dynamic young Canadian, Lord Beaverbrook, as Minister of Information, and the newspaper baron, Lord Northcliffe, as Director of Propaganda in Enemy Countries (both of them appointed in February), a powerful stream of propaganda was being aimed at Allies, neutrals and Germans. Notably as regards anti-German propaganda, it was strange that no systematic assault had been mounted before. Such a project had been proposed in 1915, but rejected on the grounds that the enemy might mistake it as a sign of weakness. Nevertheless, had this been undertaken early in the war it might, in the view of some authorities, have had valuable results. Now, from his Crewe House headquarters in Mayfair, Northcliffe was waging a psychological warfare campaign by leaflet that, judging from reports received later, was proving highly effective. He was aided by able men like Wickham Steed and H. G. Wells – a writer with idealistic aims for 'changing'

Germany – whose clearly written messages gave news sup-pressed by the German censor, included maps showing the Allies' progress and stressed the massive arrival of American troops in France. At the same time they offered hopes of a just peace for a 'democratised' Germany.[26] Bundles of the leaflets were attached to small balloons which were carried eastwards to Belgium, France and even into Germany. They were also dropped by plane. By October 167,000 a day were being re-leased over the enemy lines. Meanwhile Beaverbrook, housed in a hotel off the Strand, was directing American, French and neutral propaganda (Rudyard Kipling being in charge of the American, and Arnold Bennett of the French section). But Beaverbrook also had an interest in home propaganda – again, a field never previously concentrated on by the Government (the Press Bureau being restricted to a negative function of suppressing news that might be useful to the enemy) and left largely to the press and independent bodies. As a newspaper man, he had an acute sense of news presentation and he now, as he later put it, 'seized on the cinema', then the only medium of mass-entertainment. He used the news-reels for introducing propaganda, and was allowed by distributors to tag slogans to the end of films.[27] By these means was the enemy further discouraged and neutrals and the Home Front heartened in the war's closing months.

As if the affliction of four years' war were not enough, Britain and the other belligerents were struck in the latter part of 1918 by a plague of disease that, raging throughout the world, in a few months killed over seventy million people, more than the total casualties caused by war: the great 'Spanish Influenza' pandemic. In Britain the visitation started in mid-June, when some thirty people in Lancashire and Yorkshire suddenly died after a brief unidentified illness. Then in the last week of June, as the sickness spread to widely separated towns, the death-roll rose to over five hundred. The weekly toll of deaths steadily mounted, reaching its peak at the end of October, when the total was over 4,000. Everywhere in London and the provinces, in those autumn weeks, life was disrupted by this mysterious scourge. Hundreds of people succumbed daily, many collapsing in the streets. Schools, offices, cinemas and other places were closed, army camps were affected, telephone exchanges and postal services disorganised, police forces and fire brigades gravely reduced. Hospitals were so full that some had to stop admitting ordinary patients. Baffled doctors and medical staffs tried desperately and unsuccessfully to treat the deadly new virus, for which there was no known remedy. People wore masks in the streets, in some towns roads were sprinkled with disinfectants, queues formed outside chemists' shops for medicine. In London boroughs there was a house-to-house distribution of leaflets advising preventive measures. As the death-toll soared, the obituary columns of *The Times* swelled enormously with deaths attributed to 'pneumonia following influenza'. And in Woolwich harassed undertakers had to call in soldiers to help make coffins.[28] When the pandemic finally subsided in May 1919, the British death-toll was about 200,000. For many civilians, their resistance undermined by the prolonged strains and privations of the war, the onslaught of this new enemy was the last straw.

But with the passing of October, the end of the long struggle was in sight. As the German Army retreated eastwards under the relentless pressure of the British, French and Americans, the enemy leaders had seen the writing on the wall. An approach to President Wilson on the 4th October for an armistice (vitiated by the German sinking on the 10th of two passenger ships off the Irish coast) was rejected by the President in a stern, condemnatory Note containing proposals which the Germans themselves rejected. But now the picture of defeat was completed by widespread riot and revolution on the Home Front. There remained no alternative but to surrender. An armistice was requested, and signed at 5 a.m. on Monday, the 11th November. At 11 a.m. that day the fighting stopped. After four years, three months and seven days the guns were silenced at last and the war was over. Once again, as at 11 p.m. on 4th–5th August 1914, the booming chimes of London's Big Ben were the signal for a wild burst of jubilation. But whereas then the cheering was for war, now it was for peace. All over the country the striking of this eleventh hour, and in places the bursting of maroons, was greeted with joy and thankfulness. The people's long-endured tensions and anxieties suddenly vanished in the realisation of victory. In London the oft-described scenes of celebration on that grey, misty November day – with officers and privates fraternising, munitionettes drilling squads of officers and rankers, here a policeman inveigled into dancing on the pavement, taxis groaning under loads of flag-waving enthusiasts, the streets packed with delirious, arm-linked crowds, strangers spontaneously embracing – outdid the rejoicings of Mafeking night. It was a joyous junketing that marked, above all, the good-natured overthrow of all the authority, discipline and regulation that had pressed so heavily on the British people throughout the war years. When the carnival was over, tomorrow would be time enough to think about the forthcoming problems of peace.

Chapter 16

FRANCE

Ordeal surmounted

IT was providential for France that by the start of 1918 she had largely recovered her old fighting spirit. Otherwise she might never have been able to weather the supreme trials that faced her in this last year of the war. It is said that the time produces the man, and whereas in the case of Britain a dynamic leader in the person of Lloyd George had appeared late in 1916, it was only a year later – in the nick of time – that Georges Clemenceau had emerged to rally the nation for the final effort. As always throughout the war, while Britain was bearing a grievous enough burden of loss and privation, that of France was even more onerous. Once more she was to experience a menacing enemy drive across her devastated homeland towards Paris, an advance that would bring the Germans within forty miles of the capital – almost as close as in the darkest days of 1914. And for extra measure Paris had to undergo prolonged bombardment by 'Big Bertha' (an ordeal comparable to that suffered in the Second World War by London, under the 'V2' assault of 1945). But somehow the nation was to pull through, sustained by its indomitable Prime Minister, Clemenceau. In September, as the end of the war approached, a phrase frequently heard among the people was 'If Clemenceau says victory is in sight, it *is*.'[1]

But in the chill weeks of January, any prospect of victory seemed remote. As the front remained static under the cold of another bitter winter, Frenchmen at home were fully occupied in coping with their shortages and discomforts. As in Britain, these mostly concerned food and warmth. The winter had brought rationing of gas, electricity and coal. In most households the coal allowance went on cooking, so for heating purposes people had to rely on wood. But this was expensive, and hard to obtain owing to transport difficulties. In Paris many apartment-dwellers with central heating were left shivering when their landlords ran out of fuel. People were reduced to living in one room, with their overcoats on. Under increasing shortages, social life almost ceased. Citizens were fortunate to get an invitation from friends who happened to have a fire. For the less well-off, even clothing was now a problem. By the end of 1917 woollen fabrics had risen to prohibitive prices, and good serge or other cloth was unobtainable for less than some 30s. a yard. Linen and silk were also scarce, as were dyestuffs. To add to shopping inconveniences, the smallest coin, the sou, virtually disappeared, to be replaced by paper coupons which, as they passed from hand, became tattered and indecipherable. Then stamps were used, and as a means of giving change privately minted *jetons* were introduced.[2] Such small annoyances, it seems, were taken in good part by Parisians. But wherever people turned, there was little cause for cheer. Even the cinemas and theatres, to which they had flocked to find some warmth and comfort, were now in the name of economy closed four days a week. Nearly all the city's museums and galleries were shut, their pictures and other art treasures removed for safety. The only museum fully open was the Invalides, whose show of war trophies continued to draw crowds. Cars were virtually banned except for official purposes. Dancing was frowned on, and the British Ambassador in Paris, Lord Bertie of Thame, remarked what a pity it was that English people in Paris offended French feeling 'by going to houses where dancing takes place'.[3] With liquor sales restricted, cafés and restaurants shutting early and all but two bus routes suspended, the darkened streets were almost dead after 10 p.m. At night the dim blue lighting of the Paris tramways and Metro, it was noted, turned passengers to a ghastly hue, giving the painted street women 'the colour of rotting corpses'.[4] Railway stock was deteriorating, its broken doors and windows left unrepaired. As an air-raid precaution, train lights were turned off within twenty miles of Paris. The lighting situation was even worse in the provinces, where paraffin was unobtainable and people were using candles.

As to food, the story was one of continued shortage, restriction and soaring prices. For all but the well-off there was a still closer tightening of the belt. Milk, eggs and butter were scarce and expensive, and in Paris potatoes vanished from the shops for a fortnight after the fixing of a maximum price. A dearth of meat caused butchers to close three days a week and temporarily reduced restaurants to serving only vegetarian dishes. (In May municipal butchers' shops were to be opened in Paris, to reduce and regulate meat prices.[5]) For various reasons housewives would suddenly find themselves deprived of this item or that. Soft cheese, for instance, was banned, tinned food prices became exorbitant, loaf sugar disappeared (even other kinds being rare), and a shortage of macaroni and other pastas threatened to banish a staple dish. As a result of the severe frost, the worst scarcity was in vegetables; cauliflowers, carrots, turnips, cabbages fetched extravagant prices. The only food cheaper than in 1917 was game. It was said, with some truth, to be less expensive to eat in restaurants than at home, especially in view of the restaurants' added comforts of warmth and light. It certainly seemed true that because of the restaurants' disregard of the food regulations no customer with the money to spend needed to go short. This typified the contrast between France and Britain in the matter of wartime food control. While the multifarious regulations introduced in Britain, including the strict enforcement of maximum prices and rationing of all staple foods, ensured (generally speaking) fair shares for rich and poor alike, in France the rules and restrictions were never so stringent that they prevented the rich eating well. In addition, save for temporary emergencies, France's food situation remained less precarious throughout than that of Britain. But for the ordinary Frenchman, new limitations that were imposed from the end of January onwards meant further austerity.

On the 29th bread was rationed at 10 ounces per head

daily – the effect, it was said, of wheat shortages in Italy which had to be supplemented from French stocks. This was a blow to working people in town and country, who relied on this basic foodstuff and ate up to 2 lb a day. In Paris, for several days before, queues gathered at the bakeries to lay in stores (gone were the times when Frenchmen would eat only crisp, fresh-baked bread). There were brawls at Versailles among fiercely competing customers. The rationing order applied to hotels and restaurants as well as domestic consumers, and diners-out wanting bread had to surrender coupons. Soon after came a new decree to check 'superfluous consumption', which forbade, among other things, the serving to a customer, at a meal costing over six francs, of more than two dishes with or without vegetables and more than one bread roll.[6] (This was hardly more rigorous than previous orders.) But the diner could also command soup, hors-d'œuvres or oysters and dessert. There was also a further ban on luxury pastries, ices, chocolates and so on, which caused Lord Bertie of Thame to express satisfaction. The serving of such things 'was a scandal and ministered only to the well-to-do', he commented.[7] But 'superfluous consumption' did not appear to be altogether suppressed. In February a Paris publisher entertained guests to a luncheon consisting of: Goose sausage, *Bécasses* (woodcock) *flambées à la fine champagne, Baron de Pauillac* (beef) *à la purée de champignons, Truffes* (truffles) *en croûte, Langoustes en Bellevue, Salade Russe, Mont-Blanc* (a dessert), and three choice wines.[8]

For the average shopper the constant background to the food difficulties was the queue – for sugar, coal, petrol, chocolate, tobacco, milk, meat. Only rationing, as of bread and coal, dispensed with the endless lines. Troops on leave had a special privilege in the ranks of queuers. They could pass into shops without waiting, a right which tempted women to stop them in the street and ask them charmingly to go and find a kilo of chocolates or sugar. Food and the cost of living, in peacetime subjects only for family and domestic conversation, now became topics to be discussed on trams, in the streets, wherever people met. The papers were full of food items, featuring news of the markets and ingenious recipes for producing dishes from the commonest ingredients. Parisian housewives would eagerly follow these instructions and initiate their families into the novelties of potato-cake or boiled rice. The papers reiterated the need for economy. School children composed posters urging the public to economise, bearing such calls as: Don't Waste Bread'; 'Economise Bread by Eating Potatoes'; 'Eat Fish to Save our Livestock'; 'Split your Today's Sugar into Two to have some Tomorrow'. The press printed humorous cartoons on the food crisis, like that of the fat man running out of a restaurant, his napkin still under his chin. 'Where are you going?' a friend asks him. 'To another restaurant, to have my two dishes over again!' There were articles written by doctors claiming that meat-eating was unhealthy, and that it was preferable to exclude meat from one's diet and substitute vegetables. Efforts were made to show that war bread was superior to that of peacetime, its darker colour indicating less refinement and greater nourishment. There were regular appeals to substitute margarine for butter, condensed milk for the fresh variety and saccharine for sugar.[9]

To the various trials of Parisians were now added ordeal by air attack. There had been air-raids before, from August 1914 onwards, including two abortive Zeppelin assaults in 1915 and 1916. But their effect on the city had been slight. In January, however, the Germans launched their heaviest raid to date, using their large Gotha bombers. On the clear moonlit night of the 30th fifty Gothas flew over the city, dropping ninety-three bombs which caused damage and casualties. Next day the papers were clamouring for reprisals, while frightened citizens crowded the stations to get out of Paris. When Georges Clemenceau was informed of this he said sardonically: 'All the better! Paris will be easier to feed!' More raids followed in March, killing one hundred and twenty people, the forerunners of a dozen more, lasting through the summer. Paris now assumed the look of a city under fire. Air-raid precautions were intensified, with sandbags protecting important sites and monuments like the Arc de Triomphe and the Vendôme column, windows criss-crossed with paper strips, and communal shelters set up in every street. On the alarm people took to the shelters and cellars, remaining there until bells and bugle-notes signalled the all-clear. Cellar life became an institution. Parisians furnished their refuges with chairs, tables, even beds. New friendships were formed as cellar-occupiers invited inhabitants of higher floors down to share the shelter. More impressive, it was said, than the sound of falling bombs was the noise of the anti-aircraft barrage (whether this last was effective or not). But the most terrifying racket of all was the alarm, a strident cacophony of sirens and fire-engine horns. The public reaction to the raids was fairly stout-hearted. 'It was some time before the civilian allowed himself to admit he was frightened,' noted a participant. 'He was horribly oppressed by his own safety (compared with that of the men at the front), ashamed to go to his cellar, to have a fire and a roof and four walls. There were moments when he was ashamed of what he called his "wretched little raids".'[10]

Parisians had hardly got used to the Gotha raids when the enemy's great offensive started, causing fresh fears and misgivings. As the Germans drove forward in the fourth week of March, people studied their maps with grim memories of the perilous days of 1914. Anxiously they asked themselves how far the advance would penetrate, whether Paris would once more be endangered. But as if this were not enough, the Germans simultaneously struck them a second blow, aimed directly at civilian morale. From a battery of three extra long-range guns installed at Crépy-en-Laonnais, some seventy-five miles north-east of Paris, they began to shell the capital. Between the 23rd March and the 9th August, Parisians were to endure, in addition to their other troubles, forty-four nerve-shaking days of long-range bombardment.

The shelling began at 7.30 a.m. on Saturday the 23rd, just as the early crowds were hurrying to work. There was a shattering crash in a street in north-east Paris, followed soon after by three others in the Gare du Nord area. During the next hour there were four more explosions. There had been no alert. People looked apprehensively at the sky, but there was not a plane in sight. Nevertheless at 9.15 a.m. the air-raid sirens sounded – the first daytime alert for three years – stopping all traffic and sending everyone to shelters. In the Metro travellers dismounted from stationary trains and walked through the tunnels. Shops and cafés closed, streets were deserted. Throughout the morning there were further unexplained detonations, but after a longish pause, at 2.30 p.m. the all-clear rang out, bringing perplexed citizens out of their shelters to peer at the ugly craters in the Tuileries Gardens, the Place de la République (where two had been killed and nine wounded) and a score of other places. Paris uneasily resumed its normal life. Meanwhile the military authorities had been investigating the projectile fragments and decided they were from shells, not bombs. But as the nearest part of the enemy front was sixty-seven miles away, near the city of Laon, they were mystified as to how a gun could fire from such a distance. Concluding however that the shelling could only be from super long-range artillery and noting the rough line along which the shells had fallen, they pin-pointed the apparent source of the firing as a spot on the Crépy railway line near Laon. Urgent orders were given for a French railway battery to prepare for counter-bombardment. No more shells fell on Paris that day: during the morning twenty-five had landed, killing sixteen people, wounded twenty-nine and wrecking a few buildings. Not until next day, Sunday, did Parisians know what had really happened. They read a carefully censored version of the facts in *Le Matin* which, if it did not bring much comfort, at least disposed of the dangerous rumour that the enemy had broken through to within field-gun range of Paris.

This was the start of the capital's prolonged assault by shellfire. Carefully timed to coincide with the German spring offensive, it continued right through the period of the crucial battles in which the outcome of the war hung in the balance, ending only at the moment when the enemy fortunes began to turn. By then 181 shells had fallen on Paris, killing 256 and wounding 625 people. If the overall casualties and damage were comparatively small, occasionally there were horrifying incidents, like that of Good Friday, 26th March, when a shell landed on the church of Saint-Eglise, crowded with Easter worshippers, causing eighty-eight deaths. As to the effect on morale, this, according to Henry Bordeaux, was 'not what the Germans expected'. After the first shock, people went about much as usual, merely avoiding the most dangerous areas (the shells fell in a fairly well-defined line). 'Despite the dead, they laughed at [the gun] and called it *Baraboum*,'[11] he recorded. In the restaurants, diners showed a mixture of anxiety and brittle gaiety. But Bordeaux may have been underestimating the power of *Baraboum* as a terror weapon. If in the later stages Parisians bore the shelling with what another observer called 'fatalistic calm', at first, combined with the increasingly grave news from the front, it precipitated an exodus from Paris comparable with that of 1914. There was a general fear that the shelling heralded an immediate enemy advance on Paris. By the end of March Parisians were withdrawing their money from the banks and herding into the railway termini to escape southwards. It was said that the population of Orleans had trebled. By early April some 500,000 had left the capital, and many shops had closed. Soon, as the fighting in the north approached its crisis, the banks were sending their records and securities to safety, the Ministries disposing of their documents, and the British Embassy was arranging for the British colony to be evacuated if necessary by barge.[12] Even factories were being evacuated. For those who stayed, there were additional shelter precautions. Underground refuges with the label 'Abri' multiplied. Corday visited a 'model cellar' which contained a large, comfortably sprung divan, a table, tinned foods, a cooking stove, electric torches and alarm whistles.[13] In the streets there were more sandbags. The city's statues were protected by wooden superstructures. In May an underground theatre called 'L'Abri' was inaugurated. By now, school children had been evacuated. A cartoon showed a small boy about to leave Paris.

'That's good,' he cried. 'If it hadn't been for their guns, I'd
never have seen the sea!'[14] In June, after the Germans had
reached Villers-Cotterets, forty miles from the capital, Paris and
the Seine department were incorporated once more in the Zone
of the Armies.

The feelings of those who stayed on through the capital's
emergency were described by one of them: 'The German
advanced was terrifying. The worst days of 1914 seemed come
again, and this time we were four years more versed in war and
its horrors ... We saw an abyss ... before us. After four years
of heroism and endurance, of civilian patience, of tested faith in
victory, the solid ground beneath our feet threatened to fail ...
We never said so. People who remained in Paris kept their
flag flying ... When every day the Germans came nearer, we
held on; and when they came so near that we could no longer
blink the fact of their nearness, we held furtive consultations as
to what arrangements we could make if we had to walk out of
Paris at one gate while the Germans walked in at another.'[15]
Adding to the picture, Louise Delétang noted at Easter that
people were seen walking about the streets reading their
papers, 'as in the tragic hours of 1914'.[16]

But, as in Britain, the staying-power of some workers was
now wearing thin, eroded by war-weariness, a persisting sense
of grievance, and a strong revolutionary-pacifist streak. The
situation was bad enough in March for four cavalry divisions
to be held in the interior, to handle possible disorders. In that
month a strike at Saint-Etienne, in the Loire, was drastically
quelled by cavalry and gendarmes, with some casualties. The
young strikers were sent to the front and the wages of the older
ones raised.[17] In mid-May there was a strike at the Paris
Renault factory in which the workers protested against being
drafted to the army, the use of foreigners in the plant, the rejection of peace-offers made by the Central Powers in 1917. They
insisted, moreover, on the publication of France's war aims.
This was the demand of workers staging another strike at the
Citroën plant. The uncompromising attitude to strikes and
strikers in this last phase of the struggle reflected Clemenceau's

tiger-like determination to let nothing hamper the all-out waging of the war. It was said that, after meeting the strikers' delegates in May, he placed his car at their disposal, remarking: 'But I warn you, it is only going to Vincennes.'[18] (Vincennes was the fortress where traitors condemned to death were shot.) But if the left-wing extremists were still busy trying to undermine the war-effort, fire-eating right-wingers were also having their say. In October, to the anger of the trade-union leader, Merrheim, leaflets were circulated in the munitions factories declaring: 'People of France, your hatred is not as burning and passionate as it ought to be . . . Germany is a nation devoted to the Devil . . .'[19]

As a diversion from the momentous war news and their own drab or hazardous lives, civilians were regaled – and shocked – in these months with reports of the 'treason' trials that were the sequel to the defeatist purge of 1917. The trials continued through the spring and summer, bringing into the dock a strange assortment of characters and providing sensational disclosures of the internal danger that had been threatening France. There was the flamboyant Pasha Bolo, charged with receiving German funds to undermine the French war-effort and executed in April; the treacherous Pierre Lenoir, also in German pay; Duval, tried in April with four of his *Bonnet Rouge* colleagues and shot at Vincennes on the 17th July. As if to underline the perils to which his pacifist, pro-German propaganda had exposed the country, the enemy, mounting their third massive assault, had just crossed the Marne. In prison meanwhile was the ex-Premier Joseph Caillaux, arrested in January and finally to be tried in February 1920 for 'plotting against the security of the State abroad'. Malvy himself was arraigned before the High Court of the Senate in January, charged with a number of acts committed between 1914 and 1917 tending to favour the enemy's cause by inciting the troops to mutiny. An array of witnesses, from Ministers downwards, gave evidence for and against him. Political eulogies by Painlevé, Viviani and Briand were countered by testimony that laid bare a network of corruption and intrigue with Malvy apparently at the centre of it, even if he was not treasonably active himself. Finally, with the mutiny charge dropped, on the 31st July Malvy was found guilty on a number of only slightly lesser charges and sentenced to five years' banishment. Justice may have been done and much of the canker of complacency, defeatism and treachery that had been attacking the French war-effort rooted out; but in the process there had been an unsavoury and unprecedented washing of France's political dirty linen.

To offset these sordid revelations, Frenchmen now had the heartening knowledge that American troops were pouring into France. By the end of July twenty-seven divisions had arrived, and units were already in the battle-line.[20] In the Paris cinemas audiences were frantically applauding the figure of President Wilson on the screen. When he appeared they leapt cheering to their feet, while the orchestra played the American national anthem.[21] But in these summer weeks Parisians had little else to bring them comfort. They were still enduring air-raids and long-range shelling. Food continued to be a problem. Bread – now too often a doughy, dirty grey travesty of its former self – was so short in some districts that queues for it had to be controlled by the police. Indeed the food situation generally was, according to Corday, producing a 'return to the caveman'.[22] In every household, each member was jealously guarding his own rations of bread, sugar and the rest from other members. One novelty in the city's drab and dusty thoroughfares at this time was the renaming of streets after famous war figures: there was the Rue Guynemer (called after the young French air ace), Avenue Galliéni, Avenue du President Wilson, Avenue Georges V, Cours Albert I and many more.[23]

The 4th August, the beginning of the fifth year of war, came as a sober, solemn occasion, marked by public prayers in churches, chapels and synagogues. Within days, the prayers seemed to be answered by the momentous events occurring on the battlefront. But now, as the German Army started to fall back before the onslaught of the Allied forces led by their Supreme Commander, the Frenchman Marshal Ferdinand

Foch, and at last victory became a possibility, France was struck by the influenza pandemic.[24] For weeks all mention of it was rigorously censored, and it was not until the death by influenza of Clemenceau's son-in-law in mid-October that the scourge was mentioned in the press. By then some 1,200 people in Paris were dying of it each week, and it was taking a heavy toll all over France. In Paris, burials were being conducted as late as midnight, and funerals were so frequent that the undertakers' mutes remained at the cemeteries instead of accompanying the cortèges. But by then, too, the end of the war was clearly in sight. On the 27th October, three weeks after Germany had proposed an armistice, Austria sued for peace. Paris in these last weeks of the struggle was, as ever, a place of contrasts. Ravaged by a lethal infection, lined with queues for almost every food commodity, it was pervaded by a febrile gaiety which drew crowds to the theatres and music-halls to applaud and encore the frothiest of shows like the English review *Zig-Zag*, *The Queen of Joy*, *Faster and Faster*, *The Naked Truth* and *Pa-ri-ki-ri*, featuring the beloved Mistinguett at the Casino de Paris.[25] And always the public stood fascinated in front of the war maps, whose small flags shifted daily eastwards to indicate the Allied advance. In three months those flags had moved dramatically back to release from the enemy a vast segment of northern France; and finally, on the 11th November, they remained stationary along a line almost at France's north-east frontier. The war had ended.

On armistice morning the bells and cheers rang out all over France, in a celebration as wild and jubilant as that of Britain. At the War Ministry in Paris Clemenceau and Marshal Foch clasped each other in an emotional embrace. That night delirious crowds hauled the German guns from the Place de la Concorde, and at the War Ministry the Prime Minister was hailed by a huge concourse roaring 'Clemenceau!'. Once more, in victory, France was united; but it was a bitterly hard-won victory, whose cost for the nation would only now begin to be counted.

Chapter 17

GERMANY

Defeat and revolution

GERMANY entered the New Year with prospects that were dark indeed. Month by month the material weaknesses that were threatening to paralyse her war-industries and her whole economic life – breakdown on the railways, lack of coal, absence of oils and lubricants – were operating with an increasingly destructive chain-effect. In addition, her manpower resources were virtually exhausted, and the productive power of her workers themselves was gravely impaired by food shortage and other privations. Difficult as was the predicament of Britain and France as 1918 dawned, that of Germany was substantially worse. The fate that had seemed certain to overtake her once she had failed to achieve a quick victory now appeared inescapable.

Among the people, physical lethargy was breeding a mental despair. In these cheerless winter weeks they had little thought but for those two over-riding needs, food and peace. Peace had become a goal ever more wished-for but seemingly unattainable. As one Berliner said: 'We are like a man at the top of a steeple, whose ladder has fallen away, and who cannot get down despite all his suffering.' But the food situation looked even more hopeless. Germany was now a land stalked by hunger. For many Germans the main diet was very poor bread, swedes and – when they were available – potatoes. Meat supplies were negligible. The all-embracing ration tickets were often worthless, as the foods they authorised were not available. The most serious shortage was of fats, a lack particularly felt by the Germans, who liked fatty foods, and showing itself in a yellowish, unhealthy pallor of the face. Eggs, nominally costing 1s. each and obtainable only on doctor's orders, had almost disappeared. Vegetables, apples and pears were scarce and costly, a single cabbage fetching as much as 12s. Other fruit, like nuts and bananas, was hardly seen, while oranges and lemons were non-existent. A fashionable jeweller in Berlin, showing with a tired wave of the hand the glittering gems with which he was surrounded, said sourly to a companion: 'And yet I am hungry.' Poorer people had become cynical. An elderly guard at Ruhleben camp, watching a nearby 'victory' parade, said contemptuously: 'Bah, what's the use of that? Will it bring us any food?'[1] In January a typical meal provided by Berlin's renowned Adlon Hotel was one sardine, three thin slices of smoked salmon, soup that was little more than hot salty water, two small boiled potatoes and a substitute for 'corn-starch' pudding. There was no butter or sauces.

As spring came, growing numbers of Berlin restaurants were closing. Those remaining open had little to serve besides potatoes and swedes, accompanied by various tasteless substitute dishes. One familiar item was 'Gulasch', a stew containing mysterious and unidentified ingredients. There was also questionable sausage, largely composed of swedes, offal, horse-meat and even dog-meat. Soups were mostly of swede, onions were a rarity, and menus were innocent of fish, eggs and vegetables. Even salt was scarce, and the wines were new and vinegary. Fresh food controls had endeavoured to stop the rich enjoying black-market country supplies, but these were being evaded by the literally underground practice of fattening pigs, geese and rabbits in cellars and selling them at exorbitant prices. In May, Berlin's food scarcity was such that, according to Princess Blücher, even the capital's rare and admired kangaroos were slaughtered for meat.[2] In June, Berliners were limited to 1 lb of potatoes weekly, and often these were bad; while citizens of Munich now had little to eat but smoked meat and dried peas and beans. By August, the over-slaughtering of milch-cows had necessitated the introduction of meatless weeks.

It was now that the full physical effects of the blockade were beginning to be seen, even on the children. In earlier years it was mostly the adults who had suffered. This, as a medical officer at Chemnitz had written, was due to the self-sacrifice of the parents, and especially the mothers, in stinting themselves rather than their families. 'If one looks at the women,' he recorded, 'worn away to skin and bone, and with seamed and careworn faces, one knows where the portion of food assigned to them has really gone.' This opinion was confirmed by the Director of the Clinic for Children's Diseases at the Charité Hospital in Berlin. But by 1918 the picture had changed. The Chemnitz doctor now wrote of the children in his care: 'Thin and pale as corpses, they shoot up, mere skin and bone.'[3]

Hunger (if the worst) was only one part of the general hardship. In the accelerating run-down of the nation's resources, almost every normal activity and amenity was affected. With trains infrequent, slow, overcrowded and liable to break down, travelling was an ordeal. Berlin's public transport was in a parlous state. Buses had vanished, leaving a few ramshackle trams and a creaking, dilapidated underground service, both grossly overcrowded. The streets were almost bare of other traffic except official cars. Fuel shortage had reduced men to shaving with cold water, and the fat famine denied them shaving soap, the alternative being a dubious substitute that irritated the skin and stopped up the drains. Tobacco was almost unobtainable, and long queues formed outside tobacconists' shops for exiguous supplies. More and more shops were closing because they had nothing to sell. Chemists were almost without drugs, music shops had no strings for musical instruments and corset manufacture ceased through lack of suitable materials. Dentists were gravely short of gold and rubber, the lack of which latter material for tyres signalled the disappearance of the bicycle. Paper, cotton, leather and photographic supplies were among everyday commodities now almost unavailable.

By early summer the footwear and clothing situation was becoming disastrous. Good shoe-leather was virtually unknown, and many citizens were clattering about in wooden-soled clogs or sandals with cloth uppers. In Berlin it might be possible, by

bribing a shoemaker with a pound of butter or a few bottles o
wine, to buy shoes of passable leather for up to 150 marks, but
with a likely delay on delivery of six months. The alternative,
for which one had to queue for anything up to half a day, was an
inferior article of grey cloth and poor leather, for about 50
marks. There was a cheaper substitute, liable to disintegrate on
first wearing, of flimsy cotton-type material with a thin coat of
varnish. Clothing had grown so scarce that men were being
ordered to surrender their extra suits (two being the official
allowance). The poorer women had dispensed with stockings.
And to secure even the scant ration of sewing cotton meant,
for the patient housewife, a tedious queuing. Meanwhile
clothing prices had soared fantastically. A costume, jacket or
skirt of reasonable quality cost up to ten times the normal
figure.[4]

One beneficial effect of the fabrics shortage was a revival of
the rural skills of hand-spinning and weaving. Country people
were busy cultivating their patches of ground with flax, and
housewives were preparing the flax for spinning in the long
winter evenings ahead. From cottage cupboards, long-stored rolls
of home-spun linen were being unearthed, to be dyed and made
up into servicable dresses for the women and children. Many
villagers had taken to keeping a few sheep for the sake of their
wool, and the half-forgotten art of spinning wool into a coarse
worsted for such things as stockings was being re-learnt.
Indeed, except for lighting country-dwellers were now generally
better-off than townspeople. Their home-grown produce
afforded them more than enough food, and they could sell the
surplus at high prices. Their worst disadvantage, and this
applied specially to farmers, was the growing dilapidation of
buildings and equipment whose maintenance and repair was
impossible. Farmers were also grievously affected by the reduction of their stocks through lack of fodder, commandeering by
the military, and the slaughter of milch cows for meat. Owners
of the larger country estates could support themselves on their
own game, and if lucky could barter the excess to cottagers or
tradespeople for butter, sugar, eggs and so on.

Inflation was now widespread. Never had there been so much money about, but it was nearly all paper. Silver had been withdrawn the previous year, and notes were in circulation for as little as 1 mark (about 1s.). Gold had almost vanished, and to discourage hoarding the authorities were offering every soldier who gave up a 20-mark piece two days' leave plus the equivalent in paper money. The increased wages that were part of the upward spiral had brought the workers little satisfaction. With quantities of paper money in their hands, they soon found that they were no better off. A workman re-laying the cement floor at Ruhleben internment camp spoke bitterly about this to a British internee. 'It's true that I've got all this,' he said, pointing to a thick wad of notes, 'but what use is it to me? Could I really buy a good meal, even if I offered the whole lot?' He produced a small and unpalatable-looking piece of sausage and a lump of black bread, part of his wife's ration. The internee noted that under-nourishment had left the workman 'pitifully slow and uncertain'. He took three weeks to lay a small area of concrete, and to testify to the poor materials he was using, in a short time the flooring had crumbled.[5] The workers had other grievances too. There was mounting resentment against the war profiteer (*Kriegs-Gewinner*). Anyone wearing a fur coat or a specially well-made pair of boots was an immediate suspect, and liable to be followed and robbed, and made to walk home in his stockings. More serious was the prevalence of illicit trade, or black-marketing, by which the rich were obtaining advantages not open to the poor. This evidence that Germany's upper classes were evading the burdens being imposed on the people generally was most destructive of morale. Not only was it breeding anger against the rich and those who were doing well out of the war, but it was producing among the less privileged a weakening of their endurance and a feeling that the sacrifices they were being called upon to make were useless. The inevitable result was a breakdown of order and discipline – as shown by the increase in violent crime and thieving, especially of food, which now made it hazardous to walk alone in Berlin after dark.

In these anxious days Berliners, like the people of Paris, sought escape from their hardships in an avid search for pleasure. They crowded the handful of theatres still open (the Apollo, the State Opera House and one or two others), the cinemas and concert halls. Music indeed, from orchestras and bands, mostly manned by wounded soldiers, remained one of the few distractions still widely available – though now it was threatened by lack of strings for the instruments. Night clubs flourished, gambling was rife, and dancing, long banned, underwent a revival. Horse-racing and trotting were actually encouraged by the authorities, and photographs of it appeared in the press, to show the neutrals that Germany still enjoyed pre-war amusements. The round of diplomatic and official dinner parties continued, and in March, with a lavishness reminiscent of the famous Brussels ball held on the eve of Waterloo, Prince and Princess Blücher gave a great reception attended by one hundred and fifty distinguished guests. It was a brilliant affair, resplendent with jewels and multi-coloured uniforms, and the company was regaled with the richest foods from the Blücher country estate. The Spanish Ambassador murmured to Princess Blücher that he was sorry that the British Prime Minister was not there, 'for if he could see that supper-table he would know how nonsensical it was to talk of Germany being starved out'.[6] (The reactions of German workers, had they observed the groaning buffet, might have been different.) But even for the eminent guests, reality reasserted itself at the end of the party, when, for lack of droshkies and cars, they had to return home by tram and underground. Beyond the small orbit of Berlin's gaiety, the city at night was dead and deserted, for by 9.30 p.m. most citizens, under a self-imposed curfew, had retired to bed in apartments almost devoid of light and heat.

By day, under the spring sunshine of late March, Berlin could present a more cheerful sight. The snow and cold had gone, the streets were full of life and movement. But it still carried grim reminders of the war, with columns of marching troops, no longer singing, accompanied to their departure-station by groups of sad-looking women. And there were the streams of anxious relatives hurrying past the flower-sellers to the *Kriegs-ministerium* in the Dorotheen-strasse to read the latest casualty lists. On a more encouraging note, there were the newsboys shouting out the news of the German offensive. For now at last, in the massive assault launched at the end of March, there was cause for an uplift in the nation's wilting morale. The newspapers were already hailing the advance as a great victory, the whole city was beflagged and the bells were ringing. Elated Germans were talking of their armies reaching Calais. There was further rejoicing at the news of the long-range bombardment of Paris. To a despondent, war-weary nation it seemed that at last the tide was turning.

But there was no hiding the colossal effort that was being put forth to mount the offensive. In the previous months Luden-dorff, the army's Quartermaster General, had combed out men of almost every category who could hold a rifle or aim a machine-gun. There was now no ground of civilian indispensa-bility except essential war-production. The young men had long since vanished from the Berlin streets: now the middle-aged were rarely seen. Those not in war-factories were em-ployed behind the lines, thus relieving younger troops for front-line service. Even wounded soldiers and invalid civilians were caught in the net, being employed according to their abilities. A one-armed man, for instance, would be found a task that could be performed by a single arm.[7] It was noted at Ruhleben how the guards had steadily deteriorated throughout the war until in 1918 they were elderly men in civilian clothes carrying a rifle and side-arms. Germany was being bled white in a vast and final mustering of her manpower. And the comb-out for these last battalions would not itself have been possible if the country's normal economy had not been ruthlessly truncated, leaving men from the closed-down inessential industries available for the one thing that now mattered in Germany: the war-machine.

But (in human terms and apart from the now desperate question of material supplies) how long could the over-strained war-machine continue to function? Within the army itself, iron military discipline might retain its grip on the fighting men until they were actually faced with defeat in the field. But among the war-workers on the Home Front discipline must perforce be less easy to exercise. Though regulated and regimented to an unprecedented degree, they were still civilians, open to all kinds of influences, political and economic, from which the soldiers were immune. And their morale was being steadily undermined by physical privation, resentment at the inequality of sacrifice on the civilian front, and growing hopelessness as to the outcome of the war. More and more the cry was gaining ground, not for 'victory' but for 'peace and food'. In this atmosphere the industrial unrest that had erupted in 1917 broke out again with renewed force at the start of 1918.

In January, starting with random acts of sabotage, strikes occurred in Berlin, Hamburg, Essen, Leipzig and elsewhere. They affected most of the great munition factories, small-arms factories, car and locomotive works and Berlin's huge Allgemeine Elektricitats Werk. The number of workers who downed tools, 250,000 in Berlin alone, was enough to threaten the preparations for the coming offensive. In many places there was violence and rioting. To quell the trouble in Berlin, on the 1st February the city's Commandant, General von Kessell, put its seven biggest industrial plants under martial law and proclaimed a 'state of siege' for the capital. Though the strikes collapsed a few days later, they left a long aftermath of insecurity. It was significant that they now had a strong revolutionary tinge, as shown by the demands issued by the strikers' directorate in Berlin. These called for: alleviation of food restrictions; amnesty for political offenders; restoration of rights (for instance, of assembly) abolished under the state of war; democratisation of the Government; peace on the basis of 'no annexations and no indemnities; participation of workers' delegates at peace negotiations'.[8] An idea of the workers' grievances was later given by the Socialist politician Philipp Scheidemann (a future Prime Minister of the German Republic) who was involved in the disturbances in Berlin's working-class Moabit district. Scheidemann listed them as 'insufficient food, abolition of public meetings, impossibility of publishing complaints owing to

the censorship, and anxiety lest the war should continue indefinitely if the Government did not assume the most unequi-
vocal attitude towards peace negotiations'.[9]

The strikes were a shock for the Government and army
leaders. They came at a time when political rifts seemed to
have been healed and the parties were unanimously supporting
the High Command in the continuance of the war and putting
all their hopes in the success of Hindenburg's great offensive.
Now the nation's supreme bid for victory was seen to be
imperilled by stoppages that were not only affecting war
production but carried a disturbing hint of revolution. Even
the Socialists, aware of the potential dangers, viewed the situation with alarm. Though the strikes were hushed up as much
as possible and soon over, the presence of fifty policemen per-
manently stationed near Berlin's Brandenburger Tor in February betokened the Government's fear of further disorders. But
through this anxious spring and into the summer, as the crucial
battles raged in France and the German armies pressed on,
seemingly victorious, towards the Channel coast, an uneasy
peace prevailed in the nation's war-factories. The writing,
however, was on the wall. Nothing but the firm hope of early
victory for Germany could now hold the Home Front together.
Defeat, or delayed success, would precipitate a speedy collapse.

But even the spectacular gains of the German armies now
produced little enthusiasm. In May, the last days of which
brought the Germans to the Marne and the fall of Allied-held
Soissons, the public mood was apathetic. People declared themselves 'tired of suffering', saying that what they wanted was
food, and the return of their sons and husbands. The priests and
clergy were finding that fear was becoming a dominant emo-
tion. There was a reluctance to subscribe to the latest war loan,
though money was not lacking. Any kind of 'patriotism' was
now dead. Coupled with the apathy was a fierce resentment
against the industrialists who had grown rich out of the war.
And there was a bitter realisation of the fatal mistake made by
Germany in allowing America to enter the struggle. (The first
convoy of United States troops arrived in France in June.)

'Everyone is forced to admit', wrote Princess Blücher in May, 'that it is America that is now keeping on the war. How foolishly they laughed at the idea two years ago!'[10] After the start of the great Allied counter-offensive in mid-July she commented: 'People here may well look grave; the meaning of America is coming home to them at last. They comprehend now that it means an increase of the French reserves at the rate of 300,000 fresh, well-equipped men (i.e. Americans) per month, whilst Germany can bring up no fresh reserves.'[11]

The military tide, which seemed in the spring to be turning in Germany's favour, was now starting to sweep back against her. As August came, bringing what Ludendorff called that 'black day for Germany', the truth was starkly revealed. The German Army, now in retreat, had shot its bolt and the last great gamble seemed to have failed. The public sank into yet deeper depression, filled with one wish: to end the war. This vein of talk was heard on every street corner. In Berlin a shop-girl told an eminent German: 'We are going to stop the war now. Those in command have failed entirely . . .' More radical was a view heard in a crowded tram: 'It is high time for the Emperor to abdicate to bring about peace, and the sooner this is made clear to him the better.'[12] Worsening news from the front intensified the gloom. Attempts by the authorities to counter the general despondency only aroused the weary, under-fed population to anger. Hindenburg, it was reported, had forbidden anyone to speak of the situation in anything but optimistic terms. Meanwhile in one industrial area, the simmering restiveness of the workers had erupted into fresh trouble. In July, even before things had begun to go badly for the German Army, the miners in Upper Silesia had struck, less for political reasons than from sheer food shortage. They demanded that their working hours be cut to eight per day because they were physically unable to work longer owing to lack of food. The military authorities responded by proclaiming a 'major state of siege' and putting all the mine workers of the district under martial law. This had little effect on the angry, desperate miners, and the strike persisted into August.

By now the military situation was causing the German leaders deep anxiety. At a meeting of the Crown Council at Spa in mid-August, presided over by the Kaiser, Hindenburg reported that his armies could no longer hope to break the will of the Allies by military operations, and advocated a wearing down of the enemy by a 'strategic defensive'. But outside the council chamber efforts were made to play down the difficulties and present a less gloomy picture. The Foreign Secretary assured the Reichstag that the military position was not desperate, and the press continued to minimise the German reverses. But Germany now had not only the Allies' mounting military pressure to contend with: she was under assault from the massive propaganda offensive launched by Britain this summer. Leaflets were being showered over the German lines, and books, pamphlets and newspapers smuggled into the country through neutral channels, in a concerted campaign whose effectiveness was being admitted by commanders in the field and politicians at home. The press acknowledged the part played in the Allies' successes by this psychological warfare and lamented that there was nothing on the German side to compare with it. 'Had we shown the same activity in our propaganda,' declared the *Rheinische-Westfalische Zeitung*, 'perhaps many things would have been different now. But in this, we regret to say, we were absolutely unprepared.' Not only among the troops but throughout the Home Front the propaganda was sowing doubt and distrust. In the Bavarian Parliament the Bavarian War Minister spoke angrily of the 'wild and extravagant rumours' caused by it, and the *Berlin Lokalanzeiger* ranted that the German nervous system was being shattered by 'shameful and impudent lies'. In October a senior German officer was to report that what damaged the troops during their retreat was the 'paper war carried on by the enemy'.[13] Early in the war Hindenburg had said that the winners would be the side that possessed the better nerves. Now, in an Order dated 2nd September, he declared: 'Beside his war against us on the battlefield, the enemy has taken up arms against German morale, seeking to poison it . . . He is not satisfied with assailing our Front, but he must needs poison our home also. For he knows whence our real strength is drawn.'[14]

That 'strength' had been too long maintained and bolstered by lie and distortion. The psychological assault was now exposing to the Germans a reality that was frightening indeed. But even without it, no comforting euphemisms could any longer hide the truth of Germany's predicament. By the end of September the blows began to fall thick and fast on the Central Powers. The vaunted Western bulwark, the Hindenburg Line, was broken, in the Middle East Damascus fell, and Germany's ally, Bulgaria, surrendered. With Austria in dire straits and likely soon to collapse, the outlook for Germany was grave. The looming defeat of her armies signalled, for her leaders, the most far-reaching decisions. In order to facilitate the peace-approach to the Allies which now could not be much further delayed, it was necessary to make a show of democracy. This entailed the speedy ending of the autocratic military rule that had dominated the Reichstag and the life of the people. So, after a crucial meeting with political and military leaders on the 29th September, the Kaiser issued a momentous proclamation: 'I desire that men who are supported by the confidence of the people shall share in wide measure in the rights and duties of government . . .'[15] At the same time the Chancellor, Hertling, resigned, to be replaced by the liberal-minded Prince Max of Baden. On the 2nd October a representative of the High Command read to a meeting of Reichstag members an ominous report from his chiefs, which stated that Hindenburg and Ludendorff had decided to propose to the Kaiser that the war be ended. Next day the new Chancellor sent an armistice proposal to the President of the United States. Germany's struggle was virtually over.

News of the Chancellor's armistice approach sent a wave of relief and hope through Germany. In the streets people read their papers with a sudden rise of spirits. 'Peace smiles in the eyes of every little shopgirl in the baker's or grocer's shop as she hands you your loaf of coarse half-baked bread, or bag containing 100 grams of lard,' wrote Princess Blücher.[16] But even while the Note was being studied by the President, the Germans were wantonly prejudicing their case with the Allies. In France and Belgium the retreating troops were carrying out systematic deportation and destruction, and in the waters off the Irish coast two British passenger ships were sunk on the 10th October with the loss of over eight hundred lives. Thus on the 14th the American President rejected the Note in a cold reply which concluded: 'The nations associated against Germany cannot be expected to agree to a cessation of arms while acts of inhumanity, spoliation and desolation are being continued which they justly look upon with horror and with burning hearts.'[17] The shattering of their peace hopes plunged the people into renewed gloom and depression. In a general atmosphere of uncertainty and alarm, wild rumours circulated. With Berlin in a state of mounting unrest, armed and mounted police patrolled the streets. On the 23rd they made ready to protect the Admiralty from an anticipated mass demonstration against submarine warfare. That night excited crowds hailed the Socialist Karl Liebknecht, released after two years in prison, as he drove past the Reichstag in a flower-decked carriage en route to the Russian Embassy. Each day brought fresh signs of demoralisation, growing threats of disorder, as the long-suffering Germans finally threw off the bonds of discipline in a wholesale repudiation of the war.

At the centre of the crumbling regime stood the Kaiser – now a pathetic figure. His waning prestige had been evident in January, when malcontents had been distributing leaflets in Berlin's back streets proclaiming 'Down with the Kaiser: Down with the Government!' The police, it was said, refused to arrest the offenders, being allegedly in sympathy with them. 'Now that his time has come,' wrote Princess Blücher, in mid-October, 'one pities him. Why has he not already abdicated, instead of waiting until he's forced to go? Children in the street were now taking up the cry "The Kaiser must go", and on an autumn Sunday he was seen walking through the Tiergarten, "a white-haired broken man".'[18] When his abdication finally came, early in November, it marked the death-knell of the old Imperial Germany.

Events were now moving with gathering speed. On the 26th October Ludendorff resigned, allegedly having suffered a nervous breakdown. Next day Austria sued for peace; and this same day the German Government sent a Note to President Wilson (its fourth in the month) carrying the fateful words: 'The German Government now awaits proposals for an armistice which shall lead towards that peace of justice the President has outlined in his proclamations.'[19] But before the armistice was signed, Germany was to erupt in violence, riot and revolution, the gigantic protest and upheaval of a powerful nation in defeat, starved, spent and broken by the intolerable pressures of total war and turning – soldiers, sailors and civilians alike – against the rulers who had led it into disaster.

The final collapse was heralded early in November by mutiny among the sailors at Kiel, in protest against an Admiralty order for the fleet to put to sea. The demoralised crews, seeing this as a useless gesture to avoid surrender to the Allies, rebelled. They were joined by garrison troops and dock labourers. While the Social Democrat, Gustav Noske, was attempting on the Government's behalf to quell the trouble at Kiel, revolt spread swiftly to Lübeck, Hamburg, Cuxhaven, and Bremen. By the 8th there was rioting at Cologne, Düsseldorf, Coblenz and Mainz. In emulation of the Russian revolutionaries' example, local soldiers' councils were set up. The mounting disarray was increased by army deserters streaming back from the front. Meanwhile Berlin was in a state of upheaval with parades, processions and demonstrations in which the workers marched with soldiers. With order everywhere breaking down, Germany was rapidly sliding into chaos. On the 9th, as a means of saving the country from wholesale bloodshed and civil war, the Chancellor took upon himself to announce the Kaiser's renunciation of the throne. At the same time he proclaimed the intention to appoint a Regency, the proposed nomination of the Socialist Deputy Friedrich Ebert as Chancellor, and the introduction of a Bill authorising a general election. In Berlin the news of the Kaiser's abdication brought wild rejoicing. Red banners flew from rooftops in place of the black, white and red flag of the Hohenzollerns, and crowds of soldiers, sailors, men, women and children packed the streets, interspersed with lorry-loads of cheering, flag-waving servicemen. Here and there sporadic shooting and violence broke out as officers were attacked and their insignia wrenched off. But on the whole the tumultuous scenes in Berlin on this day of revolution almost suggested some famous victory rather than the culmination of Germany's defeat. Indeed, for the sore-tried German masses, it was victory of a kind.

But if they had triumphantly got rid of their military over-lords, the hard terms of the armistice signed two days later – and particularly that which decreed the continuance of the blockade – brought home to the German people the full bitterness of defeat. They were a nation brought to the verge of dissolution, drained of material resources, energy, pride and hope. What-ever Government now led them, it would be long before they could recover from the ravages wrought by these four years of total war.

Epilogue

THE COST AND THE CONSEQUENCES

W HEN the echo from the last shot had died and the dust from the explosion of the last shell had settled, all three belligerents – victors and vanquished alike – had one sentiment in common; immense relief that here at last was peace. But even for the victors, any sense of triumph was modified by realisation of the appalling cost of the war, not only as regards material wealth but above all in terms of human lives. In Britain, France and Germany, the best of a whole generation had been wiped out. The British dead (Great Britain and Ireland) numbered 744,000, the French 1,385,000, the German 2,300,000. In addition to these were the millions of wounded. The losses in dead meant incalculable impoverishment of the belligerents' national strength to the detriment of leadership, energy, initiative and working skill. The impoverishment would be perpetuated in future generations. This, among all the other debits, was the most grievous price imposed by the war.

But if the war far outdid all previous wars in the scale of its casualties, it also made history in other respects. It was the first 'total' war, the first conflict in which the belligerents devoted virtually their entire energies and resources, industrial, financial and psychological, to war-making. With the State assuming unprecedented powers and subordinating every national activity to prosecuting the war, the civilian populations had become almost as important as the soldiers. To supply the weapons of war and sustain the fighting forces, they had been regimented and mobilised to an unparalleled extent, their lives had been rigorously regulated and their traditional freedoms ruthlessly curtailed. This was especially noticeable in Britain, whose citizens were subjected to the unheard-of restrictions of DORA and for the first time underwent military conscription. And as an indication that civilians in the rear were no longer immune from the physical dangers of war, they had suffered aerial bombing (an innovation made possible by the development of the new weapon of war, the aeroplane) and even long-range bombardment. There was no longer, as of old, just a fighting front where the armies clashed and contended: there was now – and in this war the phrase was used for the first time – a Home Front.

In one way and another, the whole nation was involved in the struggle. Nevertheless, among all three belligerents the fact had emerged that, however closely identified with the war-effort and whatever sacrifices they were called upon to make, the civilians remained separated, indeed almost alienated, from the fighting men. This was to some degree inevitable. Civilians at home could not be expected to realise fully the horrors of actual battle and front-line conditions. The more self-centred of them were more concerned with their own day-to-day hardships and discomforts (including the relatively minor perils from bomb and shell) than with the ordeals of the fighting men. And there was another side to this picture of alienation. For the soldiers returning on leave the life of the civilian, drab though it was, seemed with all its ordinary civilised amenities to be sheer peacetime luxury compared with his own miserable existence in the trenches. This, together with the obvious inequalities of sacrifice as between soldier and civilian (for instance, as regards the enormous contrast in the soldier's and the civilian war-worker's pay), left the fighting man with the impression that he was bearing more than his fair share of the common burden.

Another factor in this divisiveness between civilian and soldier was the censorship and propaganda that were extensively employed by all three belligerents. Soldiers returning from the front found civilians entertaining a totally different picture of the war from what they themselves were experiencing. And civilians, on their side, were disappointed to discover that what they read in the papers about resounding successes did not tally with the soldiers' stories. Indeed, as the war progressed, it became clear that, as preservers and promoters of morale, censorship and propaganda had their limits of effectiveness. Censorship could not forever continue to conceal the truth and stifle criticism, and optimistic propaganda, unless backed by actual military achievement that appeared to have a decisive effect on the course of the war, sooner or later backfired. What the French called *bourrage de crâne* (eyewash) served only to produce cynicism and in the long run hinder rather than help the war-effort.

What did become plain was that the single most important element in maintaining civilian morale was sufficiency of food. The most glittering military successes counted for little against an unsatisfied stomach. Second only to food was warmth. The lack of these two basic needs (besides obviously impairing the physical vitality and productive power of the workers) sapped, like nothing else, the spirit and the will to carry on. This was seen most clearly in Germany, whose civilians suffered immeasurably worse from hunger and fuel shortage than Britons and Frenchmen. But to offset the effect of these deficiencies on the Germans was the potent factor of national character and tradition. More than the British or French, the Germans were a people conditioned by obedience and discipline. Thus they were able to endure extreme privation longer than either the French or British might have been able to do, though when their collapse finally came it was all the more catastrophic. France was fortunate in that her crisis of morale, caused by war-weariness and defeatist influences rather than physical stringency, came in 1917 and not in the year of supreme effort. The British people, less closely and directly involved in the war than the French, though brought near to starvation by the U-boat campaign of 1917, managed by a certain equability of national character to retain their fighting morale without any obvious breakdown.

For the civilians who had striven for over four years to further the war-efforts on the Home Fronts, as for the soldiers who came back, there was, at the best, disillusion, and at the worst, despair. In Germany, aflame with revolution and still subject to the blockade, blank misery prevailed. France, left with huge areas of war-devastated territory and exhausted by losses that were relatively the greatest among the three belligerents, mourned her dead and thought of little but obtaining reparations and ensuring her future security. Britain, a land that was, in the words of Lloyd George, to be 'fit for heroes', fell after a brief period of boom into economic crisis and political and labour troubles. Everywhere there was a revulsion against war, and at the same time a loss of confidence in things human and divine. Established moral values and old ideals and beliefs continued in the state of flux into which the war had cast them. But against the many adverse legacies of the world conflict, its enormous waste and destructiveness, certain benefits could be counted. Necessity being the mother of invention, the four years of total war had produced advances in the technological, scientific and industrial fields, that otherwise would have taken decades to attain. And in the social sphere, women had by their services during the war thrown off their age-old shackles of inferiority and gained a new and respected status. Moreover, in Britain at least, the old rigid class distinctions had become blurred, many working people had achieved a higher living-standard, and the power of the trade unions had been strengthened. British war-administration, though it had resulted in a hugely-swollen bureaucracy, had at least learnt lessons that would be valuable in the event of another war. But this conflict of 1914 to 1918 was supposed to be the 'war to end war'. What was certain was that if, despite everything, world war broke out again, it would be a struggle in which the civilians would be even more closely involved. *Hindsight*

REFERENCES

PROLOGUE

1. The two main European power groupings were the Triple Entente (Britain, France and Russia) and the Triple Alliance (Germany, Austria-Hungary and Italy).

2. Lloyd George, Rt. Hon. D. *War Memoirs*, Vol. 1 (n.d.). p. 33.

3. *The Great War*, ed. by H. W. Wilson and J. A. Hammerton, Vol. 1 (1914). p. 80.

4. Britain was party to the Treaty of London, 1839, which guaranteed the neutrality of Belgium.

CHAPTER I

1. Blücher, Princess. *An English Wife in Berlin* (1920). p. 7.

2. Pankhurst, E. S. *The Home Front* (1932). p. 37.

3. Playne, C. E. *Society at War, 1914–1916* (1931). p. 192.

4. Op. cit. p. 294.

5. Op. cit. p. 295.

6. Sharp, W. G. *War Memoirs, 1914–19* (1931). p. 40.

7. Blücher. p. 24.

8. *The Great War*, Vol. 4 (1915). pp. 307–8.

9. Strong, R. *The Diary of an Englishman Resident in France during War Time*. Vol. 2 (1916). p. 7.

10. Bullitt, E. D. *An Uncensored Diary from the Central Empires* (1918). pp. 152–3.

11. Blücher. p. 9.

CHAPTER 2

1. *The Great War*, Vol. 4 (1915). p. 164.

2. Op. cit. p. 314.

3. Op. cit. p. 315.

4. Strong, Vol. 2. p. 309.

CHAPTER 3

1. Riddell, Lord. *War Diary, 1914–1918* (1933). p. 138.

2. *The Great War*, Vol. 4. pp. 312, 314.

3. Lloyd George, Vol. 1 (n.d.). p. 181.

4. Pankhurst. p. 206.

5. Dearle, N. B. *An Economic Chronicle . . . of the War for Great Britain and Ireland* (1929). p. 66.

6. Sandhurst, Lord. *From Day to Day, 1914–15* (1918). p. 199.

7. MacDonagh, M. *In London during the Great War* (1935). pp. 79–80.

8. Op. cit. p. 55.

9. Pankhurst. p. 207.

10. Peel, Mrs C. S. *How We Lived Then: 1914–1918* (1929). p. 114.

11. Pankhurst. p. 278.

12. Op. cit. p. 267.

13. *The Great War*, Vol. 9 (1917). pp. 399–400.

14. Peel. p. 60.

15. Sandhurst. p. 176.

16. Pankhurst. pp. 175–6.

17. Lloyd George, Vol. 1. p. 193.

18. Op. cit. p. 194.

19. Bertie of Thame, Lord. *The Diary of, 1914–1918*, Vol. 1. (1926). p. 244.

20. Op. cit. p. 256.

21. *Annual Register*, 1915 (1916). p. 13.

22. Davray, H. D. *Through French Eyes: Britain's Effort* (1916). p. 115.

23. *Annual Register*, 1915. p. 36.

24. Graves, Robert. *Goodbye to All That: an Autobiography* (1929). pp. 187–8.

25. MacDonagh. p. 89.

26. Op. cit. p. 90.

27. Playne, Vol. 1. p. 276.

28· MacDonagh. p. 91.

CHAPTER 4

1. Galli, H. *La Guerre à Paris, 1917* (1917). pp. 421–2.

2. Fontaine, A. *French Industry during the War* (1932). p. 26.

3. Op. cit. p. 18.

4. Bordeaux, H. *Histoire d'une vie*, Vol. 5 (1959). p. 125.

5. Poincaré, R. *Au Service de la France, 1914–1918*, Vol. 6 (1930). p. 265.

6. Corday, M. *The Paris Front* (1933). p. 55.

7. An interesting exhibit, presented by President Poincaré in April, was a 'dud' shell bearing the inscription 'An Easter egg for M. Poincaré', fired by the Germans at a spot on the Belgian coast to coincide with a visit there by the President.

8. Bertie, Vol. 1 (1926). p. 116.

9. Corday. p. 54.

10. Op. cit. p. 49.

11. Op. cit. p. 53.

12. Adam, H. P. *Paris Sees it Through 1914–1919* (1919). pp. 56–7.

13. Bordeaux, Vol. 4. (1957) p. 191.

14. Poincaré, Vol. 6. pp. 121–2.

15. Corday. p. 78.

16. Sandhurst. p. 249.

17. Bennett, A. *The Journals, 1911–21* (1932). p. 136.

18. Strong, Vol. 2 (1916). pp. 259–60, 264.

19. Bordeaux, Vol. 4. p. 243.
20. Adam. p. 54.
21. Bordeaux, Vol. 4. p. 224.
22. Strong, Vol. 2 (1916). p. 272.
23. Bordeaux, Vol. 4. p. 214.
24. Corday. p. 65.
25. Fontaine. p. 42.
26. Corday. p. 81.
27. Bordeaux, Vol. 4. p. 317.
28. Corday. p. 124.
29. Op. cit. Ibid.
30. Private Notes.
31. Corday. p. 72.
32. Strong, Vol. 2 (1916). p. 103.
33. Corday. p. 74.
34. Adam. p. 50.
35. Strong, Vol. 2 (1916). p. 270.
36. Poincaré, Vol. 7. (1931) p. 335.
37. Coolidge, J. G. *War Diary in Paris, 1914–17* (1931). p. 93.
38. Sandhurst. p. 346.

CHAPTER 5

1. Chambers, F. P. *The War behind the War, 1914–1918* (1939). pp. 146–8.
2. *The Times,* 5th July, 1915.
3. Gerard, J. W. *Face to Face with Kaiserism* (1918). p. 160.
4. Butler, T. *Boche Land, before and during the War* (1916). p. 96.
5. Blücher. p. 55.
6. De Beaufort, J. M. *Behind the German Veil* (1917). pp. 46–7, 73.
7. Blücher. p. 62.
8. Op. cit. pp. 51, 54.

9. Op. cit. p. 100.

10. De Beaufort. p. 354.

11. Gerard, J. W. *My Four Years in Germany* (1917). p. 301.

12. Blücher. pp. 90–1.

13. Gerard, *Kaiserism*. p. 78.

14. Bruck, W. F. *Social and Economic History of Germany* . . . (1938). p. 140.

15. Schreiner, G. A. *The Iron Ration* . . . (1918). p. 8.

16. Op. cit. pp. 5–7.

17. *The Great War,* Vol. 4. p. 164.

18. Op. cit. p. 165.

19. Op. cit. Ibid.

20. Knight, W. S. M., and others. *The History of the Great European War.* Vol. 10 (1918). p. 199.

21. Pyke, E. L. *Desperate Germany* (1918). p. 49.

22. Butler. p. 90.

23. Op. cit. p. 82.

24. Gerard. *My Four Years.* pp. 57, 75.

25. Blücher. pp. 95, 96.

26. Mendelssohn-Bartholdy, A. *The War and German Society* (1937). pp. 27–8.

27. Blücher. p. 53.

28. Mendelssohn-Bartholdy. p. 287.

29. Op. cit. pp. 10–11.

30. Blücher. p. 95.

31. Mendelssohn-Bartholdy. p. 112.

32. Curtin, D. T. *The Land of Deepening Shadow* (1917). p. 97.

33. Bordeaux, Vol. 4. pp. 351–2.

34. Blücher. pp. 100, 102.

CHAPTER 6

1. Joffre. *Memoirs,* Vol. 2 (1932). p. 452.

1. Playne, Vol. 1. pp. 273–3.

2. Chambers. p. 257.

3. *The Great War,* Vol. 7 (1916). p. 52.

4. MacDonagh. p. 99.

5. *The Great War,* Vol. 7 (1916). p. 40.

6. Pankhurst. pp. 314–15.

7. Playne, Vol. 1. p. 280.

8. Pankhurst. p. 285.

9. Playne, Vol. 1. p. 218.

10. Lloyd George, Vol. 2. pp. 1142–5.

11. Sandhurst. pp. 337–8.

12. Dearle. p. 114.

13. Pankhurst. pp. 340–1, 379.

14. Playne, Vol. 1. p. 140.

15. MacDonagh. p. 119.

16. Playne, Vol. 1. p. 107.

17. Bordeaux, Vol. 5. p. 126.

18. MacDonagh. pp. 116–22.

19. Playne, Vol. 1. p. 237.

20. Graves. pp. 284–5.

21. Op. cit. p. 283.

22. Playne, Vol. 1. p. 243.

23. Pankhurst. pp. 308–11.

24. MacDonagh. p. 123.

25. Bennett. p. 173.

26. The Lord Chamberlain's department had its censorship troubles too. The previous December, a play called *Disraeli* had been submitted to it, in which Russia was shown as being antagonistic to Britain. The Lord Chamberlain saw the Russian Ambassador and it was agreed that all direct allusion to Russia should be removed, and 'Prussia' substituted for 'Russia'. (Sandhurst. p. 342.)

27. Chambers. p. 420.

28. Bertie, Vol. 2. p. 11.

29. MacDonagh. p. 164.

30. Peel. p. 66.

31. Chambers. p. 253.

32. Op. cit. pp. 265–7.

33. The Paris Conference was a meeting of Allied statesmen to review Allied war-making resources. Lloyd George, who was attending, was hoping for important decisions that would revitalise the Allies' war effort.

34. Playne, Vol. 1. p. 273.

35. Op. cit. pp. 337–8.

36. MacDonagh. p. 163.

37. Op. cit. p. 162.

38. Op. cit. p. 161.

39. Playne, Vol. 1. p. 251.

CHAPTER 8

1. Corday. p. 158.

2. Poincaré, Vol. 8. p. 210.

3. Adam. pp. 70–7.

4. Bordeaux, Vol. 5. p. 87.

5. Clarke, M. *Light and Shade in France* (1939). pp. 102–3.

6. Bordeaux, Vol. 4. p. 366.

7. Corday. p. 150.

8. Bordeaux, Vol. 5. p. 184.

9. Corday. p. 200.

10. Sellier, *et al. Paris pendant la guerre* (1926). p. 2.

11. Bordeaux, Vol. 5. p. 181.

12. Op. cit., Vol. 4. p. 225.

13. Corday. p. 136.

14. Sellier. p. 3.

15. Fontaine, A. *French Industry during the War* (1926). p. 54.

16. Corday. p. 173.

17. Adam. p. 107.

18. Forbes, Lady Angela. *Memories and Base Details* (1921). p. 248.

19. Delétang, L. *Journal d'une Ouvrière Parisienne* (1935). pp. 276–7.

20. Corday. p. 179.

21. Poincaré, Vol. 9 (1932). p. 23.

22. Coolidge, J. *War Diary in Paris, 1914–1917* (1931). p. 161.

23. Delétang. p. 277.

24. Corday. p. 211.

25. Bordeaux, Vol. 5. p. 225.

26. Op. cit. p. 223.

27. Corday. p. 156.

28. Gay, E. *Paris Héroïque* (1920). p. 267.

29. Delétang. p. 295.

30. Poincaré, Vol. 9. p. 18.

31. Corday. pp. 154–5.

32. Jerrold, L. *France Today* (1916). p. 252.

33. Bordeaux, Vol. 5. pp. 270–1.

CHAPTER 9

1. Riddell. pp. 154–5.

2. Knight, Vol. 10. p. 200.

3. Bullitt, E. D. *An Uncensored Diary from the Central Empires* (1918). pp. 273–4.

4. Chambers. pp. 345–7.

5. Feldman, G. D. *Army, Industry and Labour in Germany, 1914–1918* (1966). p. 117.

6. Op. cit. Ibid.

7. Knight, Vol. 10. p. 200.

8. Bullitt. p. 104.

9. Feldman. pp. 107–8.

10. Gerard. *Kaiserism.* pp. 91, 93.

11. Blücher. p. 137.

12. Op. cit. p. 146.

13. Bullitt. pp. 19, 20, 62–3, 117, 231.

14. Chambers. p. 162.

15. *The Great War,* Vol. 8. (1917). p. 385.

16. Chambers. pp. 160–1.

17. Schreiner. pp. 140–3.

18. Butler. p. 91.

19. Gay. p. 19.

20. Schreiner. p. 173. As regards the Kaiser's wartime frugality, it was, however, reported by a French newspaper correspondent, Paul Gentizon, who visited Berlin at the end of the war, that the cellars of the Royal Palace were filled with enormous stocks of food.

21. Morrison, M. A. *Sidelights on Germany* (1918). pp. 92–3.

22. Op. cit. Ibid.

23. Curtin. pp. 50–1.

24. Butler. pp. 111–12.

25. Gerard. *Kaiserism.* pp. 105, 116, 121.

26. Bullitt. p. 106.

27. Gerard. *Kaiserism.* pp. 119–20.

28. Curtin. p. 164.

29. Gerard. *Kaiserism.* p. 100.

30. Bullitt. p. 29.

31. Op. cit. pp. 154–5.

32. Blücher. p. 117.

33. Bordeaux, Vol. 5. p. 220.

34. Schreiner. pp. 148–53. Schreiner describes (p. 149) the total regimentation to which the Germans were now subject as follows: 'By now all that man needs to live was regulated:

Bread, fats, meat, butter, milk, eggs, peas, beans, potatoes, sugar, beer, fuel, clothing, shoes ... These were *directly* under control. Under the *indirect* influence of regulation, however, lay everything but water and air.'

35. Swope, H. B. *Inside the German Empire in the Third Year of the War* (1917). pp. 267 *et. seq.*

36. Curtin. pp. 329, 330, 335.

37. Schreiner. pp. 302, 318–20.

38. *The Great War*, Vol. 8. p. 390.

39. Op. cit. p. 389.

40. Op. cit. p. 390.

41. Almost at the same time the British Government was framing its much milder measure for conscripting manpower: the National Service Scheme.

42. Gerard. *Kaiserism.* p. 123.

CHAPTER 11

1. *The Great War,* Vol. 9 (1917). p. 404.

2. Dearle. p. 133.

3. Lloyd George, Vol. 2. pp. 1150–9.

4. Bennett. p. 190.

5. Dearle. p. 174.

6. Chambers. p. 425.

7. Peel. p. 105.

8. Op. cit. p. 122.

9. MacDonagh. p. 179.

10. Peel. p. 69.

11. Graves. p. 306.

12. *The Great War*, Vol. 11 (1919). pp. 337–9.

13. Playne, C. E. *Britain Holds On, 1917–1918* (1933). p. 107.

14. *The Great War*, Vol. 9. p. 407.

15. *The Great War*, Vol. 10 (1918). p. 317.

16. MacDonagh. pp. 195–6.

17. Lloyd George, Vol. 1. p. 670.

18. MacDonagh. p. 176.

19. Peel. p. 82.

20. Dearle. pp. 137, 136.

21. Riddell. p. 248.

22. Bennett. p. 196.

23. *The Great War,* Vol. 10. p. 98.

24. Op. cit. pp. 32, 33.

25. MacDonagh. pp. 194–5.

26. Playne, Vol. 2. p. 197.

27. MacDonagh. p. 233.

28. Op. cit. p. 237.

29. *The Great War,* Vol. 10. p. 318.

30. Playne, Vol. 2. pp. 246–7.

31. Playne, Vol. 1. pp. 217–18.

32. MacDonagh. pp. 95–6.

33. Playne, Vol. 2. pp. 112–13.

34. Blunden, E. *Undertones of War* (1928). p. 178.

35. Riddell. p. 296.

36. MacDonagh. p. 210.

37. Playne, Vol. 2. p. 146.

38. Op. cit. p. 148.

39. Bennett. p. 205.

40. Playne, Vol. 2. pp. 195–6.

CHAPTER 12

1. Bordeaux, Vol. 6 (1959). p. 13.

2. Britain now needed her coal for herself, and in any case shipping was scarce.

3. Corday. p. 230.

4. Op. cit. p. 239.

5. Op. cit. p. 222.

6. Fontaine. p. 113.

7. Adam. pp. 115–16.

8. Corday. p. 259.

9. Gerard. *Kaiserism*. p. 240.

10. Op. cit. p. 237.

11. *The Times*, 7th April, 1917. p. 8.

12. Sharp. p. 182.

13. De la Gorce, P.-M. *The French Army* ... Transl. by K. Douglas (1963). p. 121.

14. Delétang. p. 338.

15. Coolidge. p. 231.

16. Op. cit. p. 233.

17. Allard, P. *Les Dessous de la Guerre* ... (1932). pp. 173, 178, 181.

18. Poincaré, Vol. 9. p. 153.

19. Corday. pp. 256–7.

20. Op. cit. pp. 249–50.

21. Op. cit. p. 259.

22. Op. cit. p. 246.

23. Coolidge. pp. 195–6.

24. Corday. p. 242.

25. The soldiers were graded for exemption according to the importance of their civilian occupations in respect of national service. At the bottom of the list were: 'Art and letters, porters, bath-attendants, hairdressers, night-watchmen.' 'Behold to what a level literature and the arts have now been reduced,' lamented Corday (p. 272).

26. Fontaine. pp. 32, 34.

27. Corday. p. 235.

28. Forbes. p. 289.

29. Poincaré, Vol. 9. p. 345.

30. Bertie, Vol. 2. pp. 215, 209.
31. Delétang. p. 348.
32. Adam. pp. 128, 129.
33. Corday. p. 277.
34. Adam. p. 105.
35. Corday. pp. 300–1.
36. Poincaré, Vol. 9. p. 444.
37. Delétang. p. 366.

CHAPTER 13

1. Schreiner. p. 239.
2. Blücher. p. 158.
3. Op. cit. p. 162.
4. Davis, A. N. *The Kaiser I Knew* (1918). p. 279.
5. Gerard. p. 125.
6. Curtin. p. 352.
7. Blücher. pp. 162–3.
8. Schreiner. p. 232.
9. Op. cit. p. 182.
10. Blücher. p. 161.
11. Knight, Vol. 10. p. 202.
12. Schreiner. pp. 252–5.
13. Op. cit. Ibid.
14. Op. cit. Ibid.
15. Pyke. p. 185.
16. Feldman. pp. 326–7, 337–9, 362.
17. Mendelssohn-Bartholdy. pp. 143–4.
18. Schreiner. p. 195.
19. Bertie, Vol. 2. p. 203.
20. Gerard. *My Four Years*. p. 222.
21. Gerard. *Kaiserism*. p. 127.

22. Blücher. p. 179.

23. Op. cit. p. 160.

24. Op. cit. p. 176.

25. Pyke. p. 100.

26. Anon. *Conditions in Germany* (1917) (Pamphlet). pp. 12, 22, 24, 26, 29.

27. Lloyd George, Vol. 2. p. 1210.

28. Chambers. p. 361.

29. Blücher. p. 185.

30. Peel. p. 50.

CHAPTER 15

1. Playne, Vol. 2. p. 252.

2. Riddell. p. 303.

3. Peel. pp. 57–8.

4. MacDonagh. p. 244.

5. Chambers. p. 422.

6. Knight, Vol. 10. p. 185.

7. Graves. pp. 335–6.

8. MacDonagh. p. 269.

9. Bennett. p. 221.

10. Peel. p. 103.

11. MacDonagh. p. 246.

12. Op. cit. p. 281.

13. Riddell. pp. 323–4.

14. Lloyd George, Vol. 2. pp. 1173–4.

15. MacDonagh. p. 290.

16. Playne, Vol. 2. p. 309.

17. Op. cit. p. 332.

18. Lloyd George, Vol. 2. p. 1167.

19. Playne, Vol. 2. p. 303.

20. Op. cit. pp. 334–5.

21. Sinkings of British ships in September, at 129,483 tons, were the lowest since 1916. In October sinkings fell to 56,000 tons. (Lloyd George, Vol. 1. p. 709.)

22. Dearle. p. 216.

23. Bennett. p. 238.

24. Trade disputes for 1918 showed a general increase over those for 1917. There were 1,252, affecting 1,132,000 workers. (Dearle. p. 239.)

25. MacDonagh. pp. 316–17.

26. Chambers. p. 496.

27. Driberg, T. *Beaverbrook: a Study in Power and Frustration* (1956). p. 125.

28. Much of this information is drawn from contemporary issues of *The Times*.

CHAPTER 16

1. Adam. p. 244.

2. Sellier. pp. 19–20.

3. Bertie, Vol. 2. p. 256.

4. Corday. p. 323.

5. Sellier. p. 84.

6. Op. cit. p. 17.

7. Bertie, Vol. 2. p. 257.

8. Corday. p. 317.

9. Sellier. pp. 18–19.

10. Adam. p. 209.

11. Bordeaux, Vol. 7. p. 14.

12. Adam. p. 227.

13. Corday. p. 333.

14. Sellier. p. 83.

15. Adam. pp. 226–7.

16. Delétang. p. 381.

17. Bertie, Vol. 2. p. 277.

18. Corday. p. 347.

19. Op. cit. p. 379.

20. Falls, C. *The First World War* (1960). p. 335.

21. Corday. p. 362.

22. Op. cit. p. 367.

23. Sellier. p. 84.

24. Propaganda from the Home Front now played its part in the assault. Like Britain, only in 1918 did France start to mount a serious anti-German campaign. In May Clemenceau incorporated the existing military Aerial Propaganda Service into an extensive new *Centre d'Action de Propagande contre l'Ennemi*. In September the *Centre* distributed 14 million leaflets on or behind the German lines. (Chambers, pp. 494–7.)

25. Corday. p. 382.

CHAPTER 17

1. Pyke. pp. 11–12, 96.

2. Blücher. p. 225.

3. Richter, L., *ed., Family Life in Germany under the Blockade* (1919). pp. 15–16.

4. Op. cit. pp. 225, 228, 233–4.

5. Pyke. pp. 24–9, 33.

6. Blücher. pp. 203–5, 207.

7. Pyke. p. 147.

8. Chambers. p. 499.

9. Knight, Vol. 10. p. 206.

10. Blücher. pp. 228–9.

11. Op. cit. p. 238.

12. Op. cit. p. 241.

13. *The Great War*, Vol. 13 (1919). pp. 393, 401.

14. Chambers. p. 498.
15. Op. cit. p. 517.
16. Blücher. p. 250.
17. Chambers. p. 522.
18. Blücher. p. 253.
19. Chambers. p. 525.

BIBLIOGRAPHY

The following is a select list of the works consulted. (Among sources not specifically mentioned are contemporary newspapers and periodical publications.)

GENERAL

Annual Register, The, 1914–1918. London, 1915–1919.

CAMERON, JAMES. *1914.* London, 1959.

Carnegie Endowment for International Peace: *Economic and Social History of the World War.* London and elsewhere. 1919 *et seq.*

CHAMBERS, FRANK P. *The War behind the War, 1914–1918*: a History of the Political and Civilian Fronts. London, 1939.

CLOUGH, SHEPARD B., *et al. A History of the Western World: Modern Times.* Boston, 1964.

KNIGHT, W. S. M., *ed. The History of the Great European War, its Causes and Effects.* 10 vols. London (n.d.).

LASSWELL, HAROLD D. *Propaganda Technique in the World War.* London, 1938.

PONSONBY, ARTHUR. *Falsehood in Wartime.* London, 1936.

WILSON, H. W. and HAMMERTON, J. A., *ed. The Great War: the Standard History of the All-Europe Conflict.* 13 vols. London, 1914–1919.

WINTRINGHAM, T. H. *Mutiny.* London, 1936.

Anon. *Britain Transformed*. (Pamphlet.) London, 1916.

BELL, JULIAN, ed. *We Did Not Fight. 1914–1918 Experiences of War Resisters*. London, 1935.

BENNETT, ARNOLD. *The Journals, Vol. 2, 1911–1921*. London, 1932.

BERTIE OF THAME, LORD. *The Diary of, 1914–1918*. Ed. by Lady Algernon Gordon Lennox. 2 vols. London, 1924.

BLUNDEN, EDMUND. *Undertones of War*. London, 1928.

BRITTAIN, VERA. *Testament of Youth: an Autobiographical Study of the Years 1900–1925*. London, 1933.

CASE, CLARENCE MARSH. *Non-violent Coercion: a Study of Methods of Social Pressure*. London, 1923.

CHARLTON, L. E. O. *War Over England*. London, 1936.

CLARKE, TOM. *My Northcliffe Diary*. London, 1931.

COOK, SIR EDWARD. *The Press in War Time: Some Account of the Official Press Bureau*. London, 1920.

DAVRAY, HENRY D. *Through French Eyes: Britain's Efforts*. London, 1916.

DEARLE, N. B. *An Economic Chronicle of the War for Great Britain and Ireland*, 1914–1919, with Suppt., 1920–22. (Carnegie Endowment for International Peace.) London, 1929.

DRIBERG, TOM. *Beaverbrook: a Study in Power and Frustration*. London, 1956.

FAIRLIE, JOHN A. *British War Administration*. (Carnegie Endowment for International Peace.) New York, 1919.

FAY, SIR SAM. *The War Office at War*. London, 1937.

FORBES, LADY ANGELA. *Memories and Base Details*. London, 1921.

GEORGE, RT. HON. DAVID LLOYD. *War Memoirs*. 4 vols in 2. London, 1934.

GRAVES, ROBERT. *Goodbye to All That: an Autobiography*. London, 1929.

HIRST, FRANCIS W. *The Consequences of the War to Great Britain*. (Carnegie Endowment for International Peace.) London, 1934.

MACDONAGH, MICHAEL. *In London during the Great War: the Diary of a Journalist.* London, 1935.

MCKENNA, STEPHEN. *While I Remember.* London, 1922.

MARWICK, ARTHUR. *The Deluge: British Society and the First World War.* London, 1965.

MITCHELL, DAVID. *Women on the Warpath: the Story of the Women of the First World War.* London, 1966.

PANKHURST, E. SYLVIA. *The Home Front: a Mirror to Life in England during the World War.* London, 1932.

PEEL, MRS C. S. *How We Lived Then: 1914–1918.* London, 1929.

PLAYNE, CAROLINE E. *Society at War, 1914–1916.* London, 1931.

PLAYNE, CAROLINE E. *Britain Holds On, 1917, 1918.* London, 1933.

REPINGTON, C. A'COURT. *The First World War, 1914–1918: Personal Experiences.* London, 1920.

RIDDELL, LORD. *War Diary, 1914–1918.* London, 1933.

SANDHURST, LORD. *From Day to Day, 1914–1915.* London, 1918.

SASSOON, SIEGFRIED. *Memoirs of an Infantry Officer.* London, 1928.

STREET, G. S. *At Home in the War.* London, 1918.

STUART, SIR CAMPBELL. *Secrets of Crewe House: the Story of a Famous Campaign.* London, 1920.

SYMONS, JULIAN. *Horatio Bottomley.* London, 1955.

TAYLOR, A. J. P. *English History, 1914–1945.* London, 1965.

WARD, MRS HUMPHREY. *England's Effort: Six Letters to an American Friend.* London, 1916.

WARWICK, COUNTESS OF. *A Woman and the War.* London, 1916.

WILLIS, IRENE COOPER. *How We Went into the War.* London, 1918.

WILLIS, IRENE COOPER. *How We Got on with the War.* London, 1919.

WORSFOLD, BASIL. *The War and Social Reform.* London, 1919.

FRANCE

ADAM, G. *Treason and Tragedy: an Account of the French War Trials*. London, 1929.

ADAM, H. PEARL. *Paris Sees it Through: a Diary 1914–1919*. London, 1919.

ALLARD, P. *Les Dessous de la Guerre, Révélés par les Comités Secrets*. Paris, 1932.

ALPHAUD, GABRIEL. *La France pendant la Guerre (1914–1918)*. Paris, 1917–1920.

BARNARD, CHARLES I. *Paris War Days: Diary of an American*. London, 1914.

BORDEAUX, HENRY. *Histoire d'une Vie*. Vol. 4 *et seq*. Paris, 1957 *et seq*.

BROGAN, DENIS. *The Development of Modern France (1870–1939)*. London, 1944.

CHATELLE, A., and TISON, G. *Calais pendant la Guerre (1914–1918)*. Paris, 1927.

CLARKE, M. E. *Paris Waits, 1914*. London, 1915.

CLARKE, MOMA. *Light and Shade in France*. London, 1939.

CLERMONT, CAMILLE. *Souvenirs de Parisiennes en Temps de Guerre*. Paris, 1918.

COOLIDGE, JOHN GARDNER. *A War Diary in Paris, 1914–17*. Cambridge, 1931.

CORDAY, MICHEL. *The Paris Front: an Unpublished Diary, 1914–1918*. London, 1933.

DAWES, CHARLES G. *A Journal of the Great War*. London, 1923.

DE LA GORCE, PAUL-MARIE. *The French Army: a Military and Political History. Transl.* by Kenneth Douglas. London, 1963.

DELÉTANG, LOUISE. *Journal d'une Ouvrière Parisienne pendant la Guerre*. Paris, 1935.

FONTAINE, ARTHUR. *French Industry during the War.* (Carnegie Endowment for International Peace.) New Haven, 1926.

GALLI, HENRI. *La Guerre à Paris*. Paris, 1917.

GAY, ERNEST. *Paris Héroïque: la Grande Guerre*. Paris, 1920.

HORNE, ALISTAIR. *The Price of Glory: Verdun 1916*. London, 1962.

HUBER, MICHEL. *La Population de France pendant la Guerre*. (Carnegie Endowment for International Peace.) Paris, 1931.

HUMBERT, CHARLES. *Chacun à Son Tour*. Paris, 1925.

HYNDMAN, H. M. *Clemenceau: the Man and his Time*. London, 1919.

JERROLD, LAURENCE. *France Today*. London, 1916.

LAUDET, FERNAND. *Paris pendant la Guerre: Impressions*. Paris, 1915.

LAVEDAN, HENRI. *Les Grandes Heures, 1914–18*. 5 vols. Paris, 1915–20.

MADELIN, LOUIS. *Le Chemin de la Victoire*. 2 vols. Paris, 1920.

MILLER, HENRY W. *The Paris Gun: the Bombardment of Paris by the German Long-Range Guns*. . . . London, 1930.

OHNET, GEORGES. *Journal d'un Bourgeois de Paris pendant la Guerre de 1914*. 11 parts. Paris, 1914–1916.

POINCARÉ, RAYMOND. *Au Service de la France, 1912–1918*. 10 vols. Paris, 1926–1933.

ROSMER, A. *Mouvement Ouvrier pendant la Guerre*. 2 vols. Paris, 1936–1959.

SELLIER, HENRI, *et al. Paris pendant la Guerre*. (Carnegie Endowment for International Peace.) Paris, 1926.

SHARP, WILLIAM GRAVES. *The War Memoirs of an American Ambassador to France, 1914–1919*. London, 1931.

STRONG, ROWLAND. *The Diary of an English Resident in France during War Time*. 2 vols. London, 1915–1916.

GERMANY

Anon. *Conditions in Germany*. (Pamphlet.) London, 1917.

BLÜCHER, PRINCESS EVELYN. *An English Wife in Berlin: a Private Memoir*. London, 1920.

BRUCK, W. F. *Social and Economic History of Germany from William II to Hitler, 1888–1938: a Comparative Study*. London, 1938.

BULLITT, MRS E. D. *An Uncensored Diary from the Central Empires.* London, 1918.

BUTLER, THEOBOLD. *Boche Land, before and during the War.* London, 1916.

BRUNTZ, GEORGE G. *Allied Propaganda and the Collapse of the German Empire in 1918.* Stanford, 1938.

CURTIN, D. THOMAS. *The Land of Deepening Shadow: Germany 1916.* London, 1917.

DAVIS, ARTHUR N. *The Kaiser I Knew: My Fourteen Years with the Kaiser.* London, 1918.

DAYAL, H. *Forty-Four Months in Germany and Turkey: February 1915 to October 1918.* London, 1920.

DE BEAUFORT, J. M. *Behind the German Veil: a Journalistic Pilgrimage.* London, 1917.

FELDMAN, GERALD D. *Army, Industry and Labour in Germany, 1914–1918.* Princeton, 1966.

GERARD, JAMES W. *My Four Years in Germany.* London, 1917.

GERARD, JAMES W. *Face to Face with Kaiserism.* Toronto, 1918.

HINDENBURG, PAUL VON. *Out of My Life.* Transl. by F. A. Holt. London, 1920.

LUDENDORFF, ERICH. *My War Memories, 1914–1918.* 2 vols. London, 1919.

LUDENDORFF, MARGARETHE. *My Married Life with Ludendorff.* Transl. by Raglan Somerset. London (n.d.).

LUTZ, RALPH HASWELL. *The Causes of the German Collapse in 1918.* Stanford, 1934.

MAX OF BADEN, PRINCE. *Memoirs.* Transl. by W. M. Calder and C. W. H. Sutton. 2 vols. London, 1928.

MENDELSSOHN-BARTHOLDY, ALBRECHT. *The War and German Society: the Testament of a Liberal.* (Carnegie Endowment for International Peace.) New Haven, 1937.

MORRISON, MICHAEL A. *Sidelights on Germany: Studies of German Life and Character during the Great War based on the Enemy Press.* London, 1918.

PLESS, DUCHESS OF. *By Herself.* London, 1929.

PYKE, ERNEST LIONEL. *Desperate Germany.* London, 1918.

RICHTER, LINA, ed. *Family Life in Germany under the Blockade.*

With a Preface by Bernard Shaw. London, 1919.

ROSENBERG, A. *The Birth of the German Republic, 1871–1918.* London, 1931.

SCHREINER, GEORGE ABEL. *The Iron Ration: the Economic and Social Effects of the Allied Blockade on Germany and the German People.* London, 1918.

STOLPER, GUSTAV, *et al. The German Economy, 1870 to the Present. Transl.* by Toni Stolper. London, 1967.

SMITH, THOMAS A. *What Germany Thinks: or, the War as Germans See It.* London, 1915.

SWOPE, HERBERT BAYARD. *Inside the German Empire in the Third Year of the War.* London, 1917.

INDEX

women—*cont.*
30, 35, 151–3, 169, 228, 231,
unemployment, 31, social
position, 91–2, 152, pay and
conditions, 151–2; in **France,**
war work, 34-5, 73, 77–8, 79,
80–1, 217–18, pay and
conditions, 80, 81, 85, 139–40

York, Archbishop of, 17

Ypres, Third Battle of, 175, 184,
198

xenophobia, 20–2, 31–3, 38, 65–6,
69, 82, 93–4, 143–4, 215–16

Zeppelins, 93, 222, 235, 265;
and see air raids

12

8565 S